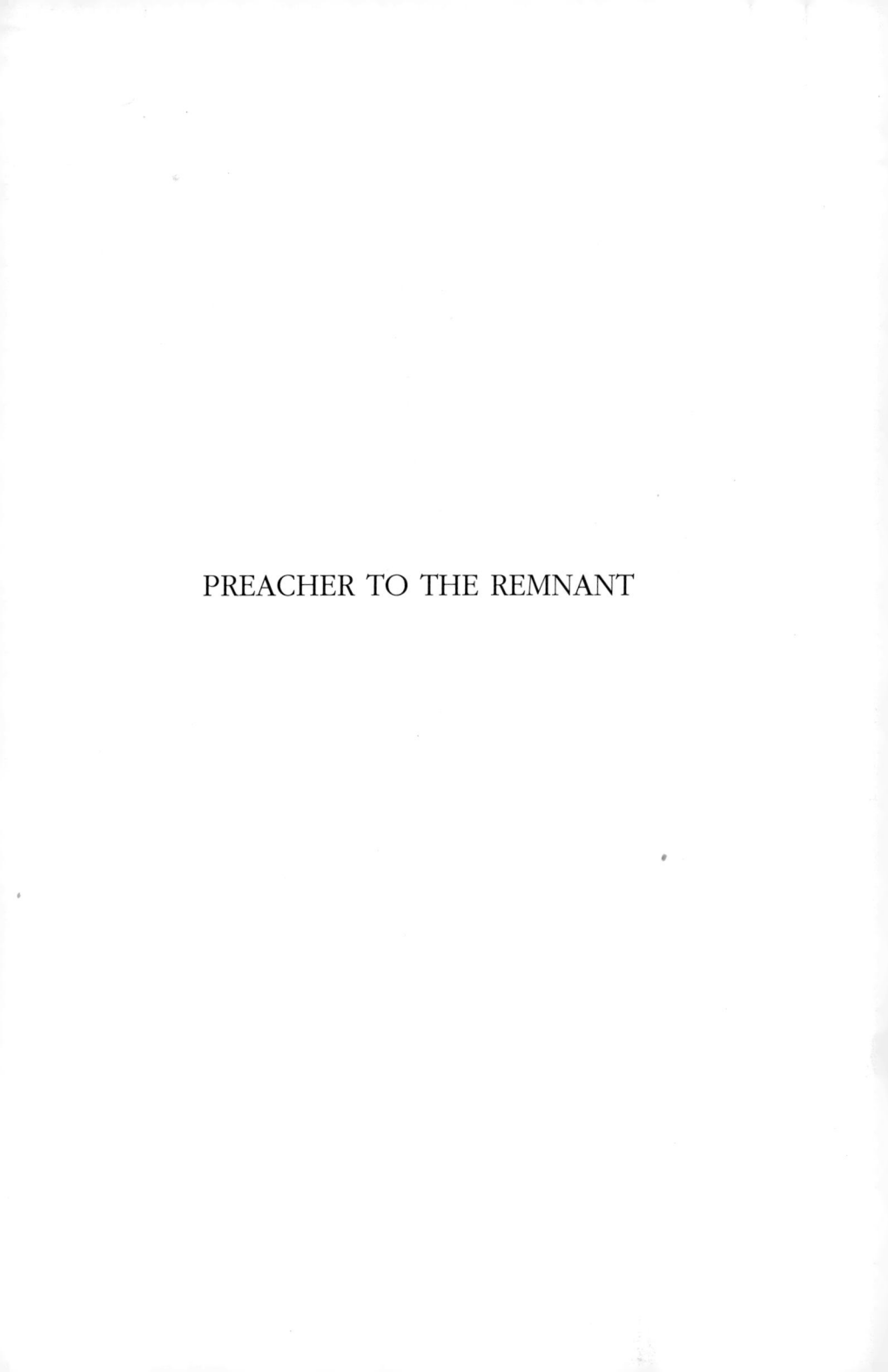

PREACHER TO THE REMNANT

PREACHER TO THE REMNANT

THE STORY OF JAMES RENWICK

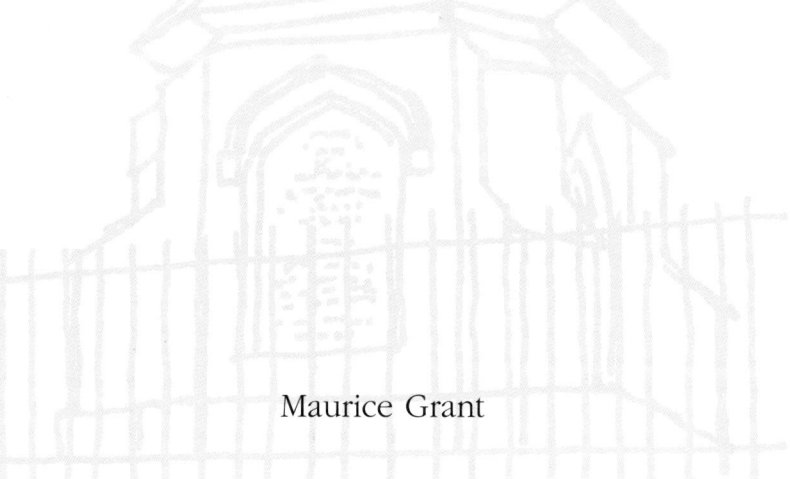

Maurice Grant

2009

Published by
Blue Banner Productions
on behalf of
The Scottish Reformation Society
December 2009

ISBN 978-0-9511484-9-5

© Maurice Grant

Printed by
Bell and Bain Limited
Glasgow

Preface

JAMES RENWICK was the last of the great trio of field-preachers who preached to the "suffering remnant" of the Church of Scotland in the persecution of the late 17th century. As the successor to Donald Cargill and Richard Cameron, it was Renwick's lot to minister in the very hottest time of the persecution, including what is often referred to as the "Killing Time" of the mid-1680s, when those who refused to conform to the state-enforced order were hunted down mercilessly by the forces of authority. As their only minister Renwick shared to the full in the trials they suffered, and for much of his ministry he was harried from place to place and forced to find refuge where best he could. As time went on, he had to endure not only the persecution of the state authorities but, increasingly, the reproaches of former friends. In the face of these twin assaults he remained utterly dedicated not only to his Divine call to the ministry, but to the upholding of the Crown rights of Christ as King and Head of the Church – a principle which lay at the heart of the historic testimony of the Church of Scotland and which had been enshrined in the Covenants sworn by all ranks in the nation.

In his own day it was common to decry Renwick as a deviant from the principles of Scottish Presbyterianism. The same charge had been levelled at Cargill and Cameron before him. It had particular reference to their disowning of the king as their lawful sovereign. Far from accepting this charge, Renwick argued that his refusal to own an earthly sovereign who had usurped the Crown rights of Christ was fully in accord with the principles of the Scottish Reformation. Like the Reformers, he knew that the liberties of the Church went hand in hand with the liberties of the people. His stand was fully vindicated at the Revolution of 1688 when the very grounds on which he had rejected the authority of King James VII were adopted by the supreme court of the nation. It is no exaggeration to say that his testimony – and particularly his death – paved the way for the religious and civil liberties we enjoy today.

The events which shaped James Renwick's career had also of course shaped the ministries of his two predecessors. To that extent the historical background in this work is necessarily similar to that in my biographies of Cargill – *No King but Christ* (1988) and *Cameron – The Lion of the Covenant* (1997). I have sought to keep any duplication to a minimum, though to make the story reasonably self-contained the repetition of some material has been unavoidable. For the same reason I have included a few of the notes to be found in the earlier volumes.

As before, I sincerely acknowledge my indebtedness to those who have assisted me in this work. My particular thanks go to the staffs of the National Library of Scotland, the National Archives of Scotland, New College Library, the Edinburgh and Glasgow University Libraries and the Ewart Library, Dumfries, for their kind attention to my various wants, and for their unfailing courtesy.

MAURICE GRANT

Contents

		Preface	PAGE	5
		Foreword		9
Chapter	1:	Birth and Background		11
Chapter	2:	Preparation for Service		23
Chapter	3:	In the Bonds of Fellowship		31
Chapter	4:	The Call to Service		39
Chapter	5:	Ordination		48
Chapter	6:	A Time of Testing		61
Chapter	7:	The Start of the Ministry		73
Chapter	8:	The Darkness Gathers		91
Chapter	9:	Into the Abyss		100
Chapter	10:	A False Dawn		111
Chapter	11:	Trial and Controversy		118
Chapter	12:	The Controversies Deepen		131
Chapter	13:	Testifying Amid Tribulation		142
Chapter	14:	The Informatory Vindication		154
Chapter	15:	The Woeful Toleration		168
Chapter	16:	A Fearless Witness		182
Chapter	17:	A Prisoner for Christ		193

Chapter 18:	Preparing for Glory	PAGE 205
Chapter 19:	The Final Testimony	212
Chapter 20:	Renwick's Place in History	220
Appendix 1:	Renwick as a Preacher	230
Appendix 2:	Renwick as a Correspondent	245
Appendix 3:	Renwick and the United Societies	251
	Select Bibliography	261
	Notes	263
	Index	277

FOREWORD

A FOREWORD, being but the porch through which the house is entered, should not long detain the reader. Having previously told the story of Donald Cargill in *No King but Christ* (Evangelical Press, 1988) and the story of Richard Cameron in *The Lion of the Covenant* (Evangelical Press, 1997) Maurice Grant does further useful service to the Church of Christ in presenting this fresh, thoroughly researched and attractively written comprehensive account of the life of James Renwick, the last Covenanting minister to be put to death for his adherence to the Biblical principles of the Scottish Reformation.

Mr Grant sets Renwick's life in the context of his times and provides readers with a clear account of the principles for which the most resolute Scottish Presbyterians contended to the end during those Killing Times. Much background information is introduced almost incidentally and with a light touch, giving a factual account of the history of the times which exposes just how partial and prejudiced many commonly accepted narratives are.

Particularly interesting and edifying is the way in which the gracious, godly and attractive character of James Renwick shines through in these pages. From extracts of sermons and letters and the comments, brief or extended, of friends and foes, an attractive portrait of this servant of God emerges quite unlike the fanatical, inhuman and rigid Renwick of popular mythology. Prepared as he was to resist unto blood in contending for the right of Christ to reign in His own Church, his love for God his Saviour overflowed in love to his fellows. He recognised as godly, and longed for fellowship in the Gospel with, many from whom his commitment to the testimony of the first and second Reformations of the Church in Scotland required him to be separate. Though he had just turned twenty-six when he was put to death he was wise and judicious and a moderating influence among his associates. He was most at home in preaching Christ to sinners and saints and searching and edifying doctrine to the people of God. Perhaps unusually in reading historical narratives we have felt our heart drawn to the subject of this book. Here is no unhealthy hagiography, but we feel in the company of one of those faithful witnesses to Christ "of whom the world was not worthy" (Hebrews 11:38).

Let the reader enter in to be instructed and inspired.

HUGH M. CARTWRIGHT

CHAPTER 1

BIRTH AND BACKGROUND

GLENCAIRN is a small inland parish in south-west Scotland. In many ways, it is typical of rural Dumfriesshire. The scenery is quiet and undramatic, the landscape for the most part green and undulating. According to a modern writer, the peaceful nature of Glencairn is reflected in the character of the inhabitants. "The people," he says, "are naturally friendly and hospitable to strangers, and their manners are agreeable, courteous and obliging. Few feuds are found between different families, and the gentle air of the district seems to engender gentle habits."[1]

Glencairn is said to take its name from the "cairns" or prehistoric stone burial mounds which in former times dotted its landscape, but of which few traces now remain. The numerous antiquities which have been found in the parish suggest that it has been inhabited from the earliest times. There is only one community of any size – the village of Moniaive, situated picturesquely in the centre of the parish.[2]

Glencairn is watered by numerous streams, the main one – the Cairn Water – being a tributary of the Nith, which it joins just above Dumfries. The land, particularly in the river valleys, is fertile, and well suited to arable farming. For generations, the staple industry of Glencairn has been agriculture. The parish was long noted for its Cheviot and blackface sheep, reared on the upland slopes which dominate it to the north and north-west.

In former times, the agriculture industry impacted on much of the life of the parish. Apart from giving employment directly, it generated a variety of cottage industries. Of these, much the most important was weaving. It was the custom for wool shorn from locally-reared sheep to be spun into yarn in local households before being woven into cloth for the use of their families. The weaver's work was well paid, and indeed it has been recorded that to become a weaver was often the height of a village boy's ambition. Entry to the craft was well-guarded, and young men were expected to serve an apprenticeship of up to four years before being regarded as competent.

By the seventeenth century, weaving had become a well-established local trade. The weaver was a valued member of the community, and his work was in constant demand. Though the work could be arduous, it provided him with a steady income, sufficient for him to maintain his household in a reasonable standard of comfort. At a time of political uncertainty and economic upheaval, the weaver's craft offered an enviable measure of stability.

It was one such man, Andrew Renwick by name, who in the mid-1600s tenanted a small cottage on the lands of Neiss, on the western outskirts of Moniaive. The Renwicks were of Cumbrian origin, but branches had by this time become established in the south of Scotland and there is no reason to think that Andrew Renwick was other than a native of Glencairn.[3] He was well-respected in the local community, not only because of the skills he brought to his craft, but because of his eminent Christian character and the transparent integrity of his life. His wife, Elizabeth Corson, was like-minded with himself. A young woman of considerable strength of character, she was to need all her resources of strength and grace in the experiences which lay before her.

Andrew and Elizabeth Renwick appear to have married around the year 1650. Through time, several children were born to them, but tragically these all died in infancy. Andrew Renwick was wont to say, when comforting his heart-broken wife, that he was well satisfied to have children, whether they lived or died, young or old, providing they might be heirs of glory. His wife too was resigned to God's will; yet she could not but yearn for a kinder course of providence. In secret, she made it her aim to cry to God for a child who would not only be an heir of glory, but would live to serve the Lord in his own generation.

So it was that James Renwick, a child of many prayers, was born on 15th February 1662. Immediately on his birth, his mother saw in him the answer she had so longingly sought; and she resolved from that moment to dedicate him to the Lord. It was not long before she came to believe that hers had been no misplaced confidence. Even at two years of age, as she later told, she saw him to be "aiming at prayer" while still in the cradle;

and from that moment she had the unshakeable conviction that God would use him in some particular way for his glory, and enable him to honour God in his generation. His father, too, soon came to the persuasion that, though his son's time in the world would be short, yet the Lord would make some eminent use of him.

In cherishing this vision for their son, Andrew and Elizabeth Renwick could have had few illusions about what lay ahead of him. James Renwick had been born at a time of deepening crisis for the Church of Scotland. Over the previous hundred years, that Church had known remarkable blessing. In 1560, the great Reformation had delivered the church and people of Scotland from the long bondage of Romanism. In no country in Europe, indeed, had the effects of the Reformation been so radical. The reform of the Church had gone hand-in-hand with a great spiritual revival which affected the entire fabric of society. A nation was, as it were, born in a day. There was a determination to conform both Church and State to the pattern of Scripture. Over the succeeding years, the government and discipline of the Church had been re-modelled on a strictly Presbyterian basis. The Church had asserted its independence of any earthly ruler, be he king or pope; and in 1592 it had had these liberties acknowledged by an Act of Parliament which was seen, in effect, as the Charter of the Church of Scotland.

These changes had been presided over by the young king, James VI, who had come to the throne in 1567 on the abdication of his mother, Mary Queen of Scots. By temperament, James was notoriously volatile. At times he appeared sympathetic to the claims of the Church; at other times he was distinctly hostile. As time went on, it was the latter characteristic which gained the ascendancy. Reared in the absolutist principles of the Stuarts, James increasingly saw the independence of the Church as a threat to the authority of the throne and to the Divine Right which he claimed as king; and he set himself to curb the Church's liberties by what means he could. James of course knew that these liberties were firmly rooted in the popular will, and with an uncertain power base he was careful not to do anything which would alienate his Scottish subjects. But after 1603, when he succeeded to the Crown of England, he felt in a stronger position to assert his will. Some ministers were only too anxious to do his bidding, and through subservient General Assemblies he introduced a series of measures designed to undermine the Presbyterian government of the church. Bishops, appointed by royal authority, were installed and given positions of influence in church and state. The right of calling General Assemblies was declared to be vested in the king. Other innovations, such as observance of holy days, were foisted upon the Church. Ministers who resisted these innovations were persecuted, and some – such as John Welsh of Ayr, the son-in-law of Knox – were banished the country. Generally however the king's measures were brought about in a way which did not irritate the popular will; and even by the time of his death in 1625 he had succeeded only in introducing a fairly modified form of episcopacy which was no doubt well short of what he would have wished.

However, the accession of James's son, as Charles I, changed the scene dramatically. Charles had the same absolutist aims as his father, but lacked his craft and guile. Spurred on by unscrupulous advisers, he sought to force the pace of change in a way which brought his subjects in Scotland to the brink of rebellion. An attempt in 1637 to impose a new Service Book and Canons on the Church precipitated a crisis, and led in Edinburgh to a popular revolt. Early in the following year, in the Greyfriars Church, citizens of all classes signed a National Covenant, pledging themselves to the defence of the Reformed religion and to resist all innovations. Copies of the Covenant were sent throughout the country, and were signed amid scenes of wild enthusiasm. Later that year, a General Assembly of the Church in Glasgow swept aside the Episcopal innovations, deposed the bishops, and restored the government and discipline of the Church to its Reformation model. At a stroke, all the corrosive work of the past forty years had been undone; and the Church now stood forth once again in her Reformation purity.

This "Second Reformation", like the first, was accompanied by a wave of spiritual fervour which swept the country. The moment too produced the men – preachers and writers of towering attainments such as Samuel Rutherford, James Durham, George Gillespie and David Dickson – who gained for Scotland an international reputation as a centre of the Reformed faith. Of this time in Scotland a contemporary writer could say: "Religion advanced the greatest step it had made for many years; now the ministry was notably purified, the magistracy altered, and the people strangely refined. Godly men were employed in all offices, both civil and military. Scotland has been, even by emulous foreigners, called Philadelphia; and now she seemed to be in her flower." He went on: "As the bands of the Scottish church were strong, so her beauty was bright; no error was so much as named, the people were not only sound in the faith, but innocently ignorant of unsound doctrine. Then was Scotland a heap of wheat set about with lilies, uniform, or a palace of silver beautifully proportioned; and this seems to me to have been Scotland's high noon."[4]

This great spiritual revival was all the more remarkable as it took place at a time of tumult and turmoil in the civil sphere, with the effects of the civil war in England spilling over into Scotland. As the war progressed, the

BIRTH AND BACKGROUND

Scottish church and people were drawn increasingly into supporting the English Parliament in their struggle against the king. This support found expression in 1643 in the Solemn League and Covenant, in which the representatives of the Scottish nation, with the General Assembly of the Church, made common cause with their counterparts in England and enlisted their support to establish the Reformed religion in England and Ireland. It was Scottish help, indeed, which helped eventually to turn the tide of the war in favour of the Parliament. But by the end of the decade the deciding factor had become the rise of Cromwell and the Army, who in 1649 had the king executed and, later, Parliament suppressed. In a revulsion of feeling against Cromwell the Scottish church and people once again espoused the cause of the Stuart monarchy, and in 1650 they had the king's son recalled from exile and crowned as Charles II.

It was an act of misguided loyalty which was to cost them dearly. In a short and sharp military campaign Cromwell crushed Scottish opposition and brought the whole country under his control. From then until 1660 he and his generals ruled the country with an iron hand. But despite the upheavals in civil affairs the condition of the Church continued to flourish. Cromwell's favoured form of church government was Independency, but he practised toleration in religion and apart from a ban on meetings of the General Assembly he allowed the Church to function much as before. The combination of Covenanting preaching and English puritan morality carried forward the spiritual momentum of the previous decade. Again of this time a contemporary could write: "Every parish had a minister, every village had a school, every family almost had a Bible, in most of the country all the children of age could read the Scriptures. I have lived many years in a parish where I never heard an oath, and you might have ridden many miles before you had heard any; also, you could not for a great part of the country have lodged in a family where the Lord was not worshipped by reading, singing and public prayer. Nobody complained more of our church government than our taverners, whose ordinary lamentation was, their trade was broke, people were become so sober."[5]

But this state of things was not to last. The death of Cromwell in 1658 spelt the end of the military dictatorship, and as civil affairs became increasingly disordered there was a general call for the monarchy to be restored. On 29th May 1660, amid much general rejoicing, Charles II was restored to his father's throne. Nowhere did his return cause greater satisfaction than in Scotland, where nine years earlier he had been crowned as the nation's Covenanted king. The Scottish church and people had been the first to affirm their loyalty to the new monarch; now the Church of Scotland looked for that loyalty to be rewarded by being confirmed in the rights she had secured for herself in the Second Reformation and its achievements.

The reality was to be woefully different. Despite all his fair promises, the new king was no friend of Presbyterianism, or of the Reformed religion – indeed, of any religion. He had himself solemnly sworn the Covenants, not once but twice, but it was only too evident that in doing so he had been motivated by self-interest and now that he was in a position of power he could show himself in his true colours. The enormity of Charles II's perjury has perhaps not always been recognised for what it was. Suffice it to quote from a declaration he signed at Dunfermline in August 1650, shortly after returning to Scotland to be crowned: "His Majesty having, upon the full persuasion of the justice and equity of all the heads and articles thereof, doth declare that he hath not sworn these Covenants, and entered into the oath of God with his people, upon any sinister intention and crooked design for attaining his own ends, but so far as human weakness will permit, in the truth and sincerity of his heart, and that he is firmly resolved in the Lord's strength to adhere thereto, and to prosecute to the utmost of his power all the ends thereof in his station and calling, really, constantly and sincerely, all the days of his life. In order to which, he doth in the first place profess and declare, that he will have no enemies but the enemies of the Covenant, and that he will have no friends but the friends of the Covenant."

Events were soon to reveal in all their starkness the falsehood and treachery behind these words. Charles had a bitter animosity towards the Reformed Church – an animosity bred of resentment at the way he felt it had so long dominated affairs in Scotland and had threatened the Divine Right which he and his forebears had claimed as theirs. There were plenty around him willing to do his bidding. Many of the influential men in the nation had chafed under the restrictions of the Covenant and were only too eager to cast off restraint and take their cue from their new sovereign. Sadly, some collaborators were to come from within the church itself – the most notable of them James Sharp, minister of Crail, who was to gain a reputation for infamy which is linked to his name to this day.

The new regime started as it meant to continue. A servile parliament declared the king sovereign in all ecclesiastical matters – meaning that he could order the affairs of the church in whatever manner he pleased. This of course had wide-reaching implications, for it meant that anyone disobeying or not conforming to whatever order the king set up for the church was defying royal authority, and so was guilty of treason. This was to be the handle by which those who could not in conscience submit to the new order were to be branded as traitors and rebels. Soon, the work of demolition gathered pace. At a stroke, all the Acts of the Covenanting

Parliaments were swept from the statute book. The Covenants themselves were declared illegal, and anyone renewing them was made subject to heavy penalties. This was an act of tremendous consequence, since it risked involving the whole nation in the guilt of perjury before God. But the Covenant-breakers went further. They struck at the heart of Presbyterianism itself. The great charter of Presbyterian church government – the Act of Parliament of 1592 – was rescinded and annulled. Legislation was passed, in an entirely arbitrary way, introducing an episcopal regime led by a hierarchy of archbishops and bishops. James Sharp was made the Primate of Scotland and appointed Archbishop of St Andrews. All ministers who refused to conform to the new order were expelled from their charges. Three of the main Covenanting leaders – the Marquis of Argyll, who had placed the crown on the king's head; James Guthrie, one of the most prominent of the ministers; and Archibald Johnston of Warriston, the clerk to the great Glasgow Assembly of 1638 – were arrested and executed.

In his last sermon in his church in Stirling, in August 1660, James Guthrie had spoken these prophetic words: "The Lord Jesus Christ is oft times, and ordinarily pleased after special manifestations of his power and glory in his church, and amongst his people, to exercise them with special pieces of trial, and troubles, and storms. After his doing of great work for their comfort, he is ordinarily pleased to raise great and dreadful storms and tempests, for their exercise and trial." He went on: "We of this church and nation would be looking for a storm: the Lord hath been graciously pleased to make glorious discoveries of his power and mercy in his word and works amongst us, now these many years, and even on that account we would be looking for a storm." And he counselled his hearers: "We would study to have our ship as light of all unnecessary burdens as we can; all things of the present world, all things beside God and our precious soul; we would have as little weight of these things on our spirits as we may, for they will sink our ship in a storm. We would be careful to make friendship with Jesus Christ that blessed pilot, that we may get him in the ship with us, for we are not able to steer our ship in a storm." Now the storm had come in earnest, and tragically Guthrie himself was to be one of the first victims of it.

With the leaders silenced, the Government no doubt expected the great majority of the ministers to conform. In the event, some 400 ministers – a third of the ministry of the church – refused to accept the new order of things and were driven out of their charges. It then became a question of how many of their congregations would follow them. Of course, many complied; but a substantial number did not. For them, as for their ministers, the years ahead were to be a time of testing; a test which was to become increasingly severe as the years passed and as the persecution grew in intensity and violence.

At first, the outed ministers, as they were called, held meetings privately in houses. However, it was not long before the numbers attending became too great for the houses to contain. So the people began to meet increasingly in the open, in the fields. These field-meetings, or conventicles as they came to be called, soon spread over the southern part of the country, starting in the south-west in Dumfries and Galloway, from there spreading to the Eastern Borders, Roxburgh and Berwickshire, then through East Lothian and across into Fife.

Of course, it was not long before the Government reacted. Fines were first imposed for non-attendance at the parish churches. Threats of imprisonment and banishment followed. Eventually, troops were sent to the disaffected areas to suppress the field-meetings by force of arms. Inevitably, these brought confrontation. It was just such a situation that led to the first serious clash of arms, in November 1666, when a party of men from Galloway, goaded beyond endurance by the oppressions of the troops, took captive the leader of the Government forces in the area and marched towards Edinburgh, where they had hopes of support. But these hopes were disappointed, and as they turned homewards they were attacked and routed on the slopes of the Pentlands by a Government force under General Dalyell. Bitter reprisals followed. The Pentland Rising, as it came to be called, was the first fruit of the Government's policy of repression; there were to be many more to come.

For the next number of years there was an uneasy peace, but as the field-meetings grew in strength the Government resorted to more and more desperate measures. Eventually preaching in the fields was made punishable by death, and hearers were threatened with imprisonment and other heavy penalties. These measures had little or no effect; the field-meetings grew in number, many thousands attending the preaching of the Word every Lord's Day, in disregard of all the penalties. As oppressive measures would not do, a new tactic was tried. In 1669, and again in 1672, the Government issued declarations of indulgence, allowing those ministers who had not given offence to the authorities to return to their charges, subject to strict terms and conditions. Sadly, this was to prove an apple of discord among many who had previously been united, and from the Government's point of view it achieved what all the oppressive measures up to then had failed to do – it divided the non-conforming ministers among themselves. For many men the prospect of being allowed once more to exercise their ministry was altogether too tempting, and numbers of them accepted the Government's terms. For others, however, to resume their ministry on terms dictated by the secular power was a betrayal of the very fundamentals of their belief. They could not, despite all the inducements, accept their liberty at the hands of a power which they saw as usurping the place of Christ. Rather than accept of such a favour, as it was held out to be, they chose to remain in the wilderness. It was a choice they made in full awareness of the consequences, for it was on these men, and their hearers, that the full fury of the Government was now directed. In 1674, and again in 1675, all the non-complying ministers were publicly declared traitors, and strict orders were issued forbidding anyone to give food, shelter or any assistance to them, at the highest peril. At the same time the penalties for attending the preaching of these men were made even more severe. Landowners were made responsible for their tenants, if they attended field-preaching, and in this and other ways the pressures on the people were made almost unendurable.

Towards the end of the 1670s the confrontation between the Government and the people gathered pace. In face of the continuing persecution a new party had grown up who believed in taking a more assertive line to defend themselves, and advocated carrying the battle to the authorities. It was by a group of such men that James Sharp, Primate of Scotland and the most hated figure of the time, was assassinated one Saturday morning in May 1679 on the road to St Andrews. This was the signal for a major conflagration. On 1st June 1679 John Graham of Claverhouse, who was later to gain notoriety as a persecutor, attacked a field-meeting at Drumclog in North Ayrshire but was repulsed with considerable loss. After this, the victors grouped together for their own defence. Alarmed at the turn of events the Government brought together a massive force which met a makeshift opposing army at Bothwell Bridge, near Hamilton, on 22nd June the same year. The result was only too predictable, but that the "Covenanted army", as they called themselves, lost the day was due not merely to the superiority of the enemy's numbers but to divisions in their own ranks. Sadly, the main cause of discord was what they should declare themselves to be witnessing against; and the main element in that discord was the Indulgence granted to ministers by the Government.

After the rout was over, the Government took severe reprisals; several of the leading figures were executed, some of them after torture, some were banished or imprisoned, some were in process of being transported to the Plantations when they were shipwrecked off the Orkneys and a great number of them perished. Others were marched to Edinburgh and confined for months in inhospitable conditions in an area of the Greyfriars Churchyard still known as the Covenanters' Prison. It is a telling commentary on the citizens of Edinburgh that as the prisoners were led into the town, through Corstorphine and the western outskirts, the roads were lined with people jeering at them and calling out "Where's your God?". It was a spirit which, sadly, was to characterise Scotland's capital city for the duration of the persecution.

Bothwell Bridge was a major setback for the non-conforming Presbyterians. After it, their cause was upheld by relatively few. But in the immediate aftermath of Bothwell there were two who were particularly prominent, and whose names left an indelible memory of faithfulness to later generations.

There was, first, Richard Cameron, the Lion of the Covenant, a man of dynamic character and passionate conviction. In his younger days, indeed, Cameron had no concern for the things of the Gospel. In worldly terms, he had made an early success of his life; a graduate of St Andrews University at the age of eighteen, and appointed schoolmaster of the royal burgh of Falkland in his early twenties, a position which not only gave him a comfortable living but guaranteed him standing and influence in the local community, where he had connections with some of the leading citizens. But Cameron gave all this up on hearing the despised and persecuted field-preachers, and soon became one of them himself. Cameron's career was one of tumult and turmoil, not only because of the persecution from the forces of authority, but also because of the controversies in which he found himself embroiled with his fellow-Presbyterians. Cameron's uncomplicated nature could not abide any suspicion of trimming or compromise.

Perhaps the most controversial action of his career was at Sanquhar on 22nd June 1680 – the first anniversary of Bothwell – when he and his adherents published a declaration formally disowning Charles II as king, and declaring war on him as a "tyrant and usurper". As a result, Cameron had to part company with many who had been his friends. But he earned for himself an enduring place as one who would never compromise the truth, however high the cost that had to be paid. His sermons, preached with intense energy and power, made a profound and enduring impression. And he himself paid the ultimate price when at Airdsmoss on 22nd July 1680 he was cut down by Government troops, fighting to the last for those religious and civil liberties he had championed with such fearlessness and courage.

Cameron's close co-adjutor was Donald Cargill, from Rattray in Perthshire, a man very different from Cameron in personality, a man naturally diffident and introspective, but yet one who evoked passionate loyalty from the people and who could say memorably as he went to his death on 27th July 1681 at the Mercat Cross of Edinburgh: "I have followed holiness; I have taught truth; and I have been most in the main things." Cargill's greatest victories were over his own temperament, as his retiring nature often shrank from the challenges he was called upon to face. He had for some years prior to the persecution held a settled charge, in the Barony Church of Glasgow, where he ministered from 1655 till his ejection in 1662. Even at his entry to the ministry there, he had had to be reminded forcefully of his duty. As a young probationer, he had gone to preach at the Barony on a Lord's Day, and had arranged to preach again on the following Thursday when it was the custom to give a weekday lecture. But after the Lord's Day services his heart so failed him with a sense of his own unfitness that he decided to cut short his stay and return home. He was on the point of leaving, with his horse ready, when a woman in the congregation confronted him: "Sir," she said, "you have promised to preach on Thursday; and have you appointed a meal to a poor starving people, and will you go away and not give it? The curse of God will go with you." One is reminded of the words Farel spoke to Calvin in calling him to his duty in Geneva. It was just the rebuke Cargill needed, and he knew it. Rather than return home, he cast himself on God's grace and urged the people to pray for him; and in due time he was successfully settled in the Barony where he pursued a much appreciated and faithful ministry.

There were to be many similar challenges ahead of him. But despite his natural diffidence, his assurance of the Divine direction enabled him to act resolutely and fearlessly when the occasion demanded. The crowning public act of his career was without doubt his excommunication of Charles II and his leading officers of state, at Torwood near Stirling on 12th September 1680 – an act which complemented Cameron's declaration at Sanquhar and which earned Cargill the bitter hostility of the authorities. But for Cargill the chief work of his life was that of the ministry. For him, it was ever a tremendous and weighty responsibility; and he trembled to think that he might not discharge it faithfully. But he came honourably through; and when after many wanderings and privations as a field-preacher he came to lay down his life his mind was at peace. "I go up this ladder," he said at his execution, "with less fear and perturbation of mind, than ever I entered a pulpit to preach."

By the time of Cargill's death, active resistance to the authorities was being carried on by relatively few. The severe repression after Bothwell had cowed the spirits of many; others had fled abroad; and for the majority of the non-complying Presbyterians the actions of disowning and excommunicating the king were more than they found themselves able to accept. Increasingly, the followers of Cameron and Cargill came to be seen as a faction, an aberration from the main body of Presbyterianism. But, for them, the issue was clear-cut. The king had declared himself supreme in all matters concerning the Church. Loyalty to Christ demanded that such a claim should be resisted. But the claim had gone further than that. The king's supremacy had been declared to be, in the words of an Act of 1669, "an inherent right to the Crown". Acknowledgement of the king's authority therefore carried with it acceptance of his authority over the Church. This was the essential point which Cameron and Cargill could not concede. In his last testimony, Cargill had made the issue crystal clear: "This is the magistracy that I have rejected, that was invested with Christ's power. And seeing that this power, taken from Christ, which is his glory, made the essential of the Crown, there is no distinction we can make that can free the conscience of the acknowledger from being a partaker of this sacri-legious robbing of God. And it is but to cheat our consciences to acknowledge the civil power; for it is not civil power only that is made of the essence of the Crown. And seeing they are so express, we ought to be plain; for otherwise it is to deny our testimony and consent to his robbery."

Cargill well knew that, after his death, there would be few who would continue his testimony. But in his last speech, he had affirmed his conviction that God would provide for the needs of the remnant. He was, as so often, speaking with prophetic insight. In the crowd around the scaffold, looking with awe on the scene before him, stood a young man of nineteen, newly graduated from university. He had never met Cargill nor Cameron, nor been associated actively with their cause. But the events of that day were to prove decisive in his life. That young man was James Renwick.

CHAPTER 2

PREPARATION FOR SERVICE

JAMES RENWICK was a child of the persecution. When he was born, in February 1662, the new order was already making itself felt. The liberties of the Church were being overthrown; the first of the new bishops had been consecrated; and the first two martyrs of the Covenant, Argyle and Guthrie, had been led to the scaffold. These events were to be the precursors of a long night of tribulation for the Reformed Church of Scotland. And yet, in God's Providence, in obscure enough circumstances, a young life was even then being prepared which would do signal service to the Church in the darkest hour of its tribulation, and be a light in the prevailing darkness.

James Renwick had already given his parents promise of his future. These hopes were reinforced as he grew into boyhood. By the age of six, he was able to read the Bible for himself. He impressed his parents by his ready obedience to them, and by his delight in secret prayer and in reading God's Word. At the same time, unusually for a child of his years, he came to entertain serious thoughts about the origins of life, and the purpose of all things. He was already, in his own way, a seeker after truth. His soul-searchings at this time are perhaps best recorded in the words of his contemporary, Alexander Shields, who had them from Renwick himself: "The Lord began to give some sproutings of gracious preparations, in his way of training him, in exercising him with doubts and debates, above childish apprehensions, about the maker of all things, and how all things were made, and for what end; and with strange suppositions of so many invisible worlds, above and beneath, with which he was transported into a maze of musing, and continued so exercised about the space of two years." Shields goes on: "By prayer and meditation on the history of the creation, in a manner and measure more than ordinary for a child, he came to quiet and composure, in believing that God made all things, and that all which he made was very good."

Yet this simple and settled assurance was not to last. In later childhood, he became assailed with doubts about the very existence of God himself. Yet so firm were his earlier convictions that he would not readily let them go. The result was an agonising inner conflict. To quote Shields again: "He relapsed into a deeper labyrinth of darkness about these foundation truths, and was so strongly assaulted with temptations of atheism, that being in the fields, and looking to the mountains, he said if these were all devouring furnaces of burning brimstone, he would be content to go through them, if so be that thereby he could be assured that there was a God." Eventually, after much soul-searching, Renwick was delivered from these temptations into greater light and liberty. "He emerged, through grace, into the sweet serenity of a settled persuasion of the being of God, and of his interest in him."

In planning their son's education, Andrew and Elizabeth Renwick were able to avail themselves of one of the enduring legacies of the Scottish Reformation. John Knox's *First Book of Discipline* of 1560 had famously recommended that "every several kirk have one schoolmaster appointed" though it was some time before this desirable objective could be put into effect. However, a significant step forward was taken in 1616 when the Scottish Privy Council declared it "necessary and expedient" that "in every parish of this kingdom, where convenient means may be had for entertaining a school, that a school shall be established, and a fit person appointed to teach the same, upon the expenses of the parishioners according to the quantity and quality of the parish".[1] This principle had been endorsed by an Act of the Scottish Parliament in 1633, which provided for a local "stent", or tax, to finance the schools and their teachers. It appears that a parish school was established in Glencairn fairly soon thereafter, for the then minister of the parish, William Brown, who died in November 1636, is recorded as having left in his will "for the maintenance of a school at the kirk, 100 merks".[2] At this school, which was around two miles from his home, it is likely that James Renwick received his first basic education. In the normal course, like other boys of the parish, he would have gone on to learn a trade, possibly the weaver's craft in apprenticeship to his father. Renwick indeed was ready to submit to this if it had been his parents' wish for him; but even at this early stage it had become obvious that his abilities lay in other directions. However, with their modest means,

Andrew and Elizabeth Renwick could not hope to give their son an academic education. But news of his abilities had spread; and such was the respect in which his parents were held that a number of influential friends stepped in to help. Who these were has not been recorded, but it is well known that several of the local landowners were sympathetic to the Presbyterian cause and indeed were to pay dearly for their allegiance as the persecution continued. These could well have been the benefactors to whom Renwick was indebted for the opportunities which now opened up to him. They were certainly to have no cause to regret their judgement.

The destination chosen for Renwick was Edinburgh, and there, probably at the age of twelve or thirteen, he went to complete his education. He may well have lodged with friends or relatives of his sponsors, but of this, as of his schooling in Edinburgh, there is no extant record. It is certainly possible that he attended the local High School, then the most prestigious of the Edinburgh schools, which was under the direct control of the Town Council. This supposition gains credibility from the fact that the head of the High School during this period was Alexander Heriot, a known sympathiser with the Presbyterian cause, who in 1679 was to be turned out of his office for refusing to conform to episcopacy. At all events Renwick acquitted himself with credit, and by 1677, when he was fifteen years of age, he was judged fit to enter university.[3] Once again he was to be providentially provided for; his original benefactors were augmented by others in Edinburgh itself, and ample funds for his university education were soon forthcoming. His father, meantime, had died on 1st February 1676, when Renwick was only thirteen, though he had lived to see two more children – both daughters – being born to himself and his wife.

It was apparently about this time that Renwick experienced another spiritual crisis in his life. His sponsors in Edinburgh, impressed with his promise and abilities, encouraged him to build up friendships with their sons, in the belief that these would benefit his studies and theirs. Renwick indeed found these friendships congenial, though for reasons he was later to regret. They drew him away from more serious matters, and enticed him, says Shields, "to spend too much of his time in playing at games and recreations". Although Renwick later severely rebuked himself for this phase of his life, there is nothing to suggest that the activities he engaged in were other than the most innocent kind. Archery, tennis and golf were among young men's favourite recreations at this time, and indeed were encouraged by the school and university authorities. But to Renwick, on sober reflection, these were vanities he could well have done without. They drove him to seek God in earnest repentance. Says Shields: "The Lord made his reflecting, at that time, on the vanities he was then too much led away with, a gracious mean of bringing him under the exercise of legal terrors; whence, through grace, he emerged into a more explicit confirmation of his interest in Christ." With this new resolve, then, he now prepared to enter university.

Edinburgh University (known to contemporaries as the "Town's College") had been founded by King James VI in 1582. Like the High School, it was under the control of the Town Council, who appointed the Principal and staff. Its curriculum was typical of the Scottish universities of the time, with a heavy emphasis on the classics and the liberal arts. The core of the teaching structure was a staff of four "regents" or titular professors of philosophy, who each took charge of a particular year's intake of students. This meant that for the entire four years of his course a student was under the teaching of the same regent, who instructed him across the whole range of the curriculum. As a member of the intake for 1677 Renwick's regent was James Pillans, a veteran and highly-respected member of the University's staff, who had been appointed as early as 1644.[4] The regent system necessarily helped to forge close bonds between teacher and student. Pillans was, of course, a conformist to the episcopal order, and he could not have held his position otherwise. But there is no evidence that he sought to impose those principles on his students; and to a young man on the threshold of life the influence of such a man as Pillans could not have been other than beneficial.

The university curriculum of the day had been fixed in the 1620s and had changed little in the intervening years. Students studied a variety of Greek and Roman authors, particularly the Greek poets and philosophers; works on logic, ethics and metaphysics, with a heavy emphasis on Aristotle; and a course on physics, including astronomy. The university regime was spartan by modern standards. Classes began at seven in the morning in winter and six in summer. For new students, a working knowledge of Latin was a *sine qua non,* as all lectures were delivered in that language and students were forbidden to speak anything else, either in or out of class. Lectures were delivered at dictation speed (and hence were known as "dictates") and after the delivery of each lecture students were closely questioned on what they had heard. A portion of class time each week was devoted to disputation, or public debate. Students were expected to attend church regularly, and were examined on what they heard, as well as being taught the Catechism. Outside the summer vacation (July-September) holidays were meagre, and extended usually to no more than a week in mid-winter.

This intensive regime posed a daunting challenge to any student, but there is nothing to suggest that Renwick was in any way overwhelmed by the pressures it brought on him. His stay at the university coincided with some tumultuous events in church and state, particularly the uprising which culminated at Bothwell and its aftermath. These events from time to time spilled over into university life. Probably the most notorious instance of this was towards the end of 1680 when a group of students, in protest against a visit to Scotland by the King's brother, the Duke of York, who was a professed Roman Catholic, staged a demonstration and publicly burned an effigy of the Pope. For this offence the Privy Council exacted heavy penalties; the university was closed for several weeks and the parents and guardians of all the students were required to give in bonds for their sons' good behaviour before classes were allowed to continue.

While these events were clearly a distraction to Renwick, they did not deflect him from his academic studies. By the summer of 1681 he was nearing the end of his university course. He had acquitted himself well, and could look forward to receiving the degree to which he was entitled. The crown of a student's career was the public "laureation" or graduation ceremony, which was an important event in the city's life and was attended by the Town Council and leading citizens. It was basically an occasion for the students to display their dialectical skills in the presence of those who could well influence their future careers. In preparation for the event, it was customary for the regent of the class to publish a list of "theses" or propositions, in the various disciplines taught, for the students to defend in public disputation. These theses were commonly dedicated to a person of prominence, and appended to them was a list of the names of the students who were being presented. For the laureation in July 1681, the usual procedure was followed. Pillans, as the regent for the year, published a list of eighty-six theses – covering logic, ethics, physics, metaphysics and astronomy – to which he appended the names of his students. These were 32 in number, arranged in order of merit; fourteenth on the list stood the name of James Renwick.

Renwick, other things being equal, would certainly have taken his place with his fellow-students at the laureation, and shared in the public ceremonial. Indeed, with twelve others, he had signed the graduation register formally applying for admission to the degree. But events were to dictate otherwise. The Duke of York, whose presence had provoked the students' demonstration the previous December, was back again in Edinburgh as the king's commissioner to the Scottish Parliament. The university authorities, anxious to make amends for the insult previously done to him, decided to frame the graduation theses in his honour. To do this, they prefaced the theses with an elaborate Latin dedication, in which they strove to excel themselves in a riot of fulsome flattery. "To the most resplendent prince," the dedication began, "his most illustrious and august royal highness James, Duke of Albany and York, the sole legitimate and most sure heir apparent of the four kingdoms of England, Scotland, Wales and Ireland; next after the glorious God, and his own brother the most serene king Charles the Second, the one, only and greatest hope of them all." The emphasis on the Duke's hereditary right was clearly prompted by the then current opposition to him in England, where an attempt had been made to introduce a Bill to Parliament barring his succession to the throne. The dedication went on to elaborate, again in the most fulsome terms, on the Divine right of the Duke's succession and, in the same strain, to equate his detractors to the heretics who had troubled the Christian Church in the early centuries.

Renwick, when he saw the terms of the dedication, was appalled. He had not yet come to the fuller understanding of the issues which he was later to have, but even now he had sufficient discernment to recognise what was being done in his name and that of his fellow-students. Despite the disadvantage it might well cause him, he decided to take no part in the public laureation. In so doing, under the procedure then in force, he was also declining to take the public Oath of Allegiance to the king, which had been decreed by the Privy Council for all students proceeding to degrees. However, while his actions may have incurred the displeasure of the university authorities, they could not seriously endanger his degree. By this time the public laureation had declined in importance, and greater store tended to be placed on a student's performance in the class examinations than on his disputing skills at the laureation. For this and other reasons, private degree ceremonies had become increasingly frequent. Renwick had clearly attained the academic standard demanded, and his degree could not reasonably be withheld from him. So it was that later that summer, he, with two fellow-students, was privately awarded the degree of Master of Arts by the university.[5]

The degree which Renwick now possessed was regarded as a passport to three professions – the law, education, and the church. There is nothing to suggest with any certainty which of these Renwick had in view. However, it is known that he embarked on further studies in Edinburgh following his graduation. It is also known that a considerable number of graduates followed the completion of their course with a period of study in divinity. This does not necessarily prove that Renwick was preparing for the ministry of the church, but it does at least suggest that he had in view a career for which a training in divinity would be a worthwhile preparation.[6]

If indeed Renwick's intention was towards the ministry, he could not of course proceed to the usual stages of licensing and ordination since that would have required him to conform to the episcopal order. However, it was well known that several of the ejected ministers had for some time been meeting in unofficial "field Presbyteries" which had licensed and ordained young men for the ministry. Indeed, Richard Cameron had been licensed in this way in 1678. There were at this time in Edinburgh large numbers of non-conformist ministers who could well have acted in the same capacity for Renwick, once they were satisfied with his credentials. Some of these had previously preached in the fields, but because of the stringency of the persecution after Bothwell they had felt constrained to lay this aside. Others were preaching under the indulgences granted by the Government; others again were meeting privately in houses. All of them to some extent had bowed to the exigencies of the times. There is evidence that Renwick was familiarly acquainted with these men and that he held them in the highest respect. He benefited also from their ministries, and he was a regular attender at the private meetings which they held in the houses of local sympathisers, and wherever else they could find opportunity. By this time, too, many of the non-conforming Presbyterians, in Edinburgh and other places, had come together in local "societies" for mutual edification, prayer and conference, in face of the difficulties of the times. Renwick joined himself to one of these, and enjoyed the fellowship it offered with others of like mind.

All in all, then, despite the pervasiveness of the persecution, Renwick's circumstances at this time were not unfavourable. And yet there was an inner dissatisfaction gnawing at him. He felt uneasily that the relative peace he and others enjoyed had been purchased at the cost of compromise, of surrender of the principles of the Reformation and Covenants. He could not but draw distinctions between his own relatively privileged circumstances in Edinburgh and the plight of those in other parts of the country who were now bereft of public preaching and who had, indeed, appealed unsuccessfully to the Edinburgh ministers to help them. Yet, as he looked around him, there seemed to be no-one to share his concern. Eventually, with some diffidence, he confided his unease to some of the ministers, but received no satisfaction. Indeed, far from acknowledging any fault, the ministers sought to justify their position from Scripture, quoting to him such texts as "The prudent shall keep silent in that time, for it is an evil time" (Amos 5:13). With this, Renwick could not rest satisfied. There was a distinction, he maintained, between the silence of submission to God's will and the silence of neglected duty. After all, Scripture had enjoined: "Ye that make mention of the Lord, keep not silence" (Isaiah 62:6). And that injunction, Renwick felt, was not limited to the public preaching of the Word; it required a public testimony against any dishonour done to Christ and his cause. The supreme dishonour was of course the action of the king and government in usurping authority over the church, from which all the other evils had flowed. And as Renwick came to see it, the responsibility for a testimony against these evils rested squarely with the ministers, who were those to whom the people looked for leadership. The ministers had not only failed to provide that lead; they were actually leading in the wrong direction. Renwick was particularly dismayed at the actions of some in openly counselling against resistance to authority and enjoining conformity to the established order. This took various forms, ranging from the signing of bonds for the peace to the payment of the Cess or tax raised for the declared purpose of suppressing the field-meetings.[7] These actions inevitably drove Renwick nearer to a breach with the ministers and the others whose fellowship he shared. And yet, he could not but hesitate. Bonds of friendship were not easily broken; and he was torn between his natural respect for the ministers and what he increasingly felt was his God-given duty.

It was just at this juncture that events happened which for ever resolved his doubts. From the time of Bothwell, and increasingly since Airdsmoss in July 1680, the streets of Edinburgh had witnessed groups of people – women as well as men – being led to execution as rebels and traitors because they dared to put the claims of Christ above the pretended authority of the king and government. Renwick could not but be impressed by the dignity with which these men and women suffered, and the firm resolution they showed in the face of death. As he well knew, these very people were stigmatised as extremists and fanatics by those with whom he was associated, and who indeed had sought to influence him against them. Yet, he found in their conduct a strong resonance with what he himself had come to believe. Their readiness to die for their principles gave these a credibility which nothing else could give. The conviction steadily grew on him that this despised remnant, and only they, were truly preserving the testimony of the covenanted Reformation. For Renwick, the decisive moment came on that July afternoon in 1681, when he saw Cargill and four others suffer at the Mercat Cross of Edinburgh. He was overwhelmed by the experience, and particularly by Cargill's last words on the scaffold. He could now no longer hesitate. From that moment, his allegiance was never in doubt. He knew instinctively that these people had what he was seeking, and that it was with them that his destiny lay. He resolved, God helping him, to be with them wherever their lot might be cast. It was a decision which was to cost him dear, to lead to many hardships and privations, and in the end to death itself; but it was a decision from which, once made, he never drew back.

CHAPTER 3

IN THE BONDS OF FELLOWSHIP

HAVING made his resolution, Renwick lost no time in carrying it out. He sought out diligently Cargill's followers in Edinburgh, who had formed themselves into their own distinctive society. In the words of Alexander Shields, who no doubt had them from Renwick himself: "He told them how much he was grieved to hear them disdainfully spoken of, and sorrowful for the want of that spirit wherewith they were acted; and he would think it a great ease to his mind to know and be engaged with a remnant that would singly prosecute and propagate the testimony against the corruptions of the time, to the succeeding generation; and would desire nothing more than to be helped to be serviceable to them." According to Shields, Renwick's words "refreshed them much" and there can be no doubt that he made an immediate, and favourable, impression. However, knowing his antecedents, and those with whom he had been connected, it would perhaps have been surprising if he had commanded universal acceptance. One or two, indeed, continued to harbour suspicions of him long after he had confirmed his credentials beyond any manner of doubt. But these were a tiny minority; and the great majority were at once convinced of his sincerity and received him warmly.

Having commended himself through his profession, Renwick was also keen to prove himself in a practical way. An opportunity soon offered. On 10th October 1681 five young men – Robert Garnock, David Farrie, Patrick Forman, James Stuart and Alexander Russell – were put to death at the Gallowlee, between Leith and Edinburgh, on the usual charge of denying the authority of the king, but in reality for asserting the Crown rights of Christ over his Church. Renwick was present at this execution, and had the distress of witnessing the indignities done to the men after death, their bodies being buried at the foot of the gallows and their heads put on public display on the Pleasance Port, one of the city gateways. To Renwick such treatment of men whom he considered martyrs for Christ was insufferable, and he urged that some decisive action be taken against it. His zeal communicated itself to the others. Under cover of night, at great personal risk, he and a few friends disinterred the bodies and reburied them in the West Churchyard. They also succeeded in taking down the heads, but since by this time the light of day had made it too dangerous to return to the churchyard they were obliged to find a resting-place for them in private ground at Lauriston, on the south side of the city, where they were reverently interred.[1]

There can be no doubt that Renwick's leadership in this exploit greatly enhanced his standing among his new-found friends. In other directions, too, Renwick began to give proof of his unmistakable commitment to their cause. It became clear to them that one of exceptional abilities had entered their ranks. To many of them his accession appeared a singular favour of Providence; and they were never to modify that opinion of him in all the vicissitudes that they were to share with him.

In the meantime, important events were taking place in the country. On 28th July 1681 – the very day after the execution of Cargill and the four others – the Duke of York, the king's brother and heir apparent, had opened a Parliament in Edinburgh. As a professed Roman Catholic, the Duke had faced strong opposition in England from Protestant interests keen to prevent his accession to the throne. The fact that he, of all others, should have been chosen to preside over the Scottish Parliament was regarded by many Presbyterians as an insult. This sense of grievance was compounded by the measures which the Parliament proceeded to enact. The most notorious of these was an "Act anent Religion and the Test", or what commonly became known as the Test Act, which was aimed at forcing all in positions of public trust to swear an oath of allegiance to the king. While this was ostensibly aimed at Roman Catholics ("Papists") as well as non-conforming Presbyterians ("fanatics") the Duke's sympathies ensured that its main thrust was directed against the non-conformists. The oath was framed in terms which made it impossible for any true-hearted Presbyterian to accept. Ironically, it began by professing adherence to "the true Protestant Religion contained in the Confession of Faith" by which it meant the old Scots Confession of 1560 – a contrived attempt to isolate Presbyterianism from the original principles of the Scottish Reformation. It then went on to adopt positions which were completely at odds with the old Confession. The Confession, in plain and distinct terms, had affirmed Christ to be the only Head of the Church. The oath, on the other hand, required acknowledgement of the king as "the only supreme governor of this realm, over all persons, and in all causes, as well ecclesiastical as civil". It declared it unlawful "to enter into covenants or leagues, or to convocate, convene, or assemble in any councils, conventions or assemblies, to treat, consult or determine, in any matter of state, civil or ecclesiastic, without his Majesty's special command, or express licence had thereto"; and "that there lies no obligation on me from the National Covenant, or the Solemn League and Covenant (so commonly called) or any other manner of way whatsoever, to endeavour any change or alteration in the Government, either in church or state, as it is now established by the laws of this kingdom". The oath-taker was thus being asked, as his price for swearing allegiance to the king, to deny the exclusive headship of Christ over the Church, and to disown the basic principles of Presbyterianism and the binding obligation of the Covenants. As events were to show, and as opponents of the oath had predicted, the oath was soon extended beyond those in positions of public trust and was made a general test of loyalty to the king and government. It came to be pressed increasingly on any – preachers and people – who were suspected of non-conformity, and so became an instrument for an even greater intensity of the persecution.

To many of the non-conforming Presbyterians, the passing of the Test Act was the final turn of the screw. For years, they had been denied the right to worship according to their conscience. They had endured a bitter and virulent persecution. They had witnessed the legacy of the Reformation and Covenants being systematically eroded and destroyed. They had seen the highest civil position in Scotland occupied by a professed Roman Catholic who had presided over a greater subversion of the Reformed religion than any that had gone before. Now, they were threatened with exclusion from society, banishment or imprisonment, unless they were prepared to perjure themselves by swearing an oath against their deepest convictions.

In the west and south of Scotland, where the non-conforming societies were particularly strong, the feeling grew that some kind of decisive action had to be taken if the Presbyterian cause was not to be wholly extirpated. But it was not immediately clear what that could be. The death of Cargill had left them leaderless and pastorless. Force of arms was out of the question. There was little that isolated groups of people, by themselves, could do. But there was strength in numbers. There were now some eighty societies scattered around the west and south, in town and country, comprising in all some 6,000 to 7,000 people. The conviction grew on many that if these resources could be pooled in some way, an effective testimony for the truth might still be made. Faced with the harsh reality of the Test Act, that conviction soon gathered momentum.

So it was that plans were matured, that autumn of 1681, to bring together all the societies in central and southern Scotland. The catalyst for this union was to be a General Meeting, which would convene periodically, and to which representatives from the various societies would be commissioned. The date chosen for the first General Meeting of the United Societies (as they were later to call themselves) was Wednesday 15th December, and the venue a bleak and desolate spot known as the Logan House, in the hills of south Lanarkshire, between Lesmahagow and Muirkirk. There, on the chosen date, around eighty men assembled. The circumstances that winter day could scarcely have been congenial, but there was a general spirit of enthusiasm, and many had travelled considerable distances to attend. They included a contingent from Edinburgh, among whom was James Renwick.

From the sequel, it is difficult to avoid the conclusion that Renwick was actively involved in the preparations for the meeting, and that it owed not a little to his own zeal and initiative. It would certainly not have been surprising if, knowing his abilities, the society in Edinburgh had entrusted him with much of the planning for it, and indeed had commended him to other societies. At all events the confidence of the societies in Renwick was clearly evident when at the start of the day's business he was appointed Clerk to the General Meeting.[2]

Renwick's appointment as Clerk was a striking demonstration of the impact he had made on the societies in the short space of time since he had joined them. Still only nineteen, he was now entrusted with a potentially vast range of administrative duties which would include not only the United Societies' minutes and internal documents but, increasingly, a range of correspondence with other bodies and churches. His appointment also meant that, as Clerk, he was thrust into the very centre of the societies' policy-making and decisions. It was an awesome responsibility, but in this as in other respects Renwick was never to disappoint the confidence the Societies placed in him.

The first business of the General Meeting – and indeed the immediate reason for calling it – was the drawing up of a testimony or declaration against the evils of the king and government, and particularly the proceedings of the late Parliament and the Test Act. This was entrusted to a committee. The draft of the declaration had been drawn up in advance, so that the committee's work was largely a formality. They duly reported their satisfaction with it to the General Meeting. The declaration was approved, and ordered to be publicly proclaimed at Lanark on 12th January 1682, with a force of horse and foot in attendance. Lanark may well have been chosen because it was there that in 1666, during the Pentland Rising, the west country army had renewed the Covenants; and the Societies may also have known that some of the local council were not unsympathetic and might not therefore offer opposition. Renwick was one of those chosen to be present – another testimony to the prominence he had now acquired.

At noon on 12th January, a day of tempestuous weather, a force of forty horse and twenty foot, Renwick among them, entered Lanark and carried out the commission of the General Meeting. They hammered a copy of the Declaration to the Mercat Cross, showing scant respect to the venerable structure as they did so, posted up copies in various parts of the town, and distributed others to curious bystanders. They then raided the local bailiff's house, from which they removed copies of the latest Acts of Parliament, carried them to the Cross, and made a bonfire of them before departing.[3]

The Lanark Declaration, as it came to be known, was the most uncompromising of the declarations of the period, but at the same time one of the most ably drafted. Its authors are unknown, but its vigorous rhetorical style bore the imprint of a skilled pen, and one apparently not unused to legal debate. It reviewed in stark terms the tyranny of the times, the oppression of conscience, and the denial of basic freedoms, and went on to vindicate the action of disowning the king at Sanquhar: "What shall the people do in such an extremity? Should they give their reason as men, their consciences as Christians, and resign their liberties, fortunes, religion, and their all to the inexorable obstinacy, incurable wilfulness, and malice of those who, in spite of God and man are resolved to make their own will the absolute and sovereign rule of their actions? Shall the end of government be lost, through the weakness, wickedness and tyranny of governors? Must the people, by an implicit submission and deplorable stupidity, destroy themselves, and betray their posterity, and become objects of reproach to the present generation, and pity and contempt to the future? Have they not in such an extremity, good ground to make use of that natural and radical power they have, to shake off that yoke, which neither we nor our forefathers were able to bear?"

The Declaration went on to vindicate the action at Sanquhar in the light of the actions of the king, and the terrible consequences which had followed: "Hath he not seated himself as supreme head over all persons, in all causes civil and ecclesiastic? – from whence have issued all the calamities, all the languishing sorrows and confounding shames and reproaches which in this day of blackness and darkness have invaded, involved, polluted and pestered the church and kingdom. And thus hath he approved himself to be the Defender of the Faith! Under which the godly party, true sons of the church and nation, have been groaning these twenty tears bygone, and in great numbers murdered and slain in the fields, led as lambs to the slaughter upon scaffolds, imprisoned and kept in irons, and with exquisite torture tormented, exiled, banished, and sold as slaves amongst savages . . . and as if it had not been enough to exercise such a tyrannical and arbitrary power himself, he by a late Parliament intends that his cruelty and tyranny should not die with himself, but that he shall in his time instate such a one (if not worse) as himself, contrary to all law, reason and religion, and in that Parliament to unhinge very Protestantism itself, by framing a Test such as no Protestant, how corrupt soever, can take . . . is it then any wonder, considering such dealings, and many thousands more, that true Scotsmen should after twenty years' tyranny break out at last, as we have done, and put in practice that power which God and nature hath given us and we have reserved to ourselves? Let none therefore object against the legality of what we have done, or are doing; for we offer to prove ourselves to have done nothing against our ancient laws, civil or ecclesiastic."

In these eloquent words the Declaration could claim to be speaking for many in the nation, even for those who did not share the principles of the Societies themselves. But the Declaration was not without its controversial side. This lay in its apparent assumption of representative, if not magisterial, power on the part of its authors. The Declaration took as its title *The Act and Apologetic Declaration of the True Presbyterians of the Church of Scotland*. It characterised those who had published the Sanquhar Declaration as "a general and unprelimited meeting of the estates and shires of Scotland" – a term redolent of legislative powers. It also appeared to assume to its own authors the status of lawmakers. "We here convened," it declared, "in our name and authority, ratify and approve what hath been done by the Rutherglen and Sanquhar declarations, and do by these presents rescind, annul and make void whatsoever hath been done by Charles Stuart or his accomplices in prejudice to our ancient laws and liberties, in all the several pretended and prelimited Parliaments and Conventions since the year 1660; and particularly the late Parliament holden at Edinburgh the 28th July 1681, by a Commissioner professedly Popish, and for villany exiled his native land, and all the Acts and laws there statute and enacted; as that abominable, ridiculous, unparalleled and soul-perjuring Test."[4]

There can be no doubt that in aspiring to such pretensions of authority the Declaration contained numerous hostages to fortune. In particular, it made it easy for opponents of the Societies – especially among the so-called moderate Presbyterians – to charge them with delusions of power, and with perversion of Presbyterian principles. Viewed in a clearer light, the claims were not without an element of the absurd. Here was a group of men, met occasionally on a moorside, purporting to enact and repeal laws affecting the destinies of church and state. Efforts were not, of course, lacking to excuse such pretensions on the ground of an excess of zeal, and to argue that at this early stage the Societies had not had time to deliberate fully on the issues. At the same time, there can be no doubt that the Declaration, as published, reflected the majority if not the collective mind of the Societies at this time. There is no evidence that Renwick, or indeed anyone else, sought to oppose the Declaration on these grounds. On mature reflection, Renwick was to decide that this element of the Declaration was indeed unwise, and he did not hesitate to say so in the clearest of terms.[5] However, there can be no doubt that the favourers of the Declaration took the assumption of magistracy extremely seriously. Renwick was to find out that when, in later years, he attempted to portray this as an aberration, he was seen by some as virtually a traitor to the foundation principles of the Societies. The controversy, indeed, was to rage long after his death.

It was scarcely surprising that the Declaration, and the events that accompanied it, should have caused a furore on the part of the government. The Privy Council, stung by this calculated affront to their authority, meditated revenge. As an immediate, public, demonstration they ordered the magistrates of Edinburgh to go in procession to the Mercat Cross on the next market day, 18th January, and there to have the Declaration solemnly burnt by the hand of the hangman. For good measure the Rutherglen and Sanquhar Declarations, the Queensferry Paper, and the Solemn League and Covenant of 1643, were ordered to be added to the conflagration, over which the compliant magistrates duly presided.[6]

The Privy Council then vented their wrath on the unfortunate town of Lanark, whom they clearly suspected of disloyalty. Although the "desperate and wicked vagabonds and villains" had stayed in the town for two hours, "yet", stormed the Privy Council, "during all this time none of the magistrates, councillors or inhabitants offered the least opposition, nor after these villains had departed did they follow after them to discover which way they went or give timeous notice thereof to the next magistrates or officers, neither have they since so much as informed themselves whence these persons came or whither they went, and so by their neglect of duty or supine negligence the said villains have been encouraged to enter the said burgh and thus affront his Majesty's authority". The punishment on the town was a fine of 6,000 merks, to be raised by a tax on the inhabitants in proportion to the value of their property. The town council protested strongly against the imposition, but in vain.

After the stirring events at Lanark, Renwick settled down to his more routine work as Clerk. There was ample for him to do, for the General Meeting had decided to circulate news and information among the Societies, as a basis for informed prayer, and as Clerk it is likely that Renwick had a leading part in preparing this. There were also preparations to be made for the next General Meeting. The first meeting had decided that such meetings should be held quarterly, and the next one had been appointed for Priesthill, a remote spot in the hills north of Muirkirk, on 15th March 1682. It was Renwick's duty to prepare the business for the meeting, and to issue notice of it to the constituent Societies. At a time when office aids were non-existent this involved much laborious effort; but Renwick clearly counted the work a privilege, and during his time as Clerk he diligently carried out all the duties that had been entrusted to him.

CHAPTER 4

THE CALL TO SERVICE

THE main business of the second General Meeting of the Societies was the appointment of a delegate, or commissioner, to represent their case to foreign churches. This had been debated at the first meeting, and there was general agreement that such an appointment was very desirable. At a time when the Societies were pastorless, and suffering severe persecution, it may have been thought strange that they should have placed such importance on sending a delegate overseas. However, it was entirely consistent that the Societies should have seen this as a priority. As heirs of the Scottish Reformation, they had a strong consciousness of the worldwide unity of the Church; and at a time when they could expect no sympathy at home, but rather continued obloquy and persecution, it was natural that they should look for support from the Church of Christ universal. The Reformed Church of Scotland had ever cherished this wider vision of the Church. Foreign churches might differ, indeed, in details of worship and administration from what the Church of Scotland practised, but where there was commitment to the Reformed Faith, and to Scriptural forms of church government, the Church had never had any hesitation in joining with such churches in fellowship. The Societies were now serving themselves heirs to the same tradition.

In considering where to send their delegate it was natural that the Societies should first look to those churches with which ties with Scotland had already been established. The most obvious candidates, and those geographically closest to Scotland, were the churches in Holland. There had been close links between the Scottish and Dutch churches since

Reformation days, and the first Church of Scotland congregation in Holland had been founded as early as 1607. There were now flourishing Scottish congregations in Rotterdam, Campvere, Amsterdam, Leyden, the Hague, Delft, Dordrecht and Middleburg. There was also a degree of mutual eligibility between the Dutch and Scottish churches. Scottish probationers were received by the Synods of the Dutch Church, and Dutch Presbyteries ordained or inducted ministers elected by the Scottish congregations in their bounds. It was thus altogether logical that the Societies should look to the churches in Holland as the first claimants on their sympathy.

There were other compelling reasons too. Over the years, the ecclesiastical links with Holland had been reinforced by more personal ones. In the periods of episcopal ascendancy in Scotland a number of Presbyterian ministers had sought refuge in Holland from persecution in their own country. In the years following the Restoration, this process had gathered pace. It had reached a climax in the aftermath of Bothwell, when many ministers and army leaders had fled to Holland to escape the wrath of the government. Among these refugees were several from the south-west, where some leading families had thrown in their lot with the persecuted church.

One particularly prominent family was the Gordons of Earlston, near New Galloway. The Gordons had long distinguished themselves as supporters of the Reformed Faith. A remote ancestor is said to have been influenced by the teachings of Wycliffe; and over the centuries the family had continued this worthy tradition. In the 1630s Alexander Gordon, and later his son and heir William Gordon, had been friends and correspondents of Samuel Rutherford. During the persecution Earlston had been a place of refuge for many, including some of the leading field-preachers. Richard Cameron and Donald Cargill frequently found sanctuary within its walls, and both of them wrote appreciatively of the fellowship they enjoyed with friends there.

Inevitably, the Gordons were to pay dearly for their loyalty. In June 1679 William Gordon, then aged 65, was on his way to Bothwell Bridge when he was challenged and summarily shot by Government troops. His son Alexander, who had preceded him, escaped very narrowly with his life, and later, for his own safety, joined the other Scottish exiles in Holland. In February 1680, in his absence, he was sentenced to death whenever captured, and his estates confiscated. Towards the end of 1681, at great personal risk, he returned home to visit his sick wife and stayed for a number of months in Scotland. It was at this juncture that the Societies were planning their first General Meeting. They saw in Alexander Gordon, or Earlston as he was commonly known, a notable recruit to their cause; and as the feeling grew that a representative should plead the Societies' case overseas, so the view crystallised that Earlston was the man. He was present at the first two General Meetings, and at the second, when the question of a delegate was again taken up, he was the unanimous choice of the meeting. Earlston accepted the appointment, and shortly thereafter he left for Newcastle to embark once again for Holland. There, some weeks later, he received a formal commission from the Societies, written in Latin by Renwick as Clerk and dated 10th April 1682.[1]

It had not emerged at this time what precisely the Societies expected of their commissioner. The commission itself was in fairly general terms and was mainly an appeal to foreign churches to accept the credentials of the Societies as contenders for the faith of the Reformation and so as just claimants on the sympathy of other Reformed churches. "If one member suffers," said the Commission, quoting the Apostle Paul, "other members suffer with it." However, from later events it appeared that Earlston saw himself as essentially a pleader for financial support for the Societies, and little more. He was later to say that he had found even this task hazardous and "little to be effectual". From all the evidence, it appears that the Societies were placing overmuch confidence in Earlston as an ambassador and that they were expecting of him more than he could, or was prepared to, deliver.

While the appointment of Earlston had been unanimous, it was soon to prove the cause of the first division in the ranks of the Societies. Some members, after the meeting, had second thoughts about the appointment and began to harbour doubts about Earlston's ability for the work entrusted to him. So strongly did this feeling grow that these members – based mainly in Glasgow – wrote to those in Edinburgh, asking that their dissent at the decision be recorded. This was refused, and some bitter exchanges followed. The next General Meeting, at Talla Lin in Peebles-shire on 15th June, was dominated by the dispute on this issue. The majority, of whom Renwick formed part, contended that the appointment of Earlston had been agreed at the previous meeting in due form, and that to challenge it now was to subvert the whole basis of proper procedure.

The majority had their way, and the dissenters were excluded from the meeting. Another note of contention was introduced when it emerged that one of the members had had his child baptised by Alexander Peden, a veteran field-preacher who was continuing to preach in defiance of the authorities but had not aligned himself with the Societies. After some acrimonious debate, the member was suspended until Peden's position had been clarified to the Societies' satisfaction. A still further note of discord was introduced by James Russel, a representative from Fife, who three years earlier had been one of the principal actors in the killing of James Sharp. Russel, described in the Societies' records as "a man of a hot and fiery spirit" queried the right of anyone to sit in the meeting who condoned the payment of customs at ports and bridges, on the ground that this was helping to sustain the persecuting authorities. Again the majority, Renwick among them, resisted this move. It was one thing, they contended, for the Societies to refuse to pay the Cess which had been specifically levied to suppress the field-meetings; it was quite another to refuse to pay well-established tolls which were part of the normal administration of the country.

The onset of these difficulties was a keen disappointment to Renwick, and as Clerk to the General Meeting he set himself to compose them as best he could. On the way from the meeting he spoke with Russel and attempted to find some common ground. Both of them were opposed to the stance which the dissenters from Earlston's appointment had taken, and it was agreed that they would each prepare papers answering the dissenters' arguments at the next meeting. Renwick also made clear to Russel that while he shared his dislike of paying dues to a tyrannical government, he could not in conscience justify making this a ground of separation between brethren. Russel heard Renwick civilly enough, but without in any way changing his position.

The next General Meeting, on 11th August, brought matters to a head. Renwick's and Russel's papers in answer to the dissenters were read, and taken up by the meeting. Renwick, in his paper, clearly spelt out the wrong done by the dissenters but did so in a charitable and gracious way which was clearly designed to encourage them back into the fold. Russel, on the other hand, denounced them as virtual traitors to the cause, and expressed himself in a way which left little hope of compromise. Renwick made it clear that while he agreed with the substance of Russel's argument he could not support the manner in which it was expressed. The meeting, almost to a man, agreed with him. Russel then tried to reintroduce the subject of payment of customs. Again, the meeting supported Renwick in rejecting this. Russel, seeing himself isolated, then handed in a formal Protestation, to which, for good measure, he added a paper demanding reform of the names of months and days of the week.[2] He then left the meeting, never to return. Russel was to prove an inveterate enemy to the Societies, and to Renwick in particular, for the rest of his life. He was ably supported by his friend and co-adjutor, Patrick Grant, who was to remain a thorn in the Societies' side long after Russel's death and who, far on into the next century, was still denouncing the Societies as traitors to the principles they originally professed.

In some ways it is difficult to understand why these apparently secondary issues should have provoked such bitter opposition as Russel and Grant were later to show. The explanation can perhaps lie in the fact that they detected in the Societies' attitude a shift from the position on magistracy, or representative power, which the Societies had taken at the time of the Lanark declaration, and which indeed the Societies were later to make more explicit. That was certainly the ground on which Grant, in particular, was later to argue in the numerous pamphlets he published against the Societies and their practices.

With Russel gone, a major cause of dissension within the Societies had been removed. A new climate of reconciliation asserted itself. The member suspended for receiving baptism from Peden was reinstated. Efforts then moved to reconcile those who had dissented over the appointment of Earlston. The newly-appointed commissioner had now reached Holland and had written to the Societies assuring them of his commitment to their interests. On hearing this letter read, the dissenters acknowledged their fault in opposing his appointment and they too were reinstated. As a token of the new-found harmony, it was agreed on both sides that all the papers relating to the incident should be destroyed. The Societies were now able to move forward with a new resolution.

Renwick, for his part, had come out of the incident with a good deal of credit. His attitude of reasoned argument, coupled with firmness, had helped to save the Societies from a potentially damaging situation. It was a combination which was to serve him well throughout his life. Russel, certainly, had still to be reckoned with, and was yet to do him a good deal of harm; but Renwick's reputation among the Societies had never been higher. And this was to stand him in good stead in some critical decisions which lay immediately ahead.

Earlston, meantime, was reflecting on how he might best discharge the Societies' commission. The commission itself was in broad terms – basically empowering him to represent the Societies' case to foreign churches – but it is clear from later events that some specific avenues of approach had been discussed with Earlston before his departure. One of these was the possibility of stimulating the interest of the Dutch churches in sponsoring young men from the Societies who might be trained at Dutch universities for the work of the ministry in Scotland. This idea at first was only speculative, and there is no record of how it originated. Nor is there any indication that Earlston himself, even if he approved the idea, knew how to go about implementing it, or that he had the necessary contacts within the Dutch churches to take it forward. However, by what can only be seen as the overruling hand of Providence, much of this work had already been done. And the preparation for it, interestingly enough, lay largely in Earlston's own family background.

Some six years before, in November 1676, Earlston had married Janet Hamilton, of the family of Hamilton of Preston in East Lothian. Janet Hamilton came from an aristocratic family who, like her husband's, had long distinguished themselves in the Presbyterian interest. Her older brother Sir William Hamilton, who was created a Baronet in 1673, had already been fined for non-conformity. Another brother, Robert Hamilton, had been for a number of years a profligate, but he had undergone a life-changing experience and had attached himself with particular vigour to the cause of the persecuted church. His background and personality brought him to particular prominence in the years leading up to Bothwell, and he played a foremost part in the major events of the time. He was on intimate terms with the leading field-preachers, including Cameron and Cargill; he acted as self-appointed bodyguard to Cameron in his various preaching tours in the south and west; and, though he had no military experience, he assumed the role of commander of the forces which opposed the government at Drumclog and Bothwell Bridge.

Robert Hamilton was a man of strong personality and convictions, and one who provoked equally strong reactions from others. He attracted many enemies. To this day his reputation is typified in the words of the family history, *The House of Hamilton,* as that of "a narrow-minded and intolerant bigot".[3] Certainly Hamilton had his idiosyncrasies. His inclination to demonstrate against any practices or beliefs of which he disapproved was a cause of particular irritation to many. His management of affairs was often amateurish and naïve and his bombastic style and behaviour did little to attract sympathisers. For the few however who penetrated the hard exterior and got to know the man more intimately, he could prove a valuable and devoted friend. Among those, pre-eminently, was to be James Renwick, who was to share Hamilton's friendship and confidence in a way which few others were ever to achieve.

After Bothwell Robert Hamilton was keenly sought for by the government and fled to Holland, where he settled initially with the other exiles in Rotterdam. Inevitably, his temperament soon got him into trouble. The ethos of the Scottish congregation in Rotterdam did not suit his strict principles, and he found it necessary on several occasions to testify against it. The particular object of his displeasure was the minister of the Rotterdam congregation, Robert Fleming, who, though not having accepted the indulgence himself, had in various writings pleaded for an accommodation with the indulged ministers. The exiled Scottish minister, Robert McWard, who had ordained Richard Cameron in the summer of 1680, regularly heard Fleming and saw no reason to withdraw from him, though trying by friendly argument to make him change his view. On this account McWard himself was ostracised by Hamilton and by some others.

This dispute caused McWard a good deal of distress, and may well have hastened his death in May 1681. For these and other reasons Hamilton became decidedly unpopular among the Scottish exiles. Eventually realising that he was looked on generally as a "pest" – the term is his own – he decided, later in 1681, to leave Holland for good and move further into the Continent. His original intention was to go to Hungary, where he planned to align himself with the then persecuted supporters of the Protestant interest. He was dissuaded however from this by Herman Witsius, the great theologian of the Covenants, whom he had gone to see at Utrecht and with whom he was on friendly terms. He then, not knowing where to turn, made the matter one of earnest prayer, when, according to his own account, it was infallibly borne in upon him that he should not leave Holland but rather go to the northern province of Friesland, where there was a particular work for him to do. On consulting with some friends he received confirmation of this choice; and Witsius, when he consulted him again, not only approved it but gave him a letter of introduction to a Friesland minister, William Brakel, of Leeuwarden, who was a noted contender for the spiritual independence of the church.

To Friesland, then, Hamilton went, and duly presented himself to Brakel. As Brakel was later to confide to him, he had initially not known how to react to Hamilton and had sought guidance in prayer, when he had received the strong impression that he should give him every recognition and encouragement. Accordingly, in Hamilton's words, Brakel showed "unspeakable kindness" to him, entertained him in his own house for several weeks, and gave him a most sympathetic hearing when he spoke of the plight of the persecuted church in Scotland. Brakel, indeed, was so impressed by what Hamilton told him that he wrote directly to the Societies expressing his strong support and concern at their plight and pledging himself to do all in his power to help them. He also gathered together a group of influential church leaders and ministers, whom he influenced strongly on the Societies' behalf. Indeed, so impressed were Brakel and his friends with the Societies' cause that they honoured Hamilton as the Societies' representative – a role he did not altogether decline – and even provided him with suitable clothes and other necessaries.

Given this encouragement, Hamilton felt emboldened to broach a subject which he had been long meditating over, but had not previously mentioned openly – the possibility of having young men from the Societies trained for the ministry in Holland. To his delight it received a ready response; and, after further explanation, Brakel and his friends offered not only to arrange for the students' training, but to help with the costs themselves. Hamilton had had no knowledge that the Societies had been thinking on similar lines; and, for some time, as the plans were matured further, he kept the information to himself. He was just about to share it with the Societies when Earlston, after arriving in Holland with his commission, told him of the Societies' thoughts on the same matter. Hamilton was impressed not only with the concurrence of the Societies' thinking with his own, but most of all with what he saw as the hand of Providence. He wrote to the Societies on 22nd August: "Amongst many other overtures my brother showed me from you, that of having our youth educated for a new nursery of ministers did not a little astonish me, it being of a long time both my great work and exercise here, and I proposed it, and the Lord had made it acceptable at the very first moving of it."

The news of what had been no more than a speculative idea left the Societies equally surprised. To some extent, indeed, they appear to have been caught unprepared. Hamilton, in his letter, wrote that "four or five" students would be expected at first, and that these "are to stay by Mr Brakel, or else in some college here in the winter, and then receive ordination in the spring". This was confirmed shortly afterwards by Earlston, who wrote "of a door opened abroad for teaching young men at a university", for which he gave the credit to Brakel, and asked that "there might be some young men presently sent over, in order to the following of their studies there, where afterward they might come to get the benefit of ordination, when fit for the same".

Clearly, there was little time to lose. The next General Meeting was not due until 2nd November, but was hastily brought forward to 11th October, when it convened in Edinburgh. The names of six young men were before the meeting, of whom it was agreed that four would be selected for sending to Holland. They were James Renwick; John Flint; William Boyd; John Smith; William Hardie; and John Nisbet.[4] Of these, all but Boyd and Nisbet were present. Prayer was offered for guidance, and each of the young men was invited to make a personal statement to the meeting. A hat was then produced, and six slips of paper put into it, four being numbered, and the rest blanks. The numbered papers were for those to go abroad; the blanks for those to remain. Each of the young men was then asked to draw out a slip of paper for himself, the two absentees being represented by members of the meeting. Renwick, when his turn came, drew one of the numbered papers out of the hat. The successful candidates with him were Flint, Boyd and Nisbet, with Hardie and Smith drawing the blanks. In this apparently capricious way the preaching career of James Renwick was launched on its course. But the assembled commissioners could, and no doubt did, reflect on the words of Proverbs: "The lot is cast into the lap; but the whole disposing thereof is of the Lord."

CHAPTER 5

ORDINATION

THE General Meeting had good cause to be satisfied with its work. But, unknown to them, that work was not yet over. The meeting was about to disperse, and the commissioners to depart to their homes, when a messenger unexpectedly arrived with a letter. It was from Earlston in Holland, and its contents threw the meeting into consternation. Their worst fears had proved true. Russel and Grant had written to Earlston complaining about the conduct of the Societies' meetings, and portraying these in the most unfavourable light. Naturally enough, Earlston sought an explanation. The Societies' indignation at Russel and Grant was matched by a desire to justify themselves to their Commissioner. It had been a major plank of their strategy to send faithful information of themselves to foreign churches; and it was essential to act quickly if that information was not to be poisoned at its source.

The meeting decided on urgent and effective action. Written assurances would not be enough; a face-to-face contact was necessary, through a trusted representative. The meeting did not take long to decide who that should be. Their choice fell on James Renwick. In an immediate reply to Earlston, to be carried by Renwick, the Societies wrote: "Your letter came unto our hands, which unto us was both grieving and astonishing; we therefore have found it to be indispensably our duty to concredit and send the bearer hereof, Mr James Renwick, who was present with us at all our conventions since we parted with you . . . referring you to our acts enacted at all our conventions, and to his information according thereunto; and requiring that you would not give ear to the base calumnies and misinformations of any person or persons . . . testifying our adherence to all duties, and our separation from all the sins which our faithful worthies Mr Donald Cargill and Mr Richard Cameron taught to be grounds of separation, according as the bearer hereof can and will testify; we likewise leaving you to his information in several particulars which we cannot now here insert." The letter was signed by George Hill, who acted as praeses of the meeting, and by twenty other members.

Renwick had not expected to leave for Holland until the second week of November. As it was, however, he now had to sail more or less immediately, and with little preparation for his journey. It was a challenging role for a young man of barely twenty, who before this had probably not been outside his native Scotland. But Renwick was very conscious of the trust placed in him, and he gave himself willingly to fulfil it. Details of his journey have not survived, but he appears to have left for Holland soon after the Edinburgh meeting and to have arrived in Rotterdam before the end of October. He went immediately to Leeuwarden, where he met Earlston and his brother-in-law Hamilton. His mission appears to have been altogether successful. Earlston was reassured, and agreed to continue to act for the Societies' interests. Hamilton for his part took an immediate liking to Renwick. "I found my heart greatly tied to him" he was to write later to the Societies. It was the beginning of a friendship which was to endure for the rest of Renwick's life.

In discussing with Earlston and Hamilton, and seeking to vindicate the Societies' position, Renwick had perforce to disclose various matters of business which had been before the General Meetings. In doing so, Renwick was well aware that he and others had taken an oath not to divulge any of the Societies' business to others except under a solemn promise that they in turn would not disclose it to third parties. He apparently judged that it was no breach of this oath to disclose such of the Societies' affairs to Earlston and Hamilton as would vindicate them from Russel's aspersions, without formally seeking an assurance that they would not pass it on. However, on coming to know of this, Russel and Grant accused Renwick of perjury, maintaining that he had revealed what he had solemnly sworn to keep secret. There was nothing to suggest that Renwick had passed on anything of consequence, and he clearly regarded Earlston and Hamilton as so closely involved with the Societies that he could not reasonably impose the pledge of secrecy upon them. In due course the Societies were to see the oath as counter-productive, and were formally to abolish it. But, for the moment, Russel and Grant had been given another opportunity against Renwick; and they were to exploit it to the full.

Renwick might have expected that, having satisfied Earlston and Hamilton, he could then remain in Holland to prosecute his studies; but that did not prove possible. In the haste of his departure there had not been time to make all the arrangements necessary, particularly to obtain the testimonial which was essential for his ordination and to collect the money for his upkeep. Back, therefore, to Scotland he had to come. After a frustrating delay at Rotterdam, where his ship lay for several days becalmed, he eventually set sail on 24th November, arriving in Scotland ten days later. Two of his fellow-students, Flint and Boyd, had meantime left for Holland, where they arrived on 17th December. It was indeed a strange providence which had kept Renwick from accompanying the two others on the ship. Renwick, who was always one to look for meanings in providences, remarked to a friend that as they did not depart together, he doubted if they would come home together. They were words which were destined to prove prophetic.

His testimonial and other matters attended to, Renwick left once again for Holland around mid-December. He arrived probably just before the end of the year, when he joined his two friends at Groningen. The university there was relatively new, having been founded only in 1614, but it had already attracted some of the most distinguished theological professors in Europe. Over the next four months Renwick and his colleagues were to sit at the feet of these men, studying doctrinal and practical theology and applying themselves to the original languages of Scripture.

The academic life was not of course new to Renwick, but the circumstances now were very different from his previous experience in Edinburgh. Then, he was apparently pursuing his studies with no particular goal in view. Now, his call to the ministry was an everpresent reality, and the plight of the remnant in Scotland lay heavy on his heart. His letters at this time suggest almost a feeling of frustration that his studies should be diverting his thoughts from what he saw as the overwhelming concern of his life. "When I set about my ordinary studies," he wrote, "I find my mind taken off other things that ought to lie weighty upon me. . . . I am at present in a confused, anxious, and disconsolate condition. . . . O let us earnestly labour to get a sympathising frame of spirit kept up, with that poor, afflicted, scattered, and broken remnant in Scotland; for I observe this palpably, that I am never in any sort of a good frame but when they are lying near my heart, and when their afflictions are touching me. O mind sweet Scotland . . . cry and wrestle with the Lord that he would preserve a remnant." It was scarcely surprising that one of his colleagues should have noted, and indeed commented critically upon, the fact that he appeared to read little, but spent most of his time in prayer and meditation. At the same time it is clear that his studies were by no means neglected, and that he pursued them with a conscientiousness that was ever typical of him. "The three students chosen by you to the pastoral office are busy at their studies," wrote William Brakel to the Societies on 19th February; "by God's grace we hope you shall see them the next year, and hear them preaching."

That Brakel should have assumed a further year before Renwick and the others could return to Scotland is not surprising. After all, they had been at their studies for barely two months. Even with the concessions which their circumstances dictated, it would have been unprecedented for the Church in Holland to find them qualified for the ministry after so short a period. But events were to show that, in one case – and one alone – the Church could be persuaded to set aside its ordinary procedures and to agree to an arrangement which was wholly exceptional. The case was that of James Renwick.

That Renwick came to be treated exceptionally from the rest – and indeed from any other by the Church in Holland – was undoubtedly due to the influence of one man, Robert Hamilton. Hamilton had been much impressed by Renwick when he met him briefly the previous autumn, and when Renwick returned to Holland to pursue his studies he had taken pains to get to know him more intimately. "I was very inquisitive," he wrote later, "to know of two things from him; first, how it was betwixt him and the Lord, as to his state and interest, and second, as to his inward encouragement and call from the Lord as to his undertaking in that great work of the ministry. To both which I had great satisfaction from him; as also, of his lively uptakings of the Lord's way with his church and people in this day; all which were engaging to me."

After Renwick went to Groningen he kept up a regular correspondence with Hamilton and his sister Jean, who continued at Leeuwarden. A letter Renwick wrote on 22nd February 1683 made a particularly profound impression on Hamilton. In it, Renwick told of his continued inner conflicts over the competing claims of his studies and his devotional life, and his consciousness of the condition of the remnant in Scotland. "Yet," he wrote, "the Lord makes me even feed many times upon this, and that even with great joy, that as he is dealing with his church this day, so is he dealing with me; yea I see not one circumstance in the one but I also see it in the other; yea, and is not this great matter of joy? The Lord forbid that I should desire to be otherwise dealt with than his church is." He went on: "There are some things good in themselves, and good when made right use of; but to me they are as Saul's armour to David. I can put them on, but I cannot walk with them; and I cannot say but I could put them on, unless I should lie of the Lord, who, blessed be his name, hath given me, in some measure, a disposition."

These words intrigued Hamilton. Could Renwick be hinting that, even now, he was ready for some major undertaking, one which Hamilton himself would have a hand in? A few days later, Hamilton's sister Jean showed him a letter which Renwick had written to her some time earlier. In this, Renwick had unburdened himself of his thoughts on his own future and the condition of the church in Scotland. "O that he that hitherto hath condescended would condescend to let me know what course he would have me to take, and make me willing to follow the same. . . . There are many things that are very discouraging; but there is comfort, Jesus Christ is a king, and seeing he is a king, he will have subjects; yea, he shall reign until he put all his enemies under his feet. Shall not the pleasure of the Lord prosper in his hand? He will see of the travail of his soul and shall be satisfied. And may not our souls feed upon the ravishing thoughts of the pureness of that church which he will have in Scotland?"

Hamilton was impressed not only by Renwick's concern for the remnant in Scotland, but by his obvious spiritual maturity and understanding. He had replied promptly to Renwick's first letter, and he now took upon himself to reply to Renwick's letter to his sister, though without taking up the question that by now lay heavy on his mind. However, the issue was not to be long delayed. Writing later, Hamilton records: "The evening after, going out to walk, I was strongly overpowered with the impression that Mr Renwick was presently to be ordained, and that I must lay out myself therein; and, as I thought, got to great certainty, that whatever difficulties should be in the way, they should be removed." The idea that a divinity student of barely two months' standing should be put forward for ordination was indeed so novel that Hamilton might well have wondered whether he would be taken seriously in broaching it. So sure however was he that he determined to lose no time in putting it to his trusted guide, William Brakel. Brakel's response was all that Hamilton could have wished. "He no sooner heard of it," Hamilton wrote later, "but he was as one out of himself, with the great satisfaction and joy he had in it; which helped to my strengthening." Once again, Brakel showed himself a true friend. He agreed to write personally to Renwick, supporting the proposition that Hamilton now felt ready to put to him.

Renwick received both letters one day in early March. The effect on him at first was overwhelming. Replying to Hamilton, he wrote: "I received your letter with worthy Mr Brakel's, which were very surprising to me . . . the sense of the work, together with my own unfitness, came so upon my spirit, that I began to give place to this resolution, that I would desire some more time . . . upon the other hand, when I considered the afflicted and affecting case of the remnant, I say, when I considered how the glorious truths of God were wronged by cruelty against them, I thought it would be an honourable thing, the Lord calling me thereto and fitting me therefor, if it were but to give one public testimony against the same. . . . But oh a weighty work indeed! Who is fit for opening up the mysteries of salvation? Who is fit for declaring our sweet Lord Jesus Christ prophet, priest and king in Zion? Who is fit for dispensing those glorious benefits of the Covenant of Redemption? O who is sufficient for these things? And why is he calling poor unworthy nothing me out to such a great and glorious work? I think that he is saying that the excellency of the power may be of himself, and not of me. So, having the mouth of all objection stopped, I offer myself in all trembling, fear and humility; yet having great reason to believe in him for all things, though I be altogether unfit. . . . O Sir, desire all to wrestle with the Lord, that he would carry on his own work, and get glory to himself in fitting instruments, and in making his people a zealous people, a holy people, a self-denied people."

This "very satisfying and refreshing letter", as Hamilton termed it, was followed by two others which he had certainly not expected. Unknown to him, Renwick had shown his letter to Flint and Boyd, who, as Hamilton later wrote, "on what grounds I know not, resolved to concern themselves alike in the affair as if the letter had been written to all of them". So it was that Hamilton, to his embarrassment, found himself with two unsolicited aspirants for ordination. "This," he noted, "was both surprising and weighty to me, on many accounts; for the Lord, from my very first hearing of them named, led me in a quite contrary way as to them than to the other." Sadly, this was to be the beginning of a long train of troubles for Hamilton, troubles that were soon to extend to Renwick himself.

For the moment, however, it had to be assumed that all three students would go forward together. This was reflected in a letter Brakel wrote to the Societies on 14th March. "The omnipotent God," he wrote, "has so touched the hearts of those three students, that they being moved with love to the Church of Scotland, now standing in need of pastors, have resolved presently to pass their trials, and to seek their mission and confirmation from a certain Presbytery, and without delay to return to Scotland, so that I hope after one or two months you shall see them and hear them preaching."

Hamilton of course was determined that Renwick, and he alone, should go forward; and he now had to bend his efforts as much to dissuade the other two from proceeding as to remove all the possible obstacles from the way for Renwick. He decided to apply himself first to Boyd, whom he saw as the more amenable of the two; and without undue difficulty got him won over. Boyd, indeed, appears to have cherished his own doubts about his suitability for ordination at such an early stage, and Hamilton's approach merely served to reinforce his misgivings. From that point therefore only Flint and Renwick were in view for ordination.

Brakel had promised to do all in his power to assist the ordination, and he proved as good as his word. His reputation was high among his fellow-ministers. But even then the way was by no means easy. Brakel's first thought was that the ordination might be carried out by the Classis or Presbytery of Emden, now a part of Germany but then a town and district in Northern Holland. However, Hamilton had doubts about the doctrinal soundness of the ministers of Emden, suspecting that one of the leading ministers had embraced Cocceian principles, then in vogue, about the relevance of the fourth commandment, and distrusting also their position on the church's spiritual independence of the state. He demurred therefore to agree to Brakel's proposal. Brakel was none too happy, feeling that Hamilton was being over-sensitive, but eventually Hamilton persuaded him to appeal to the Presbytery of Groningen, whom Hamilton considered more orthodox, to carry out the ordination. The ministers there however were reluctant, and suggested that the Professors at the University, where Renwick and the others were studying, might be asked instead. Hamilton duly approached the Professors, only to find that one of them was a professed Cocceian. Brakel, when told of this, reverted to his preference for Emden. Hamilton however discovered that the Presbytery of Emden would not confer ordination without a testimonial from all the Professors at Groningen, including the one with Cocceian principles; and this too he found unacceptable.

In this impasse, with his relations with Brakel becoming increasingly strained, Hamilton decided to appeal to Johannes à Marck, Renwick's divinity and church history professor at Groningen. The move proved providential. À Marck was sympathetic, and undertook to use his influence with the local Presbytery. First, however, he would need testimonials from Scotland for each of the students. Hamilton happened to have Renwick's with him, and produced it. The professor was willing to accept it, but a local minister who was with him objected that it was not in proper form to put before the Presbytery. Hamilton thereupon made an impassioned appeal, pointing out the privations the Societies were under, and that it could scarcely be expected that they could produce anything more sophisticated. The professor supported him, and the minister gave way. Together, they agreed to put Renwick's case to the Presbytery of Groningen.

Hamilton had good reason to be satisfied with the outcome of the interview. But there still remained a delicate task before him. He had effectively cleared the way for Renwick; now, however, he had to reckon with Flint. The task of dissuading Boyd had proved relatively easy, but Flint, who was a strong-willed young man, was to prove an entirely different proposition. Though Hamilton used all his powers of persuasion, Flint was unmoved. "I told him," wrote Hamilton later, "I could give him no encouragement to it; but on the contrary, from the first time that I had seen him and Mr Boyd, I was made to tremble at their coming over upon such a design. As also, that the letter that Mr Brakel and I wrote to Mr Renwick was no way designed for him. I again begged him, as he loved his own soul, that he would not venture on such a weighty work rashly. Notwithstanding of all, he said he would go forward; so I, not without great heaviness of mind, was forced to countenance him." There appeared to be nothing for it, if Hamilton was not to lose face with the Dutch, but that Flint should be ordained along with Renwick; and so Hamilton, much against his will, had to go along with that presumption for the time. He wrote to à Marck, who gave him a joint testimonial for Renwick and Flint, and to Brakel, who supplied individual testimonials for each of them.

On 19th April the Presbytery met, with Hamilton, Renwick and Flint in attendance, and the two students formally applied for ordination. Their testimonials were produced and sustained. Each was asked to speak and to give an account of himself. Renwick contented himself with a brief, personal, response. Flint however, in typical fashion, took occasion to criticise the forms and ceremonies in the Dutch church, and what he saw as their undue subservience to the civil magistrate. This might hardly have seemed calculated to gain the goodwill of the Presbytery, but Flint was probably aware that some of the ministers were not unsympathetic to his views, as indeed they were later to show. Flint and Renwick were then asked to withdraw while the ministers deliberated.

The ministers well knew that what they were about was something entirely novel. They were being asked to ordain two men to the ministry of another church, in another country, about whose circumstances most of them were unaware. They could point to no precedent or authority for such an action. They had to take account of the possible consequences. Were they to go ahead, they might well expect to be called to account, not merely by the higher church courts, but possibly also by the civil authorities. Not surprisingly, several of them were uneasy. It was at this point that interventions by two senior ministers – Philingius and Albringha – proved crucial. Both men had heard – probably from Johannes à Marck, possibly also from William Brakel – about the sad condition of the remnant in Scotland, and they used all their powers of persuasion to move their brethren. The effect in the end was decisive. A wave of emotion swept through the Presbytery. Hamilton recorded that by the time the meeting ended the ministers were affirming, some of them with tears, that "it was the Lord's cause, and cost what it would, if all the kings of the earth were against it, they would go on in it" and that "no cost, pains nor charges might be looked unto in such a noble cause". Renwick and Flint were called back in, received with great cordiality, and told of the Presbytery's decision. The ordination was fixed for 10th May, three of the ministers being appointed to conduct the necessary "trials", or preliminary examination. And, as a final but not insignificant gesture of goodwill, the ministers insisted that they themselves, and not the students, would pay the standard fee of twenty guilders which was usually payable by each ordinand for the use of the church at Groningen.

Hamilton had good cause to be pleased with the outcome of the meeting. But one thing continued to trouble him. He still could not reconcile himself to the thought that Flint, about whom he harboured serious doubts, should go forward with Renwick to ordination. Flint, certainly, had acquitted himself well before the Presbytery, and had shown no little courage in what he had said. The Presbytery, too, had been impressed with him, and had cleared the way for him to be ordained. For Hamilton to argue now that he should be held back could alienate the Presbytery, and could even jeopardise the ordination of Renwick. However, such were Hamilton's misgivings that he simply could not let the matter rest; and so he determined to make yet another appeal to Flint. Reports had reached him that Flint had been speaking disparagingly of Renwick since the Presbytery meeting, so that he felt it all the more pressing to confront him.

Summoning Flint to his house, Hamilton urged him "with all tenderness", as he reported later, "to lay it to him what an extraordinary work he was about, and how extraordinary his call to the land was; and that in all, I thought it required more than an ordinary case, frame and walk, of which I could see no evidences in him". Flint, not unnaturally, reacted strongly to this blunt speaking. He could of course see, and had seen for some time, that Hamilton was partial to Renwick, and his sense of resentment now boiled over. Though his heart had been set on ordination, he saw that his own interests would be best served by letting Hamilton have his way. He knew too that if he were to withdraw without obvious reason the Dutch Presbytery could well refuse to ordain Renwick alone; and so Hamilton's best plans would be frustrated. So, he told Hamilton, he would not now be going forward for ordination, nor would he be having anything further to do with Renwick. For good measure he went on to attack Renwick's character, charging him indiscriminately with neglect of his studies and with showing "a spirit of supremacy" towards his fellow-students, and maintained that he and Renwick could never agree. Hamilton, feeling that Flint had now shown himself in his true colours, forthwith sent for Renwick, and in Flint's presence rehearsed the interview. Flint tried to back-track on some of his wilder statements, but stuck resolutely to his decision not to go forward to ordination. Hamilton had got his way, though at a cost which he – and Renwick – were to discover fully only afterwards.

For the moment Hamilton had the sensitive task of breaking the news to the Presbytery. His first move was to write to his old friend, William Brakel, seeking his help and advice. Brakel however was dismayed at the thought that Flint should be held back, and he represented the lack of credibility which Hamilton – and those he represented – would suffer as a consequence. Hamilton was now in a quandary. He did not wish to expose to the Presbytery the divisions which existed between him and Flint, and between Flint and Renwick; but on the other hand if he did not convince the Presbytery that there was a valid reason for Flint's absence it was not at all unlikely that Renwick's ordination would be jeopardised. For days, Hamilton wrestled with the dilemma. Flint for his part was anxious to hide his own motives from the Presbytery, and decided to feign illness. Eventually, on 9th May, with the ordination due on the following day, Hamilton in desperation sought an interview with the Moderator of the Presbytery. This was granted, but the immediate result was not encouraging. The Moderator, who had heard that Flint was indisposed, said that if Flint were able to do no more than sit on a chair before the Presbytery, it would be sufficient; but otherwise he hinted strongly that the Presbytery would not ordain Renwick alone.

With matters now at a crisis, Hamilton was forced to tell more of the truth about Flint; and, once he had done so, the Moderator's attitude changed in his favour. "He seemed presently satisfied," recorded Hamilton later, "and undertook most Christianly the management of the business, and that Mr Renwick should be ordained." Hamilton, berating himself for his lack of faith, next went to one of the senior and influential ministers in the Presbytery, and enlightened him fully about Flint. He too was understanding, though he thought it might reflect less badly on Hamilton and the church in Scotland if Flint were to go through with the ordination, even if he were held back from returning to Scotland until he was found more acceptable. Hamilton however, after consulting with friends, decided this was not an option. "After some time," he wrote later, "laying it before the Lord, he was pleased to let us see that it was but a temptation, and that upon no account were we to offer him a sacrifice of that we could not take to ourselves. After this, all our fears and scruples were removed, and we fully determined to lay it all on the Lord, and the management of events and consequences on himself." Hamilton then went back to Flint and pleaded with him to tell the Presbytery the whole truth. His faith was not misplaced; Flint, now keen to be rid of a burden which was weighing heavily on him, went to the Moderator and confirmed all that Hamilton had said. The Moderator now was fully satisfied, and the way was cleared for Renwick's ordination. Hamilton was left to wonder at what he saw to be no less than a Divine intervention. "Oh wonderful love and condescendency!" he wrote to the Societies, "and noble Governor, who can ply, and does ply, the hearts of all as he will! O my dear friends, who is too mean to have such a God as their God? so condescending, so loving, so mighty, and so powerful, that he can do in heaven and earth what he will."

So preoccupied had Hamilton been with Flint's case that he had given relatively little thought to the ordination itself, now only a day away. It was important however that both he and Renwick should know beforehand what the form of the ordination service would be, and particularly what vows Renwick would be required to take. When he put this point to the senior minister, he was given an answer that at once disturbed him. Renwick, he was told, would have to subscribe the Confession and Catechisms of the Dutch church, as was mandatory in all ordinations; otherwise there was no prospect of the Presbytery ordaining him. Hamilton asked to see a copy of the Confession, and found his worst fears confirmed. The Dutch church had not had the thoroughgoing reformation of the Scottish, and there were vestiges of pre-Reformation practices – ceremonial, liturgy, and the role of the civil power in the church – which were reflected all too plainly in the Confession. Hamilton, on seeing this, urgently consulted Renwick. Together they had to accept that Renwick could not subscribe the Confession, since to do so would be to compromise basic principles of the Scottish Reformation and Covenants.

The whole of the ordination process now appeared to be in jeopardy. But having come thus far, Hamilton was not going to give up readily. With single-minded zeal he went round the ministers of the Presbytery and pleaded with them that, if Renwick was to subscribe anything, it should be the Confession and Catechisms of the Church of Scotland. This had never before been done in the Dutch church, and the request may well have seemed presumptuous, if not contrary to all church order; but such was Hamilton's persistence, and the ministers' regard for his cause, that they eventually assented. The final obstacle in the way to Renwick's ordination had been overcome.

Early on the morning of 10th May Renwick, with two friends of Hamilton, James Gordon and George Hill, met at Hamilton's lodgings in Groningen. Gordon was a merchant in Rotterdam whose house had long been a refuge for Scottish exiles in Holland; Hill, who was an elder of the Church of Scotland, had come over to Holland after Bothwell and had been of considerable service to Hamilton. Hamilton had obtained special permission from the Presbytery that the two of them, with himself, should be witnesses to the ordination. After prayer, the group left for the church, where at ten o'clock Renwick was due to be called before the Presbytery. Hamilton was impressed to find that, when the appointed hour came, Renwick was called in not only by the Presbytery officer, but by one of the ministers themselves. His "trials for ordination" then began. Aware as they were that this was an exceptional case, the ministers were concerned that the examination should be no mere formality. The trials continued until two in the afternoon, with Renwick being examined exhaustively on a range of subjects. He presented a Latin sermon, which he had been asked to prepare beforehand, on words in the Epistle to the Philippians, chapter 1, verses 28 and 29: "And in nothing terrified by your adversaries: which is to them an evident token of perdition, but to you of salvation, and that of God. For unto you it is given in the behalf of Christ, not only to believe on him, but also to suffer for his sake." The text was handled "practically and methodically", as the Presbytery minutes record, and the sermon was sustained by the Presbytery. Next, Renwick was examined on "all the heads of Christian doctrine, proposed didactically and polemically" to which he answered "fitly and learnedly". Finally, he was tested in the original languages of Scripture – Hebrew and Greek – in which he showed himself "sufficiently learned".

The examination over, the Presbytery unanimously resolved that Renwick's trials be sustained. Hamilton and his two friends were invited in to witness the act of ordination. Renwick was asked the customary questions, and then had the formula of subscription read to him. This, the Presbytery assured him, was nothing more than an assent to the Scottish Confession and Catechisms, as had earlier been agreed. However, wishing to be absolutely sure of his ground, Renwick asked for the document to be read again, and then a further time, and even went so far as to demur about part of its phrasing. This was taken in good part by the Presbytery, and without further ado he signed the document. He then knelt to receive the solemn imposition of hands. This was performed, noted Hamilton, "in a most solemn, and a most tender way; and the whole time our friend was upon his knees, the most of the whole meeting were joining with the tears in their eyes". After being given the hand of each member of Presbytery, in token of their fellowship, Renwick, as the custom was, gave a brief speech of thanks – "a most serious, grave, and taking discourse", as Hamilton termed it – and so the formal act of ordination ended.

The Presbytery however had been so impressed by the occasion, and by Renwick's bearing during it, that they could not lightly let him and Hamilton go. In a singular gesture of respect they invited both of them to meet the members of Presbytery informally, and to dine with them before leaving. It was an occasion for solemn thankfulness and rejoicing. Hamilton was given a place of honour at the Moderator's right hand. The Moderator, addressing himself to Hamilton, "declared the great satisfaction the whole brethren had had in Mr Renwick, that they thought the whole time he was before them he was so filled with the Spirit that his face did shine; and that he never had seen such evident tokens of the Lord's being with them as in this affair all along, and so blessed and praised the Lord for what he had seen". Another of the company was equally moved. "He had been twenty years a minister in that place, but had never seen nor found so much of the Lord's Spirit accompanying a work, as that."

Hamilton, at the Moderator's request, gave an account of the condition of the remnant in Scotland, to whom Renwick would shortly be ministering. The Presbytery were, he recorded, "all so affected, that you would have thought they were both weeping and rejoicing; grieving for our case, as they said; and rejoicing that the Lord had honoured us in such a noble piece of service; promising to mind us both in public and private, and also offered themselves anew again for the same service, whatever might be the hazard". Writing later to Earlston, Hamilton was to record: "We were so filled with the wondrous condescendency, care and love of God toward us and his own cause and remnant, that we shall never be able to express it."

CHAPTER 6

A Time of Testing

JAMES RENWICK was now an ordained minister. He had the authority not only to preach, but to administer the sacraments and to perform all the other functions of the ministry. But, as he well knew, his ordination had come about in highly unusual circumstances. Indeed, on the face of it, it had broken all the established norms. Renwick was but twenty-one; the usual minimum age for an entrant to the ministry was twenty-five. His theological training had lasted but four months. Most critical of all, he had been ordained by ministers of a foreign church. There were of course precedents for men from Scotland to receive ordination overseas; Richard Cameron, after all, had been ordained in 1680 in the Scots Church in Rotterdam. But two of the three ministers who ordained Cameron had themselves been ordained ministers of the Church of Scotland. Here, no Scottish minister had participated in the ordination. Was it therefore competent for Renwick to regard himself as a minister of the Church of Scotland? The Dutch ministers themselves had no hesitation on this score. "We do grant," their certification ran, "to the illustrious Mr Renwick, in the Church of Scotland warring under the cross, and by whom he was set apart to this ministry, the liberty of preaching the Word of God, administering the sacraments and using the power of the keys, praying from our hearts that the Lord God our Heavenly Father may himself confirm this his servant confirmed by us; that he may pour out upon him abundantly the gifts of his Holy Spirit, uphold him in constancy, strengthen him with patience against all troubles and persecutions, make him a fruitful and blessed labourer, and keep him long in the church, that by his ministry the groaning Church of Scotland may abundantly obtain heavenly consolations, and may continually grow in faith, filled with the fruits of righteousness which through Jesus Christ are to the glory and praise of God, until she be carried out of this spiritual warfare into heavenly triumph."

Alexander Shields, Renwick's first biographer, was in no doubt about Renwick's credentials as a minister of the Church of Scotland. Certainly, Renwick had not been ordained by the Scottish Church. But, argued Shields, to hold that the ministry of the Church of Scotland was limited to those ordained within that church was to deny the catholicity of the Church of Christ. The minister's first relation was to the Church of Christ universal, not to a particular church. As such, he had power to exercise his ministry wherever the authority of Christ was acknowledged. And this catholicity, too, was the basis or principle on which one church could ordain members of another, without violation of the other's rights. "It was never doubted," says Shields, "but in a case of necessity another constitute church might lend her helping hand to furnish ministers to, and ordain these who were members of a broken church; this being one part and proof of the communion that should be in the church universal, for particular churches thus to co-operate to one another's hands." And, of course, in Renwick's case the Dutch church had not carried out the ordination of their own volition; they had performed it on the specific application of members of the Church of Scotland, by whom Renwick had been first "set apart". Renwick thus, argued Shields, had every reason to be received, and accepted by, those in Scotland as a validly ordained minister.

These were telling arguments, and Renwick himself was to have ample cause to draw on them in the years ahead. Indeed, the circumstances of his ordination were to remain a source of contention for the rest of his life. There can be no doubt that much of this arose not from any concern for church order, but simply from the malice and spite of enemies. Shields comments tellingly: "It was their interest, when they could not otherwise shift his reproof, to seek to invalidate the power of the reprover; when they could not otherwise darken his ministry, sealed upon the hearts of hundreds, to cast dirt upon his ordination." Sadly, in the case of many, this was all too true.

The opposition of enemies indeed began to show itself immediately the ordination was over. Early the next morning, when Hamilton was still in bed, a letter was delivered to him by an express post. It was from William Brakel at Leeuwarden. In it, Brakel conveyed the startling news that Scottish ministers at Rotterdam – specifically George Barclay, Robert Langlands and Thomas Hog the younger – were preparing to bring accusations against Hamilton, Renwick, and the other students, charging them with various serious offences. The ministers, Brakel noted, "take it in ill part that certain Scotsmen are studying divinity in Groningen, foreseeing that they will receive the calling and confirmation in the ministry and so to return to Scotland, which they judge to be to the hurt of the Church". The main accusations were that the Societies had set themselves up as a magistracy, usurping lawful government and holding that all were to be "cut off" as open enemies who did not acknowledge their authority; that they were not pure in religion; that they had no power to call ministers; that the power to examine and ordain students was one that properly belonged to the Church of Scotland, "and that it was not lawful for any Hollandish Presbytery to pluck that right out of their hands". The ministers, Brakel reported, "say that all these things can be proven more clearly than the light at noon-day" and they would shortly be sending him full details of the accusations and proof. "Perchance also," he added, "they will do this to the Presbytery of Groningen; it may be also they will print them that all may know these things."

The accusations themselves were serious enough, but what particularly disturbed Hamilton was that Brakel himself appeared prepared to give them credit. On the first accusation particularly, Brakel commented: "if this accusation be true, truly I disapprove of that thing, and I will not have a hand in the mission of your students because it would be the defence of a very evil thing, and to be mocked at and hated by all, both the world and the godly." He went on to counsel Hamilton to "deal warily" with the Groningen Presbytery "lest they shall say they were deceived when they shall hear these sayings". Either, he suggested, some valid reason should be found for seeking a postponement of the ordination, perhaps by saying that further testimonies were being sought from Scotland; or the Presbytery should be frankly told what the accusations were. Brakel however was at pains to assure Hamilton of his continued friendship. "Take no suspicion," he wrote, "that I am either changed in love or in my judgment about your affairs; for it is the part of a friend to search all things thoroughly."

Had Brakel's letter arrived a day earlier, it could have had a serious effect on Renwick's ordination, for Hamilton would have had little alternative but to show it to the Presbytery. As it was, however, it arrived out of time. Hamilton was mystified that, though the letter had been sent by express, and would normally have arrived three days earlier, it had failed to reach him before the ordination. He could account for it only by a Divine intervention: "The Lord in a wonderful way stopped it, but what way we could never yet learn. . . . O his wisdom! Infinite wisdom and power!" In the event the ministers, hearing of the ordination, appear to have decided not to pursue the charges any further; and Brakel, though promised further information at Amsterdam, heard nothing more, and so, wrote Hamilton, "returned more our friend, and Scotland's friend, than ever".

However, Hamilton's troubles were not yet over. That same day, in the evening, two visitors from Scotland arrived in Groningen. They were none other than Renwick's old antagonists, James Russel and Patrick Grant. Their purpose was apparently to stop Renwick's ordination, but again of course they came a day late. Hamilton was inclined to attribute this, too, to Divine intervention. He was concerned however at the potential for trouble should they decide to stay any length of time in Groningen, and his fears were certainly not misplaced. Though frustrated in their purpose, they lost no time in demanding a meeting with Hamilton to discuss their grievances. This took place on 15th May – only five days after the ordination – with Renwick and Flint also present. Russel and Grant demanded assurances that, if their allegations were proved, Hamilton and Renwick in particular would accept due censure. Renwick for his part countered that, if on the other hand Russel and Grant failed to prove their point, they should be prepared to accept the censure they were prepared to impose on others. The meeting ended without agreement, and with Russel and Grant more firmly entrenched in their positions.

It particularly troubled Hamilton that Flint, and to a lesser extent Boyd, appeared to be showing some sympathy for Russel and Grant, hinting that they had been unfairly treated by the Societies. Shortly afterwards, Hamilton heard that the two students were giving part-time instruction to Russel and Grant. Hamilton, now greatly concerned, wrote to the Societies pressing that both Flint and Boyd should be recalled. "Now," he urged, "we are keeping fire in our own bosoms, and, if the Lord prevent it not, putting weapons in madmen's hands." However, by the time the Societies acted, the damage had been done. Flint, continuing to harbour resentment against Hamilton and Renwick, had seen in the newcomers the opportunity he wanted. He made overtures to Russel and Grant, and was willingly received into their company. From then on he joined with them in their attacks on the Societies, and on Hamilton and Renwick in particular. With his keen mind, and his undoubted intellectual ability, Flint proved to be a particularly dangerous enemy. He devoted his talents to helping Russel and Grant in their efforts to prejudice the Dutch church against the Societies, and with his knowledge of Latin – the international ecclesiastical language of the time – he was able to give them a credibility that they might not otherwise have had. Over the next few years this triumvirate was to be a fruitful source of trouble to Renwick, and to compound the difficulties he faced from the more open persecution which awaited him.

For the moment, however, Renwick was at last able to turn his thoughts to going home to Scotland. It was a prospect for which he longed and prayed. "I cannot tell," he wrote to Hamilton, "what may be before my hand, but my longings to be in Scotland I cannot express. I would spare no pains or travel, and fear no hazard. . . . My longings and earnest desires to be in that land, and with that pleasant remnant, are very great." And again: "I do not think but difficulties and trials are abiding me, but if He be with me I shall not care. I hope that you will be praying that He would endue me with zeal, courage, resoluteness, constancy, wisdom, tenderness, and humility, and give a door of utterance that with all boldness I may speak all his words, and that he may follow the same with his rich blessing. Oh that I could praise Him and commend Him to all flesh!"

Renwick indeed may have expected that, with his own earnest desire to do God's work in Scotland, and the pressing need of the remnant there, he would have a quick and easy passage home. It was not however to work out in that way. Indeed, Renwick was to be faced, before he saw Scotland again, with such a series of frustrations and setbacks as were to try his faith to the utmost, and call on all his resources of submission and patience. Never once, however, did he allow himself to lose his sense of his calling, or to question the wisdom of Providence. Certainly, on some occasions he was mystified by the way that events unfolded. But his response on those occasions was always to submit to the will of God for his life. This period of testing, he came to realise, was a special preparation for a very special work. Indeed, the more difficulties that were cast in his way, the more he came to see that he was being prepared and fitted by the Lord. "I think," he wrote to Hamilton, "the work is the liker His work that there are so many difficulties in the way of it. Oh that He would help me to submit to His holy and wise will!"

It had been arranged that George Hill, who had been present at Renwick's ordination, would accompany him on his journey, and that together they would seek a passage from Rotterdam or Amsterdam from where ships regularly plied to Scotland. Renwick and Hill left Groningen towards the end of May, taking with them a lengthy letter from Hamilton to the Societies, giving a full account of the events leading up to the ordination. Renwick proceeded to Amsterdam and then on to Rotterdam, while Hill made a detour to Utrecht. His purpose in going there was to meet Andrew Cameron, the youngest brother of Richard Cameron, who was then a student at the university. The Societies had had hopes that Cameron might be won over to their cause, and Hill's visit was to sound him out on that possibility. He apparently hoped, too, that Cameron could be persuaded to meet Renwick before Renwick left for Scotland. Cameron, however, was not impressed by the Societies, and showed all too clearly that he did not share his brother's principles. Hill was able to do no more than secure a promise from him that he would meet Hamilton, but he showed no interest in seeing Renwick. Hill confided to Hamilton: "I fear that he is not as yet acted by that spirit of true zeal which the Lord confers upon those that he will make use of in this day to contend for his rights and prerogatives. It may be that he be fitting him for some other thing, but for preaching at this day I think it would not be for the strengthening of the hands of the poor remnant, though I think indeed he has both grace and parts." Cameron's meeting with Hamilton proved unproductive, and he remained on in Utrecht. Renwick for his part suspected that Cameron, far from being an asset to the Societies, would be more likely to be a liability; and in this too he was to be proved correct.

By mid-June Hill was in Amsterdam, where he set about trying to secure a passage home for himself and Renwick. In the meantime an event had taken place which was seriously to complicate matters for them both. Alexander Gordon of Earlston, who had been acting as the Societies' Commissioner in Holland, had gone home to Scotland in early May to report to the Societies on his efforts. He had been able to give them an account of matters as they then stood regarding Renwick's ordination, and other contacts with the Dutch church. The Societies, as their minutes record, were "extraordinarily well satisfied with all his proceedings" and decided to renew Earlston's commission. Earlston duly set out on his return journey. However, for reasons which he did not divulge to the Societies, he decided first of all to travel to London, where he had been having contacts with John Nisbet, who had still not taken up his studies in Holland. Renwick, on hearing of Earlston's London visit, recorded his misgivings in a letter to Hamilton. "I hope," he wrote, "he knows his errand and call thereunto, though I cannot see it . . . the Lord counsel him and lead him, for that land is a valley of snares, especially at this time." Renwick too was doubtful of Nisbet, and of what he might be planning: "I hope", he advised Hamilton, "you will not meddle with J.N."

Renwick's suspicions were to prove all too true. After returning from London to his base at Newcastle, Earlston, accompanied by an attendant, Edward Aitken, sailed for Holland on 31st May. Earlston had with him the Societies' Commission and other papers in a sealed box. The ship was just off the mouth of the Tyne when it ran aground on a sandbank, and all on board had to be taken off by boat. The incident aroused the attention of customs officers, alert to illegal traffic with Holland, and the passengers were asked to declare themselves. In a panic, Earlston threw the box containing the papers into the sea. Unfortunately for him it floated, and was speedily recovered by the officers. In it were found not only the Societies' papers, but private correspondence of a compromising nature with Nisbet and others which suggested that Earlston was involved in a conspiracy to overthrow the Government. He and Aitken were promptly arrested and sent back to Edinburgh, where Earlston was interrogated by the Privy Council. His cause was not helped by the discovery some weeks later of the Rye House Plot, which had planned to assassinate the king and his brother, the Duke of York. There was no evidence to connect Earlston with the plot itself, but his association with disaffected elements was viewed seriously by the authorities. In the event he narrowly avoided execution, and was kept close prisoner, briefly in the Bass but mainly at Blackness castle, for the next five years.[1]

From the Societies' point of view the episode meant not only the loss of their Commissioner, but the disclosure of their private business to the authorities. However, the more serious aspect of the affair was that the Societies were now seen as in some way implicated in the various machinations to which Earlston had unwisely been a party. It helped to give credibility to the views of those, both within the church and outside, who saw the Societies as some sort of revolutionary faction committed to the overthrow of established authority. The affair had particular consequences for Renwick, whose signature as Clerk was appended to Earlston's Commission, and it was the means of bringing his name before the authorities for the first time. Among the interrogations put to Earlston by the Privy Council was "what a person Mr James Renwick is who subscribes as Clerk to the said Commission; and if that was his own true or only a borrowed name; and if the same was borrowed that he would declare what his true name is, and where his place of residence was, and if he knows what is become of him since, or where he now is". Renwick of course was at this time out of harm's way; but the consequence was that, even before his return to Scotland, he was a marked man in the eyes of the authorities.

Earlston's wife had been with him in Holland, and on hearing of his plight she immediately made plans to return to Scotland to be with him. George Hill, now in Amsterdam, secured her a passage in a ship that had recently crossed from Bo'ness, then one of the usual Scottish ports for Holland. But when he tried to arrange a passage for himself and Renwick, the master absolutely refused. He suspected – apparently on information – that the Scottish authorities would view Renwick and Hill as disaffected persons, and he made clear that he was not prepared to bring himself into trouble by carrying them. It was to be one of many frustrations that Providence was to put in their path.

Renwick meanwhile had remained in Rotterdam, while he waited for Hill to join him. Here he had some contact with the ministers who had earlier tried to stop his ordination. Little information survives of his debates with these men, apart from Alexander Shields' comment that he "sustained a very sore assault from them, though thereby he was neither driven from, nor discouraged in his designed duty". It is fairly clear however that the unexpected delay in his departure, together with his confrontations with the ministers, was imposing a continuing strain on Renwick at this time. The news of Earlston's arrest was a further blow, which Renwick felt keenly. Hill mentions a letter from him in which he describes how he "went out of the town for quietness and has found no convenience, but all outward dispensations contradicting him".

It was to be some time before Renwick could emerge from this sharp trial. In letters about this time he told Hamilton: "Oh dear Sir, I cannot express the case I am in, partly with our dear friends falling into the hands of our Lord's enemies, and partly with my being so long detained from my brethren. O that the Lord would be pleased to provide some occasion which might be my duty to embrace! O that he would help me to submit to His holy and wise will, in keeping me so long here. I am not a little sorrowful at the very heart, that I am not in Scotland. . . . The Lord Himself knows, that nothing that ever I was trysted with was such an exercise to me, as my being detained now out of it is." Renwick's longing was intensified by the news reaching him of the continuing persecution, and the increasing numbers being condemned to prisons and to scaffolds. Yet, despite all outward circumstances, Renwick never lost his assurance that God was, indeed, working all things well for his cause in Scotland. And so, as he often did, he was able to rise from his despondency to a note of triumph: "His house is a costly house, and it is well worth costly cementing. Courage yet, for all that is come and gone; the loss of men is not the loss of the cause. What is the matter though we should all fall? I assure all men that the cause shall not fall."

On 18th June Renwick was joined in Rotterdam by Hill, and a few days later they succeeded in securing a passage to Scotland. But yet again they were to be frustrated. On coming on board they found that the ship was tenanted by a disorderly crowd of passengers whose language and conduct made conditions aboard highly unpleasant. Worse still, the ship was unable to set sail, having to await a favourable wind. Renwick and Hill inevitably attracted attention by their dress and conduct, and the other passengers, guessing their sympathies, did their best to bait and annoy them, pressing them to drink the king's health, and threatening to report them if they did not comply. At last, with the ship still becalmed and with no prospect of respite, Renwick and Hill were forced to leave the ship and return to their quarters. It was a bitter blow. However, yet again Renwick displayed no resentment. "Blessed be the only holy and wise Lord," he wrote later, "I have been kept by his grace from murmuring and quarrelling against Him, because I saw so much of Himself, and of His holy and wise purposes toward me, in the circumstances I stand in, in every step."

There was no immediate prospect of an alternative passage to Scotland. However, on enquiry, Renwick and Hill found a ship in the harbour about to sail for Dublin in Ireland. They decided that, rather than choose the uncertainty of waiting, they would go to Dublin and seek a passage from there to Scotland. The calm weather continued, but after a further few days' delay a light wind sprang up and the ship was able to set sail.

Renwick and Hill may have thought that, though their journey would necessarily be prolonged, the worst of their difficulties were now at an end. However, it was not to be. Scarcely had they left port than the favourable breeze developed into a strong north-easterly gale. The ship was small, and by no means strongly built. It was driven by the gale towards the coast of France, and for a time was in imminent danger. With considerable effort the master managed to reach the shelter of the English coast, where he decided to put into harbour. The port he chose was Rye in east Sussex, just to the east of Hastings. Here there was promise of shelter while the storm abated, and the ship was to remain at Rye for several days.

But while Renwick and Hill had escaped one danger, they were immediately confronted with another. The plot against the king had been newly discovered, and all the ports were being closely watched. A ship newly come from Holland, which was seen as a refuge for disaffected persons, was bound to attract suspicion. Renwick and Hill, on going ashore, were so conscious of being watched that they thought it prudent to return as soon as possible to the ship. But a further wait ensued before the ship could leave, and after some days a party of customs officers came on board and demanded of the master who they were. Renwick and Hill, listening with some trepidation in the cabin, heard the master say that he did not know; which, thought Renwick, was the surest way to increase the officers' suspicions. Yet, he recorded later, "when they came to us, they by the holy wise Lord were so restrained that they were suffered to say nothing but ask how we did". Renwick for his part, though assured of his calling to Scotland, was completely resigned to the will of God. "All this time," he wrote later, "we still concluded that we were already apprehended, seeing no probability of shunning it. But blessed be the

Lord, it was no way terrifying to me; for, notwithstanding of His other special assistance, I saw so much of His hand in it that I could not quarrel, but was much refreshed with that word, It is the Lord, let Him do what seemeth Him good."

Still further troubles, however, awaited Renwick and his companion. On the following Lord's Day the master of the ship asked them to accompany him ashore to church. This was a civil enough request on the face of it; yet Renwick and Hill strongly suspected that it was a ruse to expose them as disaffected persons, so that, on their refusing, as they felt bound in conscience to do, the master could report them to the authorities. Their suspicions were confirmed when, at the time of service, the master suddenly took sick; an event which they ascribed to a direct intervention of Providence. "The Lord so struck him," wrote Renwick, "with his own hand, that he was not able to go and tell that we would not come." Renwick was now more than ever convinced that, however adverse the course of Providence might have seemed up to now, there was a Divine purpose in it all.

By the next day the weather had sufficiently abated for the ship to resume her voyage, and the remainder of the passage to Dublin was achieved without mishap. On arrival there, Renwick and Hill set about looking for a ship to take them to Scotland, and made it a matter of earnest prayer. To their delight an opportunity arose within a few days, and they urgently applied for a passage. But while the master of the ship agreed to take Hill, he would on no account take Renwick. Faced with this dilemma, disagreeable as it was, they agreed that Hill should go on alone, so that the Societies should not be left waiting any longer for news from Holland, and that Hill could deliver Hamilton's letter. And so, around mid-July, Renwick saw his friend leave for Scotland, while he was left on his own in Dublin.

This latest reverse would have daunted many of weaker faith; and even Renwick himself was put momentarily at a stand. "It was," he admitted later, "a piece of exercise to me to know what might be the language of it; at the time I could not see it fully." In the event, Renwick was to remain in Dublin for around six weeks. These were by no means days of inactivity, as a subsequent letter from him shows. There was a small Scots Presbyterian congregation in Dublin, and Renwick, naturally enough, sought this out. He found that the minister had been preaching by licence from the British Government, but had recently had that permission withdrawn, and had submitted to be silenced. Renwick made clear his sympathy with the people in their distressed condition. He strove to instruct them about the evils of acknowledging state interference, as a wrong done to the Crown rights of Christ, and he even preached to some of them at their invitation. The minister, on hearing this, sought a public disputation with Renwick, in which Renwick proved more than a match for him. The minister then demanded a second meeting, to which he brought several of his colleagues to support him. Renwick's account of this is graphic: "He asked, how came I to draw away his congregation and to preach to them without his call, and satisfying him anent my ordination? To which I replied, that I denied him to have a congregation, and did only labour and desire to draw the people from sin to their duty; and for accepting his call to preach, that I ought not nor would not, because I could not own him as a faithful minister of Jesus Christ, for he had betrayed the cause of the Lord. And for satisfying him anent my ordination, I told, when I met with faithful ministers of Christ, I should subject myself to them, but him I declined as competent to require that of me; and also, that I behoved first to be satisfied anent his entry to that congregation, the exercise of his ministry during his continuance therein, and now his yielding it up at the enemy's command – all which had to be reconciled with the work of God, our engagements, and the duty of a minister." The result was, perhaps, not surprising: "Which when he heard, he grew mightily passionate, falling out in bitter reflections; and I, perceiving the dishonour done to God thereby, told him that I would speak no more to such men in such a frame, and so departed."

Renwick had made some bitter enemies by his plain speaking. But he had also made not a few friends. On some, the seriousness of his manner, and the earnestness of his teaching, made a powerful impression. He recorded in a letter to Hamilton: "All the people of this place were following men who did not follow the Lord, and thought they were right enough. Yet now some of them are saying, We have been misled; we never knew before this that we were standing betwixt the Lord's camp and his adversary's." Between Renwick and some of these people there was forged a strong attachment. When he eventually left them, they felt quite desolated. They besought him, he wrote later, "with tears" to stay, saying that "their necessity was greater than Scotland's necessity" and they were only comforted by a promise that, if he possibly could, he would return at some time to see them. It was a commitment which, sadly, he was never to be able to fulfil.

Renwick eventually left Dublin towards the end of August. He had been through varied experiences in the three months since his ordination. Events had not gone as he had planned them, but he had been taught many valuable lessons. He had learned the need for patience, and resignation to the will of the Lord. His stay in Dublin had been a valued training-ground for his future ministry. He had found himself having to engage in controversy, which, though naturally distasteful to him, would yet stand him in good stead in many a difficult situation. He had been able to comfort and guide the Lord's people. Looking back on the experience as he left, Renwick felt much cause to praise God. "The Lord," he wrote, "has had a special hand in my coming to this place, for he has not suffered me to be idle; and, blessed be his name, he has kindled a fire which, I hope, Satan shall not quench. O, what shall I say? Blessed be the name of the Lord, who lets me see that He will see of the travail of His soul and be satisfied, and gives me many confirmations of His calling me to this work, wherein my desire is only to be faithful. It is good keeping the Lord's way, for He will not leave nor forsake."

CHAPTER 7

THE START OF THE MINISTRY

THE Scotland to which Renwick was returning was a land riven by persecution. Certainly, the persecution had already continued for all of twenty-two years; but of late it had taken on a new and more terrible aspect. The determination of the authorities to root out all traces of religious disaffection, and to enforce adherence to the episcopal order, was now extending to all classes of society. From the highest to the lowest, there was no respite from the all-prevailing policy of repression. Attendance at the parish churches was rigorously enforced. Landowners were held responsible for the non-attendance of their tenants, and parish ministers were required to give in lists of absentees. Spies and informers were everywhere active. Troops were stationed in various parts of the country to enforce the Privy Council's orders. Families were being ruined by exorbitant fines, and by arbitrary quartering of troops. Military commanders, such as John Graham of Claverhouse, had powers of summary jurisdiction in their districts. Strict orders were given that the discovery of any field-meetings be notified at once to the nearest magistrate and commander of the standing forces, on pain of being held art and part with those present. Landowners were made liable to heavy fines for field-meetings on their ground, even if they had no prior knowledge of them.

Under the weight of these repeated onslaughts many had been forced into submission. Field-meetings had continued in a desultory fashion to around the end of 1682, but had now virtually ceased. Some of the last remaining field-preachers had been captured and sent to the Bass Rock; others had sought refuge in Ireland or on the Continent. House-meetings, relatively unmolested before, now became targets for the authorities. Even the indulged ministers began to find that their licences were no defence against persecution. As time went on, the net was drawn ever tighter. Increasingly, mere opinion was taken as sufficient evidence of guilt. It became the common method for suspects to be asked ensnaring questions – Was Bothwell Bridge rebellion? Was the archbishop's death murder? Will you pray for the King? Negative answers to these questions were a sufficient ground for condemnation. The prisons were rapidly filling. Torture was being used to secure confessions. By the end of 1683, increasing numbers – of all classes – were being sent to the scaffold. A reign of terror was extending itself inexorably across the land. Soon, it would reach a climax virtually unparalleled in the annals of a Christian state; a persecution which was to become known to generations of Scots by the terrible name of the "Killing Time".

The Societies, for their part, had been meeting regularly in Renwick's absence. They had of course their share in the persecution, and on at least one occasion their meeting was discovered and several of their members arrested. With the discovery of Earlston's papers they came also to be viewed as disaffected persons, and potential enemies to the state. But as well as persecution from the government they were subject to continued attacks from those within the church who saw them as extremists and isolationists, unwilling to hear any ministers save those they chose themselves. It was to disarm some of this criticism that they decided, shortly before Renwick left for Holland, to draw up a call to some senior ministers who had formerly been active in the fields, inviting them to preach to them. Preparation of the call was entrusted to Renwick and John Flint, and to John Smith, one of the two students who had been chosen to stay in Scotland. Renwick and Flint left their contributions with Smith on their departure, and Smith was commissioned to draw the three papers together. Unfortunately, Smith by this time was seriously ill – and indeed was shortly to die – and he was clearly not able to give the task the care and attention it deserved. For the Societies, the result was a disaster. The final document was so infelicitously phrased and intolerantly worded that it caused resentment wherever it went, and it eventually had to be recalled. Though it was soon replaced by another, the damage had been done; and for years the Societies had to endure the reproach from which they had sought in vain to free themselves.

Renwick had of course been keeping himself informed of events in Scotland, and he had no illusions about what awaited him. But he was utterly convinced that his destiny lay in his native land. The "pleasant remnant" as he liked to call them, were languishing without the preached gospel. Upon him, as he was increasingly being brought to see, lay the responsibility not only of supplying that need, but of raising once again the standard of the gospel which had fallen. It was a commitment he now regarded as a sacred trust.

Renwick left Dublin in late August on a ship bound for the Clyde. Yet again, his passage was by no means easy. All ports were still being closely watched, and masters of ships were required to give up the names of passengers. Renwick's name was now known to the authorities through the papers found on Earlston, and it would clearly have been unwise for him to land at a recognised port. Knowing this, and not wishing to court unnecessary danger, he applied to the master of the ship to be put ashore before the vessel reached harbour. The master was understandably suspicious, and made considerable difficulties; but eventually, perhaps with the inducement of a reward, he was prevailed upon to agree. On a night in early September, as the ship made her way up the Firth of Clyde, Renwick was put ashore at a point which he described later as "a hillside some few miles below Greenock" and which has traditionally been taken to be in the area of Cloch Point, between Gourock and Inverkip. After an absence of nine months, and after many vicissitudes, he was once again back in Scotland.

In the nature of things, it had not been possible for Renwick to give any notice of his arrival, and he was obliged to travel many miles before he could make contact with the Societies. It was obviously a time of great hazard and danger, compounded by his lack of knowledge of the country, but within some days he had succeeded in contacting some old friends. It was an occasion for mutual rejoicing. The Societies now had their minister, and Renwick had his life's work before him.

Renwick, despite his recent ordeal, did not allow himself much respite. The needs were great, and he was keen to lose no time. In agreement with friends he decided to make his way to Edinburgh, where some of the more influential of the Societies were, so that he could plan with them the way ahead. The Societies had met in General Meeting on 1st August, when Hill had delivered to them Hamilton's letter, and they were due to meet again on 3rd October. Clearly, this was the date at which Renwick was now aiming in order to present himself to them and to receive their formal call.

By mid-September, Renwick and a group of friends were on their way across central Scotland towards Edinburgh. News of his arrival had spread widely, and on arriving in the neighbourhood of Kirk o' Shotts, which was a noted centre of support, the party was joined by numbers of people from the outlying villages. Some of them brought young children for baptism. Renwick, though not yet having received his formal call, was nevertheless an ordained minister, and he saw no difficulty in yielding to the people's request that he preach to them and baptise the children. The meeting was conducted around a house with many of the hearers gathered outside on the moorland. Two days later Renwick and his friends were in the neighbouring parish of New Monkland, at a lonely spot known as Little Drumbreck, where they met in similar circumstances and again Renwick preached. They then went on their way towards Edinburgh, which they reached safely some days later.

Renwick had much to tell in his next letter to Hamilton, which he wrote from Edinburgh on 26th September. Particularly striking were his first impressions of the circumstances in which, as he well knew, he was destined to spend his life's ministry. "In coming through the country," he wrote, "we had two field-meetings, which made me to think that if the Lord could be tied to any place, it is to the mosses and moors of Scotland." Renwick had sensed an empathy with the very environment around him – with the lonely moors and mountains of south central Scotland with which he was later to become so familiar. In them he could sense not only an identity with the Church in her desolation, but also a solemn and powerful sense of the presence and majesty of God. It was almost, indeed, as if these very moors and mountains had been designed as a natural theatre for the people of God to meet in a time of their sorest need. For pilgrims to these lonely moors today, there is a resonance in Renwick's words which is not readily forgotten.[1]

Renwick could scarcely have expected, given the numbers accompanying him, that the meetings would not have come to the notice of the authorities; and so indeed it proved. However, so late were the meetings reported that the Council found themselves able to do very little. On 8th November they considered a complaint by the King's Advocate, Sir George Mackenzie, that "Mr James Renwick, traitor, and pretended clerk to the treasonable conventions lately kept at Edinburgh and to the treasonable commission given to Gordon, late of Earlston" had held the two meetings reported, and going on to castigate severely the local magistrates and landowners for failing to report the meetings in due time. The Duke of Hamilton, as sheriff-principal for Lanarkshire, was exonerated on showing that, when he did receive word, he had arrested several suspects and sent them as prisoners to Edinburgh. The local landowners were not so fortunate; the Laird of Dundas, on whose land the Kirk o' Shotts meeting was held, was fined fifty pounds sterling, and the Trades of Glasgow, the owners of the land at New Monkland, incurred a similar penalty. Dundas subsequently got his fine remitted on showing that he had "turned out the tenant and demolished the house". The affair did however have a more tragic sequel when John Whitelaw of New Monkland, one of those arrested by Hamilton, was executed in Edinburgh on 30th November on the ground of having been at Bothwell. Whitelaw had joined in both of Renwick's meetings, and Renwick obviously felt his loss keenly.

The fact that Renwick had already been stigmatised as a "traitor", without any proof, was typical of Mackenzie's arbitrary methods. The only evidence, indeed, which the King's Advocate could have produced for this was Renwick's signature to Earlston's commission, which had been among the papers captured at Newcastle; and, even then, Earlston had not been found guilty of any treachery. But it showed that, even at this early stage, Renwick was a marked man in the eyes of the authorities. It was a threat which was to hang over him for the whole of his preaching ministry.

Renwick now had but a few days to prepare for his formal meeting with the Societies and his acceptance of their call. His feelings at this time can be gauged by a letter he wrote to two noblewomen in Leeuwarden, the van Heermaen sisters, who had been a source of support and encouragement to him while in Holland. "Since my departure from you," he wrote, "the Lord has been pleased to tryst me with several difficulties, that he might have occasion of manifesting himself, in bringing me through the same. In fire or water I dare not say He has left or forsaken me; and though perils by sea, and perils by land, and the snares of enemies to the cause and cross of Christ, have been many, yet He has wonderfully brought me hitherto through the same, and frustrated the expectations of the wicked; and not only has been at great cost and pains to lay obligations on me to be for Him, but also has taken many ways to train me up for the work that He has laid upon me, in the circumstances of the times wherein my lot is fallen. O blessed be his name, who will see of the travail of his soul and be satisfied, and who is that good Shepherd, out of whose hand none shall pluck the sheep; for the gates of hell shall not prevail against his church, and no wonder, for it is a rock, and built upon a rock. O come, let us enlist ourselves under his banner, and take his part against a lukewarm generation, and resolve upon trials, for, I think, He loves none whom he lets want them. But consider for whom it is. It is for His name's sake, who is the chief among ten thousand, and is altogether lovely." In the same letter he wrote of the "unspeakable privileges" of Christ's people. "Shall we not stand still, struck with wonder and admiration, having our mouths filled with the praise of Him who left the glory of heaven, and the bosom of the Father, to come down, and to take upon Him our nature, that we might be partakers of inconceivable privileges, and be restored to a more happy and sure estate than what we fell from? It is angels' work to desire to look into this, and it will be our work throughout all eternity. Should we not study to be more in it now?"

It was in such a spirit that Renwick now prepared for the General Meeting of the Societies. The meeting had been fixed for Darmead, a lonely spot in the moorlands of North Lanarkshire, where Cameron and Cargill had frequently preached. Darmead had the advantage that, being remote from the main centres of population, it offered greater security from detection; and the moorland terrain, particularly in wet weather, was often impossible for mounted troops to negotiate. Thither it was that, on 3rd October, Renwick made his way.

The Darmead meeting was an important event for the Societies. It marked the first fruit of their policy of sending young men overseas for ordination – a policy, indeed, which some had opposed – and it opened for them the prospect of once again having a preaching ministry settled among them. There was therefore a very high degree of interest in the meeting, and commissioners from a large number of Societies attended. The meeting opened with prayer, and thereafter Renwick was introduced. He gave a full account of his ordination, and produced his certificate signed by the Dutch ministers. He was then, in the words of the Societies' minute, "called and received as their minister, which he accepted and embraced". Renwick went on, as was expected of him, to give an account of his principles, setting out how he saw his future ministry, and stating his mind on some of the controverted issues of the time. The basis of his remarks was a document called his Testimony, which he had prepared in Holland just before his ordination.[2] In the introduction to this document, which he probably did not read out at the meeting, he included some rare words of personal testimony. "I have been cast upon his care," he wrote, quoting the twenty-second psalm, "from the womb even until now. I had few to care for me, neither could I care for myself; but He cared for me, and has brought me through many difficulties and damping discouragements, and has plucked my feet out of many nets that have been laid for me; yea, when as for a long time I fled and ran away from him, yet he still pursued and gave not over until that he overtook me, and made me turn my face toward himself. He took me by the hand and tenderly led me, he himself only being my teacher; for he took such a way in it that I could see no man's hand in it but his own. O when I look back upon the length of time that I was little concerned with the glory of God, and with the precious immortal soul, that word sounds in my ears, 'What profit had ye then in these things whereof ye are now ashamed, for the end of these things is death?'. But by the Lord's grace now I am what I am. If any have reason to proclaim him a merciful and gracious God, surely I have reason to do it. And now he is calling me to carry his name, and when I ask, why is it that at such a time, when I am so weak, so unfit, so empty of human learning, he calls me forth? He answers me, that the excellency of the power may be seen to be of himself, and not of me. He will have me to receive all from his own hand, and to have nothing in me, or without himself, whereunto I may trust; for it will be 'not by might nor by power, but by my Spirit, saith the Lord'. O his Spirit, his Spirit! Where that is, there will be nothing wanting."

It is likely that Renwick intended this introductory section, with its words of personal testimony, to be seen only by Hamilton and some trusted friends. The more public part of the document, which he read out at the meeting, was for the most part a fairly straightforward statement of his beliefs, and an affirmation of his adherence to the principles of the Societies. In that respect, indeed, the document was largely a recapitulation of the Lanark Declaration, placing particular emphasis on the reasons for disowning the king, and justifying the civil disobedience for which the Societies had now become distinctive. Renwick expanded on the document with some stirring words of personal commitment. He was, he said, firmly prepared to be judged by his faithfulness to the principles he was now declaring. If in the future anyone had a complaint against him, let him prove it by showing his departure from these principles. If anyone had any scruples in hearing him, on the basis of these principles, let him say so now. He implored his hearers' help in prayer for the great work he was being called to, and went on to pledge himself "to hazard life and all for the testimony of this day, which I am ready to seal with my blood".

In this ringing affirmation Renwick could not fail to carry his audience along with him. But it was when he came to speak more pointedly of the conduct of ministers that he entered an area of greater controversy. Particularly contentious was a passage where he stated not only what sort of ministers he could not join with in fellowship, but went on to name specific individuals, instancing in some cases their faults. These were mainly men who had continued field-preaching since Bothwell, but had now mostly fallen silent. Among them was Alexander Peden, now in Ireland, whom the document specifically condemned for "refusing to come out to the work of the Lord, and being useful to his people in this sad day".

From a reading of the document, which was not published until many years later, it is difficult to avoid the conclusion that this passage and probably others of a similar character owed more to Robert Hamilton than they did to Renwick, and indeed some of them carry hints of Hamilton's strident style. To make matters worse, the list of names had apparently been prepared some considerable time earlier, so that by the time that

Renwick came to use it some of those named in it were dead. Predictably, opponents sought to make as much capital out of this as they could. The word swiftly went around that Renwick had "excommunicated all the ministers of Scotland, some of them after they were dead". Strong offence was also taken at a critical reference to Robert McWard, one of the most prominent of the ministers exiled in Holland, who had died some two years earlier. The criticism was made in the context of the disagreement McWard had had with Hamilton, with whom clearly the affair still rankled. Many questioned however why Renwick, who had not known McWard personally, should appear to go out of his way to cast a posthumous slight on one of the most respected ministers of the persecuted Church, and a pre-eminent witness for her cause and interests.[3]

While therefore Renwick's testimony drew praise from many, its effect also proved divisive. One result of the day was that several left the Societies, and others who saw the Societies as exclusive and intolerant felt that they had had their view vindicated. Renwick initially appears to have been unrepentant about the storm the document caused. Writing to Hamilton on 14th November, he said: "Some whom I expected to be cordial with, I have not found them so; neither should I, in the way that they are upon. And this has been chiefly occasioned by my testimony; which, as it has, by the Lord's goodness, been refreshing, encouraging and strengthening to some, so it has made others vent more what they were. And herein I rejoice, yea and will rejoice, there being not an article in it but what I am more and more confirmed of, because it has a tendency to the siding of us either for or against the Lord." In later years however he was to retreat considerably from this position. He conceded that he had been unwise to mention particular men's names; and in his final letter to Hamilton he accepted that the "manner of expression" had been "in some things too tart" and asked that the document be destroyed. For the time being, however, it offered an opportunity to opponents which they were only too ready to grasp; and Renwick was to find the document being used against him in many of the controversies that lay ahead.

Now that he had been formally called by the Societies, the way was clear for Renwick to begin his public ministry. It had been the tradition of the Scottish Church that, before any work of great moment was put in hand, there should be a solemn season of fasting and prayer. So it was that, in consultation with the Societies, Renwick decided that his first public day's preaching should be in the context of a public fast, at which he would set out the causes of God's displeasure with the land and church, and seek the Divine forgiveness through prayer. This appears initially to have been fixed for a date later in October. Renwick could well have expected that, after all the difficulties he had surmounted, and now that he had the call of the people, he could at last embark on the work on which he had set his heart. However, yet another frustration awaited him. His health, which had hitherto been robust, broke down, and he was compelled to spend some weeks in inactivity before he could take up his public preaching. The privations he had endured, both on land and sea, were no doubt responsible for this, and the controversy surrounding his testimony no doubt contributed not a little. While the delay was clearly a severe test of his faith, he bore it in a spirit of calm resignation. Before now, he told Hamilton, he had been leaving everything in God's hand, "except bodily strength, thinking that there was enough of that in my own"; now, he had been made to see that even that was a gift of God, "that so his name may get the more praise". It was in that spirit of complete submission that he now set about his life's work.

The public fast, conjoined with Renwick's first public preaching, was eventually re-arranged for Darmead on 23rd November. Once again, the remoteness of Darmead proved its worth, and the meetings of the day were undisturbed. Renwick followed the traditional practice of giving a "preface" or general introduction, followed by a "lecture" and a sermon, with a further sermon following in the afternoon. With his preface he incorporated the "causes of a fast" in which he enumerated the defections in church and state since 1649, and besought his hearers to humble themselves for those sins before the Lord. This was very much in the spirit of the public fasts kept by Cameron and Cargill, and it signalled Renwick's wish to be seen to be following in the same tradition. He was to make this abundantly clear later in his preface, when he told his hearers of his mission "to lift up and raise the fallen standard of the gospel that did fall in this our land when that valiant chariot-man, Mr Donald Cargill, fell; yea, that very part of the standard which he held". Renwick went on to suit his actions to his words. Following a brief lecture, he gave out as the text for his sermon the words from Isaiah 26, verse 20: "Come, my people, enter into thy chambers, and shut thy doors about thee; enter thou for a little moment, until the indignation be overpast." As many of his hearers would have known, this was the very text from which Cargill had preached his last sermon, at Dunsyre Common on 10th July 1681. No clearer signal could Renwick had given of his desire to follow in the footsteps of the man whose memory he revered, and to raise once again the standard that Cargill had so nobly carried. But, as Renwick was careful to point out, this was no mere hero-worship. He had no desire to be seen to be following the examples of mere men, however praiseworthy; "no, no; for we desire only to follow them, in so far as they followed the Lord".

It had been frequent practice with the field-preachers to take the same text in the forenoon and afternoon, with the preacher developing different aspects of his chosen theme. Again, Renwick followed in the old tradition. His forenoon sermon was warmly evangelical. Using the words of his text as an invitation to all, he told them:

"There is both ability and willingness in the Lord to give you whatsoever your necessity requires. *There is ability.* What would you have? Salvation and deliverance? Then he is able to save to the uttermost all that come unto him. Lift up your eyes, and behold a wonder which you cannot know, and put forth this question, 'Who is this that cometh from Edom, with dyed garments from Bozrah? – this that is glorious in His apparel, travelling in the greatness of His strength?'. And His answer will be to you: 'It is I that speak in righteousness, mighty to save.' Gainsay it who will, the pleasure of the Lord shall prosper in His hand. He shall see of the travail of His soul, and be satisfied.

"And now, methinks, I hear some of you saying, All this is true; we can set to our seals to it. But is he willing? This is our question. *Willing he is indeed.* He is not more able than he is willing. What are all His promises, but declarations of his free willingness? What are all his sweet invitations, but to tell you that he is willing, and you are welcome. 'Let him that is athirst come, and whosoever will, let him come, and take of the water of life freely.' Ah ! what say you to it? Give us your seal to his willingness also. Go, say you, why not? you have it. Then come away, there is no more wanting, save, Come; we know he is willing, and we set to our seal to his willingness. But is He willing to receive me? Satisfy me in this, and then I will be right. Ah cheat! you are taking your word back again now, and lifting off your seal. If you except not yourself, he will not except you. His invitation is to all: 'Every one, come; he that thirsteth, come; He that hath no money, come.'

"Now, why will you be so ill to yourselves, as to debar yourselves? for he does not do it. You may as well and as rationally say that you are not a body as to say he debars you. His invitation is to every one. Now assent to this; and then, before you except yourself out of this invitation, you must first say you have not a being, neither of soul nor body. We say, for you to think that He excepts you, it is all one as to deny yourself to be one of the children of Adam.

"Come, what would you have that is not in Christ? Oh! that sweet invitation, Come! we cannot tell you what is in it. There is a depth in it that all the angels in heaven cannot fathom. It is no less than Jesus Christ, who was delivered for our offences, and was raised again for our justification, spreading forth his arms and inviting you. He is opening up himself – his all-sufficiency and super-transcendent excellency – and calling to all poor, needy things, Come, here is enough for you; give in your desires, and you shall have them satisfied to the full. What, then, have you to say to the bargain? Come, come; it is a rich commodity, and there is no sticking at the price; only receive and have – the easiest of all terms. There is no more required at your hands.

"This is a free market. We must invite all to come. You who are enemies, lay down your arms against him, and come. You who are upholding his enemies, and complying with them in their sinful courses and abominations, quit the putting of the sword into God's enemies' hands, and come. You who have given bonds to the adversary; break your covenant with hell and death, and come; break your sworn allegiance to the devil, and come and swear a new allegiance to Jesus Christ, and you shall never rue it. You who compear before their courts, and pay them fines, whereby you both acknowledge them who are robbers of God, and call your duty your sin, quit these courses, and come. You who go to the curates, leave these perjured blind guides, and come. You who go to the indulged, leave these traitors to God. You who go to the backslidden, silent ministers, leave these betrayers of the cause, and deserters of the cross of Christ, and come; leave all these, and follow him: he is a true guide, and will be so to you. You who any ways seek or take the enemy's protection, leave it, and come; come to him, and you shall find chambers indeed both for safety and delight. All you that are strangers to him, come; you that are in nature, come; and you that know Him, come. We must preach this word 'Come' to you so long as you are here, until you be transplanted out of this spiritual warfare into celestial triumph. Oh! sirs, come, come, ask what you will, and he shall give it. Oh! come, come!"

In issuing this fervent Gospel appeal, Renwick was indicating in the clearest terms what the priorities for his ministry would be. Certainly, he would deal with the sins of the land, the state of the Church, and the persecution of the people of God; but his first concern was to bring the claims of the gospel before his audience, and to proclaim the excellence and suitability of Christ as Saviour. From that aim, despite all the distractions besetting him, he never would be diverted or deflected.

His afternoon sermon was on the same text, but with a different emphasis. It was a solemn, searching examination of the "marks" or characteristics of the true Christian, and the characteristics of the hypocrite. The first part of his sermon was devoted to showing how close it was possible to approximate to Christ, and yet not truly "come" to him. To illustrate his theme he instanced various classes of people who, though professing much, fell short of the true standard. The first class were those "who come not from all sin; leaving all sin, and taking up all Christian duty". "Remember," he warned, "if you entertain any one idol, it will keep Christ out. Many say of some idol-sin, that they do not quit, as Lot said of Zoar, It is a little one. But remember what David says, If I regard iniquity in my heart, the Lord will not hear me. O remember this, you who have any one predominant whose head you clap! Your right-hand and your right-eye sins must be cut off and plucked out, before you enter into the kingdom of heaven. I say, if you entertain any predominant sin, it speaks out this, that you would as well entertain all sins, if your inclination were as bent upon them." Another class were "those who rest upon their apprehended sorrow for sin". "Remember," he said, "remember Esau; remember Judas. Your building upon your sorrows and tears is like a man that builds upon a flow-moss." Others again were "those who have common gifts, and rest there". It was possible for one in this condition even to edify the people of God, and yet to be without grace himself. "God will give gifts to persons for the behoof and advantage of others; but when he gives grace, it is ever for their own advantage." The essential missing ingredient in all these cases was self-denial. "Do what they will, and come as great length as they can, they never come to Christ who are not fully denied to themselves, and positively rest only upon Jesus Christ for justification and sanctification."

The true believer, on the other hand, bore unmistakable evidence of the grace imparted to him. Again, Renwick gave various distinguishing marks by which this grace could be known. "If you be come to Christ, then you will find in you a hatred of sin naturally, and a desire to all good, though often you may fail in the performance; you will find a love to all the ways of holiness; you will find a self-denial, and a daily taking up of the cross, against your own inclinations, you will find his Spirit leading you, teaching you, convincing you of sin, ruling and commanding you; you will find an admirable change in you, a new spirit without guile, a new judgement, new desires, new affections, love, hatred, sorrow, joy, new senses, eyes, smelling, ears, taste and feeling." He went on to give some "rules how to apply these evidences". "Though you find them not all, yet if you find one or more of them really, then comfort yourselves." "If you find not what formerly you have found, labour more to renew the same, than to seek a sight of the old." "When you find marks and evidences, do not rest upon them; for though you have them they may soon be gone." "Do not pursue so much to satisfy your sense for the present, as to have a solid well-grounded assurance for the time to come." "Be not so desirous to know what you are, as what you should do. Spend not your time in questioning your state, as you do, but use the means of real union and communion with Christ; this is the shortest and surest way." "Judge not yourselves by the measure of your graces, but by the sincerity of them." "Compare not yourselves too much to the saints, but judge yourselves by the Word." "When there is a serious wrestling against corruption, though not meeting with any sensible victory, yet cast not away your hope. Paul tells you, Romans 7, how far a child of God may be enslaved by a body of sin." He added: "Remember, you have to do with God in a Covenant of Grace. All your debts are paid; all the promises are yours; in this life you have strength against temptations; in death, assurance; in the day of judgement, boldness. O come away, the chambers are every way pleasant, and every way safe."

Renwick's hearers went away from Darmead highly impressed. They had heard a memorable day's preaching. The dearth of two and a half years without a preaching ministry was finally over. They had once again among them a man who would declare the whole counsel of God. The hearts of many were knit to him from that day forward. They would support him, come what might. As they well knew, the business of hearing him would be hazardous. His name was now well known to the authorities, and there was every likelihood that their pursuit of him would be intensified. The reports of his field-preaching had aroused their indignation, and already there were signs of increased military activity. Indeed, on the very day of the Darmead meeting it was known that troops had been ranging the surrounding country. For Renwick and his hearers alike the prospect could only be one of increased hardship, difficulty and danger.

Nor was the open persecution the only hazard. By now, winter was closing in, and with it all the inconveniences for outdoor preaching. Renwick would no doubt have been thankful, as would his hearers, if conditions throughout the winter were favourable for him to preach and for them to hear. The reality was very different. The winter of 1683-84 was the most severe in living memory. Snow had fallen as early as September, and from mid-November to March there was a persistent severe frost with frequent heavy snowstorms. In these conditions Renwick passed the first months of his preaching ministry. George Hill, who accompanied him around the country, later wrote graphically of the conditions he faced: "We went through a great part of the south this winter, in the very deadest time in the year, when the frost was so cruel that it froze our feet to our shoes; and travelled the most part in the night, for we could get no travelling in the day for the enemy followed our track all the way, and was several times very near us." However, the effect on Renwick's audiences was the reverse of what might have been expected. Invitations to preach came to him from many quarters, and the calls on his time became pressing. Nor was he in demand only for preaching. Since the death of Cargill, many of the people had kept their children unbaptised rather than have them baptised by the parish ministers, and these now came to Renwick for baptism. In the first few months of his ministry he reckoned to have baptised no fewer than 600 children, and the numbers then became so great that he gave up counting.

But the enthusiasm for Renwick was by no means universal. By the moderate Presbyterians – those who had opposed Cameron and Cargill – his coming was viewed with unalloyed dismay. They had chosen what many of them knew to be the path of compromise; and Renwick's ministry made them uncomfortable. It challenged their consciences and rebuked their unfaithfulness. They sought to justify themselves by questioning his credentials and disparaging his ministry. The fact of his ordination abroad was exploited to the full. He was depicted as an intruder, an interloper into the ministry of the Church of Scotland, with no mission save to cause trouble. A common device was to denounce him as a deviant from mainline Presbyterianism, the representative of a faction bent on separatism in the church and sedition in the state. Not content with attacking his principles, his critics did not hesitate to scorn his abilities. Unable to appreciate his spirituality, they claimed that he merely copied other men's sermons, or had gained all his so-called experience from books. Replying to this latter criticism, his biographer and friend Alexander Shields aptly commented: "If ever any preacher was innocent of this alleged crime, he could not be guilty, since he was in his continual wanderings under the greatest disadvantages that ever any laboured under, to consult or make use of books; and had fewer to make use of than ever any in his condition and capacity."

It would be idle to pretend that Renwick was not hurt by the barrage of criticism. Writing to Hamilton early in 1684, he confided: "My case is singular, and my trials no less such. We have enemies now on all hands." Hamilton for his part had been having his own share of trouble, and so Renwick encouraged him, as he sought to encourage himself: "Let not difficulties damp you. There is nothing that falls out but what is in kindness both to the remnant and to you. Regard not the reproach of tongues. Are not these the badges of your honour? Our lot must not be thought strange, for the Lord's people heretofore have met with the like. Remember, 'Ye have need of patience'. As malice of opposites to the cause increases, let our love thereunto and to one another increase."

Hamilton, meantime, had become embroiled in yet another controversy in the land of his exile. Though he had been based since 1681 at

Leeuwarden, in Friesland, he had not forgotten his earlier contendings with the Scottish Church at Rotterdam, and their dismissive treatment of him while there. More recently he had been particularly incensed by their attempts to block the ordination of Renwick, and in his letter reporting on the ordination he had suggested that the time might now be ripe for a public denunciation of the Rotterdam ministers, and an exposure of their conduct. The Societies, guessing at his intention, replied that, if anyone was fitted to such a task, he was the man. Taking his cue from this, Hamilton composed a draft "Protestation" which he showed first to William Brakel, and then, apparently, sent over to the Societies for their agreement. It is not certain that all in the Societies were happy with his work; but such was Hamilton's influence, and the Societies' feeling of indebtedness to him for his recent services, that they were clearly reluctant to stand in his way. At a General Meeting on 28th November 1683 they agreed the Protestation in the general form in which Hamilton had drafted it. Hamilton duly had it published, and it appeared under the Societies' name in May 1684.[4]

The Rotterdam Protestation, as it came to be known, caused something of a sensation. It roundly berated the Rotterdam congregation for their "abominable, sinful and apostatising courses", their "errors, lies and falsehood"; for having a "hireling" such as Robert Fleming as their minister; for giving sanctuary to ministers – some of whom it named – who had "treacherously deserted" their flocks in Scotland; for maligning and reproaching the witnessing remnant, joining with their persecutors, and refusing to help or support them as refugees in Holland; and, not least, for their behaviour towards the Societies' "right honourable and faithful delegate, Robert Hamilton, against whom your hands have been active and your tongues whet like swords, and bended like bows to shoot at him your arrows, even bitter words".[5]

All this no doubt gave satisfaction to Hamilton, but it caused the Societies no little embarrassment. The document had certainly had the Societies' stamp of approval, but it had not been seen by the bulk of their members, many of whom – perhaps even Renwick himself – were unaware that it had been published in their name. Its truculent style and the sweeping nature of its allegations were particularly commented upon, and their opponents were to find it a convenient weapon to use against them. The naming of individual ministers was seen as a particular wrong, for which the Societies were widely condemned. Later, when confronted by two of these ministers, in circumstances where some kind of accommodation was being mooted, Renwick found himself having to admit that the combining of individual names with a mass of untargeted allegations had been "an oversight" and "an injury" though he did maintain that there was not one allegation that could not be sufficiently proved against one or other of those named. Generally, however, he tended to distance himself from the document, which he clearly felt had been unhelpful to the Societies' cause.

The Rotterdam Protestation was not the only source of discomfiture for the Societies in Holland. Over in Groningen, James Russel and Patrick Grant had not been idle. They had now been joined by Russel's brother Thomas, who had gone over to Holland to prosecute his studies. During the months since Renwick's departure, they had made it their business to campaign vigorously against the Societies, and particularly to denigrate Hamilton as the Societies' Commissioner. Their activities naturally excited a good deal of controversy. A meeting was eventually called, with some Dutch churchmen present, at which Hamilton publicly challenged his opponents to make good their allegations against him. The meeting proved extremely acrimonious, with Hamilton walking out at one point but eventually being prevailed upon to return. The Russels and Grant charged him with self-aggrandisement, and with exaggerating the plight of the Societies for his own ends. He had, they alleged, told the Dutch churches that there were some 6,000 witnesses for Christ in Scotland wandering on the hills without shelter night nor day, and that there were as many as 16 students waiting to be sent over to Holland should places be found for them. He had also, they charged, grossly over-rated Renwick's abilities to the Dutch churches. This had induced the Presbytery of Groningen to ordain him on insufficient grounds. Furthermore, they alleged, Renwick did not even meet the basic Scriptural requirements for the work of the ministry, not having sufficient experience for his personal piety and other qualities to be properly tested.

The fact that such allegations could be made, in the presence of Dutch witnesses, was sufficiently damaging in itself. But the Russels and Grant went further. In January 1684 they sent an elaborate document to Johannes à Marck, Renwick's old professor at Groningen, and other Dutch ministers, rehearsing their charges against the Societies and against Hamilton and Renwick in particular. To give the document an enhanced standing they enlisted John Flint's asssitance to turn it into Latin. The document repeated the old charges against Renwick – association with the guilt of the Societies in admitting men whom they had formerly voted to exclude, and conniving at perjury by passing information to Hamilton without requiring him to take the oath of secrecy.

On receiving the document Johannes à Marck immediately passed it to Hamilton, who copied it to the Societies. A General Meeting had been arranged for 21st February, shortly after the document was received, but so seriously did the Societies view the issue that they deferred the meeting to 20th March, so that a full reply could be prepared. This dealt with the allegations point by point, and fully exonerated Renwick from the charges against him. The reply was approved by the meeting and translated into Latin before being sent to the Dutch ministers. The outcome, from the Societies' point of view, was highly satisfactory: the document was, according to their minutes, "very well accepted of" by the Dutch church, and the allegations against Hamilton and Renwick were not further pursued.

At the same General Meeting the Societies decided that a firm hand had now to be taken with the Russels and Grant, and with the two students – Boyd and Flint – who still remained in Holland. Letters were duly sent to Boyd, Flint and the others, requesting them to come home. The letter to Boyd merely spoke of the need for a "clear understanding" between him and the Societies, and in response to this he returned at the beginning of June. Flint and the others were dealt with more severely, the Russels and Grant being charged with groundlessly separating from the Societies and misrepresenting their cause to the Dutch churches, and Flint with aiding and abetting them. Flint duly returned in July or August, but in a very resentful frame of mind, and set himself up as a preacher independent of the Societies' jurisdiction.

The Russels and Grant sent back a vitriolic letter of defiance, reproaching the Societies in the bitterest terms, and particularly attacking Robert Hamilton, against whom they catalogued a long series of allegations, extending over the whole period of his association with the Church. Renwick, whom they saw as very much a protégé of Hamilton, did not escape their venom. Not the least of Hamilton's crimes, they told the Societies, was "his bold attempting to build the Kirk of Scotland with perjury, by obtaining (through his subtilty) the admission of your perjured minister to the ministry, by holding him out to both the godly and the ministers here to be such a godly, pious, experienced young man that there was scarce any like him; notwithstanding he could know nothing certainly of him (not having time to try) except that he was an obstinate defender of perjury and other gross sins. . . . His parts are and were well enough known by the judicious ministers here, whose bowels of tenderness yearning towards the lamentable desolation of Scotland moved them to let him pass, Mr Hamilton having an outward deportment amongst them, as he had been an Israelite indeed, and then crying him up to the skies for piety; but how irrationally may be seen easily, seeing that scarce one and a half years before, he was amongst the midst of the enemies, and not three months in one judgement, so wavering at every wind of doctrine, not apt to teach, but a novice, puffed up with pride." The bitterness of this invective reflected not only the writers' animosity at Renwick but also their frustration at having failed to make an impact on the Dutch ministers; and the allegations in themselves were so extreme that the Societies did not see fit to dignify them with a reply. With that the exchange ended for the time.

For Renwick, while of course encouraged by the Societies' support, it was yet another trial to be borne in his Master's work. With typical discretion he avoided becoming personally involved with the Russels and Grant, leaving his defence entirely in the hands of the Societies. James Russel he regarded as the main author of the campaign against him. He made clear to Hamilton: "Lest advantage should be taken against the cause by reason of suspicion in that head, I thought fit to tell you that that part of our reply to James Russel's information which related to myself was not at all penned or drawn up by me." Otherwise, all he permitted himself was the rueful comment: "I must say, that man James Russel has been a costly James Russel to the poor Church of Scotland."

CHAPTER 8

THE DARKNESS GATHERS

THE year 1684 was to usher in a persecution even more terrible than what had gone before, though it was near the end of the year before this broke in its full fury. Renwick, meanwhile, continued to respond to the many calls that reached him from across central and southern Scotland. To avoid detection, more and more of his meetings had to be held under cover of night. Sometimes he was sufficiently fortunate to have the shelter of an outbuilding or barn, granted by one of his sympathisers. At other times there was no alternative to meeting in the open air, even in the harshest of weathers. On occasion, when conditions were particularly extreme, he and his hearers sought refuge in the local church; but these instances were relatively few. The relative comfort which this brought was of course offset by the greater risk of discovery, a risk which was to prove all too real on some occasions.

It became common, too, for many of his hearers to carry arms. This was a safeguard which Renwick encouraged, and which he himself practised. It was dictated by the necessity of the times, and was intended only for legitimate self-defence. Renwick believed that the worship of God was a duty incumbent on every man, and that those who sought to prevent the exercise of that duty could legitimately be resisted by every possible means. His friend and biographer, Alexander Shields, was to deploy telling arguments for this practice in his work *A Hind Let Loose,* published in 1687. Shields argued cogently, in terms which would clearly have been supported by Renwick, that defensive arms were justified not only by the law of nature, but by the Word of God and the practice of Christians in all ages of the Church.

After the long winter of 1683-84, the coming of spring and summer made conditions more agreeable for outdoor preaching. Renwick had preached intensively throughout the winter, but to relatively small groups in well-protected locations, and his preaching had not come particularly to the notice of the authorities. Now, however, he ventured to hold larger meetings in the open fields. What was probably the first of these was held at Cairn Hill, on the borders of West Lothian and Peebles, on Sabbath 1st June. The meeting went on all day and was undisturbed, mainly because none of the local people reported it to the authorities, a failing for which several of them were later punished severely. A larger meeting on the following Sabbath at the Black Loch, on the borders of Lanarkshire and Stirlingshire, proved particularly eventful. After the success of the previous week, the day was awaited with eager anticipation. Colin Alison, then a young man and later an influential member of the Societies, records how he and several others travelled from Glasgow all night to arrive in time for the meeting, which appears to have started at about eight in the morning. Renwick began with his usual "preface", but when he was in course of giving the "lecture" word came that a householder in the district had been seen riding off towards Glasgow to alert the troops. Renwick calculated that he had time to finish his morning's work, and so proceeded with the lecture and the subsequent sermon. In the normal course he would have preached again in the afternoon, but at this point he advised his audience to disperse. This was done in good order, leaving only the pegs for the "tent", from which Renwick had preached, still in the ground.

In the meantime, word of the meeting had reached the redoubtable General Tam Dalyell, commander of the forces in Glasgow. He immediately sent a party of twenty foot-soldiers and twenty dragoons, under Lieutenant Winram, a noted persecutor, who reached the spot by late afternoon. By then, however, all evidence of the meeting had disappeared. Indeed, so thorough had the evacuation been that the troops did not realise that a meeting had taken place at all, and, on seeing the tent-pegs, thought that the site was merely being prepared. The troops set off in pursuit, but by eleven in the evening, with darkness falling, and the dragoons unsure of their way in the moorland, they were compelled to abandon the hunt for the night.

Renwick and his hearers, meantime, had kept together all day for their own safety, and after passing south-westward through Shotts and Cambusnethan had come to the Clyde just south of Hamilton at around ten o'clock, when some crossed the ford and the rest dispersed. There, by ten the next morning, the troops finally had to admit defeat. Winram wrote disconsolately to Dalyell: "I find they have passed the water, but at present can get no further account of them. . . . I am now convening all the country people about this ford to try if I can know which way they have gone; and, if I can learn it, I resolve to follow them this night more; and if not, I am resolved to come into Glasgow with the party, who are very much fatigued." For Renwick and his friends, it was a remarkable deliverance. Colin Alison recorded: "Though the soldiers came to the place some hours after the meeting dismissed and ranged the country thereabouts, yet there was not so much as one brought in prisoner with them. . . . Blessed be the Lord for his care of me."

The Privy Council, predictably, reacted with rage and indignation. The fact that a body of a hundred men, some of them armed, had managed to pass undisturbed through the country, almost in some kind of triumphal procession, was, they declared, a "reproach" and a "scandal" for which they were determined to exercise vengeance. Having failed to apprehend any of those at the meeting, they vented their spite at those who had failed to give notice of Renwick and his party as they passed through their land. Once again, the Laird of Dundas found himself having to answer for permitting disaffected persons to gather on his estates. However, the Council's particular animosity was directed at William Vilant, the indulged minister of Cambusnethan, for not reporting the party's presence in his parish. Vilant was certainly not known for any sympathies to Renwick or the Societies, and on a previous occasion he had earned a famous rebuke from Donald Cargill for a slighting reference to his and Richard Cameron's continued preaching in the fields. Vilant, however, to his credit, deliberately failed to inform on Renwick's party, even though he was well aware that they had passed by his church on their way from the meeting. On being taken to task by the Council he claimed that he was not covered by any instruction to report rebels, and in any event, as a minister, he was not obliged "to inform in a sanguinary matter". Having also admitted some minor breaches of his licence Vilant had his indulgence rescinded, and was committed to prison and then forbidden to exercise his ministry in any part of Scotland.

Dalyell had been disappointed of his prey, but the experience led him to intensify his troop movements in the whole area under his control. On the following Thursday, 12th June, Renwick had arranged to meet in the moors with some members of the Societies. They had scarcely gathered when they saw a party of troops making their way towards them. At once they parted, and took refuge in a small defile where they felt they would be safe. In the meantime the commander of the troops sent out small parties to search. After a little time in their refuge, Renwick and his friends saw four foot-soldiers making directly for their position. In this extremity they decided that attack was the best form of defence, and four of their number went out to engage the enemy. There was an exchange of fire, in which one of the soldiers fell mortally wounded. At the noise of the shots the main body of troops rallied, and set off for the pursuit. There was no way for Renwick and his friends to flee except in the direction from which the troops were coming, so that they expected an instant confrontation. However, after committing themselves to God they went forward, and wonderfully succeeded in avoiding the enemy. Not only so, but after finding another place of refuge where this time they remained undisturbed, they were able to transact the business for which they had originally gathered.

Further deliverances were in store. The following Saturday night, 14th June, Renwick and some friends were just south of the Clyde near Lanark, where they had gathered in a barn for worship. They had scarcely begun when they heard in the distance the sound of a party of troops approaching. Considering that it would be more dangerous to leave than to stay, they decided to set lookouts at the door and go on with the meeting; and after some time the danger passed. Knowing that the troops would be ranging the country on the Sabbath, in search of any field-meetings, Renwick and his friends decided to stay in the well-wooded countryside where they were. But next morning they had word that a party of troops was within two miles of them, making straight for their position. They crossed to the north bank of the Clyde, where they expected greater safety. This time, however, unknown to them, a party of mounted soldiers was directly in their way, and coming towards them. Neither side had yet seen the other, but just at that point a remarkable thing happened. A local sympathiser had noticed the danger, and ran towards Renwick and his party waving a white handkerchief to warn them. Swiftly they hid themselves in some woodland, and stayed there until the troops went past. Even now their troubles were not over. They had scarcely resumed their journey when they met a trooper on horseback, who, on seeing them, instantly rode off to Lanark to give notice to the garrison. Again they expected an early confrontation; but they made what speed they could to get into the moors, and the threat of attack never materialised.

These varied deliverances, all within the space of a week, convinced Renwick that he and his friends had been watched over by a special Providence. He wrote shortly afterwards to Hamilton: "In all these tumults and dangers, the Lord's goodness was so manifested to his people that he not only hid them under his wings, and preserved them, but he also kept their spirits from the least fear, confusion or commotion. . . . He has given us proofs of what he can do for his people in the day of their strait; and he gives us good cause to commit to his faithfulness the management and raising up of his seemingly buried work, and the carrying through of his people." Renwick had seen in this series of deliverances an evidence of God's care of his own; and he took this as a pledge of the greater work that God would yet do in raising up his cause and interest in Scotland.

However, the sheer physical trauma of these events was having its effect upon Renwick. He had suffered bodily weakness following his return to Scotland; now it was beginning to afflict him again. He wrote to Hamilton: "For mine own part, though the enemy should not get me reached, seemingly this tabernacle of clay will soon fall; for I am oftentimes variously and greatly distempered in my body. But while the Lord has anything to do with me, I shall continue. Through his grace, it is all my desire to spend and be spent for him in his work, until my course be ended." He went on, as he often did, to reflect on the insignificance of present troubles compared with the glory that lay ahead: "The incomparableness of time's trials and sufferings with the loveliness of Christ, and the glory that shall be revealed hereafter, makes me sometimes that I see neither trouble nor danger. . . . O what a life will it be when we shall neither sin nor sorrow, when we shall lay down our arms and take up the palm of victory and triumph in our hands, and follow the Lamb with songs of praise in our mouths! O the full and sufficient satisfaction that is in the matchless pearl, Christ! Let us bestow all our love, our whole affections, upon him. Love's eye is so much taken up with contemplating the beloved, that it cannot see dangers in the way, but runs blindly upon them; and yet not blindly, it knows for whom, and for what it so ventures. Faith at length will vanish into sight, and hope into possession, but love is the Christian's continual companion, and a brave companion it is; for it is no burden to love when there is the lasting enjoyment of the beloved, and the full and continual assurance of immeasurable love again, as it is when love is made perfect."

For the moment, however, the realities of the persecution had to be faced. The situation, indeed, was growing ever darker. The reports of Renwick's field-preaching, and the presence of armed men about him, were used to justify an intensity of the ever-growing measures of repression. Increasingly, the authorities were showing a determination to root out the very last vestiges of opposition. Since the start of 1684, they had been pursuing their policies with a ruthlessness which brought some parts of the country virtually to desolation. As the year advanced, their measures became more and more extreme. Sweeping judicial powers were granted to the army commanders. With the prisons filling, large numbers were sentenced to be transported to the plantations. Torture by a new device, the thumbscrew, was introduced to force confessions. For merely refusing to answer captious questions about Bothwell, or the killing of Sharp, increasing numbers – in groups of up to five at a time – were brought to the scaffold. Many landowners, for having even the slightest contact with alleged rebels, were imprisoned, or subjected to crippling fines. Informers were regularly employed to report on those suspected of disaffection. In the western and southern shires, vast numbers of people were brought to local courts and closely questioned on their loyalty to the government. Strict searches were made for any who might have been at Bothwell, or were suspected of having harboured rebels.

It was as a result of one such search, on 29th July, that a party of soldiers were conducting nine men as prisoners from Dumfries to Edinburgh. At Enterkin pass, a narrow defile in north Dumfries-shire, they were suddenly surprised and overwhelmed by a body of men, who freed most of the prisoners and wounded one of the soldiers fatally. The authorities reacted with predictable fury. The area was saturated with troops, and ruthlessly searched. Graham of Claverhouse, with a troop of dragoons, came upon three young men who were resting in the fields after having met for prayer and fellowship, and immediately seized them as suspects. Brought to trial in Edinburgh on 15th August, they were condemned on the most slender evidence and sentenced to die in the Grassmarket the same day, with only four hours to prepare for death. No privacy was allowed them, and they were forced to spend their waiting time in the common hall of the prison. All three of them, so harshly dealt with, left vibrant testimonies giving full expression to the reality of their faith. "We bless the Lord," they wrote, in the little time allowed them, "we are not a whit discouraged, but content to lay down our life in cheerfulness and boldness and courage, and if we had a hundred lives, we would willingly give them all for the truth of Christ." One of the three, Samuel McEwen, was from Renwick's home parish of Glencairn. Touchingly he wrote: "I bless his holy name that ever he honoured me, a poor country lad, having neither father nor mother alive, to witness for him. . . . It was my desire, though most unworthy, to die a martyr, and I bless the Lord, who has granted me my desire. Now this is the most joyful day that ever I saw with mine eyes. Welcome, my sweet Saviour; into thy hands I commit my spirit."

The treatment of the three convinced many that a new and terrible phase of the persecution was about to begin. In a sermon on 16th August Renwick said: "I think we never heard of a generation of persecutors whose spirits were more set on edge by hell's fury than these; they persecute without compassion, they pursue without pity; they have given up not only with Christianity, but with very human reason itself. . . . " And he wrote agonisingly to Hamilton: "Now the adversary is most cruel . . . many are apprehended, men executed upon the very day when they receive the sentence of death. . . . O what means this hot furnace? Surely it is not to consume, it is to purge and refine. O for grace, for grace to endure to the end!"

At this time Lady Gordon of Earlston, the sister of Robert Hamilton, was in Edinburgh attending on her husband, who still languished in prison. Like many others who could remember better times in Scotland, she found it almost impossible to believe the scenes now unfolding before her. She had witnessed the treatment meted out to the three, and had been deeply affected by their dying testimonies. She wrote poignantly to her brother: "The furnace is seven times hotter than ever: they are in such fury, that the like was never seen in our day. . . . It is sad and heavy to see the case of this land: O Scotland, Scotland! What will the Lord do with her? Is he not to turn her to a field of blood, and to make her a byword and a hissing amongst the nations? Dear brother, if I could blacken many sheets of paper and were to sit by you many days, you could not be made to know the sad case of this land; but who dare say but in the midst of wrath he is remembering mercy, in giving strength and boldness to poor despised creatures in taking them, as it were, off the dunghill, in honouring them and manifesting his power, and letting his sovereignty be seen to all beholders, in carrying them gloriously through. I saw three go away; they were condemned at twelve and died at four, they got no more time, and were most cruelly handled, two of them being but eighteen years; but glorious, glorious was the sight that I saw, the Lord pouring out in the view of the world a double portion of his spirit, and letting his promises be seen to be made out."

Renwick, on the day after the Enterkin rescue, was on his way to a General Meeting of the Societies. The venue for the meeting appears to have been Auchengilloch, a remote spot in the hills between Muirkirk and Strathaven. It was a dangerous time to be in the open, for the Enterkin rescuers were being sought far and wide, and a troop of soldiers was known to be based at Sorn Castle, not far from Renwick's line of route. To accentuate the danger, the Privy Council had on 22nd July issued a proclamation calling for the pursuit and arrest of those seen in arms after the Black Loch meeting in June, and ordering the names of their resetters to be given in to the authorities. Renwick certainly knew of the dangers surrounding him, but he was keen nevertheless to attend the meeting, which had some important matters of business to transact. Among these was the commissioning of Thomas Lining, a young man, to go to Holland for study and subsequent ordination. Renwick, in a letter to Hamilton, confided that Lining was "the most hopeful lad, by appearance, that we have" and he was eager to hear the testimony that Lining had promised to give in at the meeting, which would determine the Societies' decision regarding him.

Renwick was being accompanied to the meeting by three friends, who, like himself, were on foot. The weather was warm, and, as they walked on, Renwick grew increasingly weary. Providentially the party was recognised by a local sympathiser, who, seeing Renwick in some distress, lent him a horse for the remainder of his journey. The party had not progressed much further when they caught sight of two soldiers on horseback in the distance. Confident they could hold their own against only two men, they went forward on their way. However, when they came closer, they found to their consternation that the two were an advance party of a group of some twenty dragoons from Sorn, who were now almost upon them. Too late the men with Renwick sought to escape; they were quickly pursued, wounded and captured. Renwick himself rode off at what speed he could, with the soldiers in hot pursuit. He several times came under fire, and was in imminent peril of his life. Before him lay Dungavel Hill, a grassy eminence of some 450 feet. Goading on the horse, Renwick reached a point near the top of the hill, where he dismounted, to try to find a hiding-place. Finding none, he tried to mount the horse again, only to find that it would not stand still for him. In this extremity, he thought of shooting the horse with the one shot he had left, lest the enemy should gain an advantage by capturing it. But on quick reflection he decided to keep the shot for a greater emergency, and instead goaded the horse with a short sword, so that it bolted, in the hope that it might at least save his saddle-bag and the confidential papers it held. Renwick's confidence was not misplaced; while he did not recover the papers, they at least did not fall into the enemies' hands.

Renwick, now surrounded on all sides, had no option but to continue climbing the hill. The bare grassy slope gave no opportunity for hiding, and his only thought was to lie flat on the ground in the hope that, somehow, he could avoid detection. But just over the brow of the hill he came upon a cairn, or heap of stones, and within it a den, or hide, which the local herdboys had made for themselves while herding sheep. Into this he crept, before the soldiers could come into view. It was indeed a fragile refuge, and humanly speaking hopelessly exposed; but Renwick had a strong presentiment that it was God's special provision for preserving him. He wrote later of the calm submission to God's will which he experienced when there, and of the verses of Scripture which came to him. Among these were the words in the sixth Psalm: "Depart from me, all ye workers of iniquity, for the Lord hath heard the voice of my weeping." These words he repeated about a hundred times, until he came to a complete assurance of his safety. Another passage was from the ninety-first Psalm: "For he shall give his angels charge over thee, to keep thee in all thy ways." This, he recalled later, came to him so powerfully that he actually lifted up his head to see the angels, until, he added, "considering my folly in that particular, I was made to laugh at my own witlessness". The soldiers, meantime, scoured the hill on all sides looking for him, but were remarkably restrained from finding his hiding-place. Eventually, after some fruitless hours, the search for him was abandoned. Renwick waited until sunset, praising God for his deliverance, before he decided it was safe for him to move. He did not know anyone in the surrounding countryside, and prayed that he would be led to safety. In this too his faith was not misplaced; he had travelled only some four miles when he met a faithful sympathiser, who sheltered him in his house. Here, a night or two later, he kept a house-meeting, while the soldiers continued to search the surrounding country. He recorded later: "Twice that night I very wonderfully escaped, as it had been even out of their very paws.... O time would fail me to relate the Lord's works of wonder for poor unworthy me."

Renwick not surprisingly missed the General Meeting he had been heading for, and this no doubt caused him considerable disappointment. However, he was pleased to learn that in his absence the General Meeting had approved Thomas Lining's testimony, and that he was shortly to leave for Holland. Lining duly went over in August, settling in Leeuwarden where Hamilton was stationed, and over the next two years studied privately with a Dutch minister before going on to the University of Groningen. He was to fulfil Renwick's expectations of him, and to make some amends for the disappointments the Societies had suffered with the earlier students.

CHAPTER 9

INTO THE ABYSS

RENWICK was by now a prime target of the authorities. He had come to their notice the previous September, shortly after his return from Holland, and in June the two large field-meetings at Cairnhill and Black Loch had brought him prominently to their attention. The latest incident at Dungavel, and unconfirmed reports of his further field-preaching elsewhere, convinced them that drastic action had to be taken against him.

On 19th August, the first steps were taken towards declaring him a public enemy and rebel. The initiative was taken by the Privy Council, who instructed the King's Advocate, Sir George Mackenzie, to prepare a process against Renwick before the Justice Court, summoning him to appear to answer for his conduct. This process involved what were known as "Criminal Letters", an indictment listing the various crimes of which Renwick was accused, and which would form the basis of a criminal trial. The indictment was duly submitted to the Court on 27th August. Framed in the king's name, it rehearsed no fewer than eleven Acts of Parliament which Renwick was alleged to have contravened, ranging from raising rebellion against the king to preaching without lawful authority. As was not uncommon, the narrative part of the indictment owed as much to Mackenzie's imagination as to the facts. It ran: "It is of verity that the said Mr James Renwick, shaking off all fear of God, respect and regard to our authority and laws, has presumed to commit and is guilty of the said crimes, in so far as he did rise and join in arms with the rebels at Bothwell Bridge in the month of June 1679, and continued in open and avowed rebellion with them till their defeat; and then having fled and made his escape, he skulked up and down the country with parties of the said rebels, killed and murdered our soldiers and loyal subjects, issued forth treasonable declarations and proclamations against us and our authority, and committing all acts of high treason and rebellion. And at length to shun justice he fled to England, Holland and other foreign countries, and having returned to this kingdom he without any lawful ordination or authority took upon him to be a preacher; and having convocate to himself a great number of the said rebels in arms, especially those who are declared fugitives, printed and intercommuned, he rode up and down the country with them in arms, in hostile and military posture, and kept several field conventicles with them and other traitors and rebels in arms, at all which conventicles there were great numbers of armed men in open hostility and rebellion against us and our authority."

This part of the indictment was apparently framed to depict Renwick as some kind of public terrorist, as a public danger to the state. The charges were of course ridiculous, but to Mackenzie the end clearly justified the means. It obviously mattered little to him that at the time of Bothwell, Renwick, as a youth of seventeen, was pursuing his studies in Edinburgh; or that the "armed rebels" with whom he was marching up and down the country were attenders at his field-meetings as they gathered and dispersed. It was however when he turned to the subject of Renwick's preaching that Mackenzie was, as usual, at his most vituperative: "The said Mr James Renwick did take upon him to preach, pray and expound Scripture, and to baptise children, though he was neither lawfully ordained nor authorised, and did at all these meetings and at all times and in all companies belch and vomit forth these treasonable and seditious doctrines and positions, that we were no lawful king, that we were a tyrant and usurper, and an enemy to Jesus Christ, that our subjects were loosed from and did owe no obedience to us, that it was lawful to kill us and all our judges, officers and soldiers; did declare and denounce war and threatened plagues and judgements against us and them; that it was lawful for our subjects to rebel and rise in arms against us, their sovereign prince, for maintenance of the Covenant and because we had established episcopacy. And that we had lost all right to the crown and government of these kingdoms, and that we should be deposed and suspended therefrom, and that neither we, our Council nor judicatories had any power or jurisdiction over them, nor did owe us any allegiance or obedience; and vented, published and spread abroad several treasonable papers, sermons, proclamations and declarations maintaining the horrid and unchristian positions and doctrines above-mentioned, infecting thereby our subjects and people with the poison and contagion thereof, so as several of them have maintained and owned the same in face of our judicatories and on gibbets, declaring that they had been instructed therein by the said Mr James Renwick." All of this was of course a gross distortion of Renwick's principles and teaching, but again Mackenzie was typically cavalier in his use of the facts.

The indictment was duly approved by the Justice Court and was proclaimed at the Mercat Cross of Edinburgh on 30th August. As was the custom, the proclamation was made by one of the pursuivants, or heralds, of Court, with sound of trumpet and all due ceremony. Following the reading of the indictment Renwick was publicly summoned to appear before the Justice Court on 16th September; in the meantime to find security for his appearance and to lodge it with the Court within six days; and, if he did not comply, to be publicly proclaimed an outlaw and a rebel against the king's authority.

Renwick, needless to say, did not appear on the due date. The Court, meeting again on 19th September, took formal note of his disobedience and went ahead with the next stage of the process. This was the drawing up of "Letters of Denunciation", the vehicle for declaring an accused person an outlaw and rebel. Mackenzie had the document ready for the Court's approval, which was readily granted. The next day, again with all due ceremony, the proclamation was made at the Mercat Cross. In accordance with custom, the proclamation was prefaced by three blasts on a horn, the term "put to the horn" being synonymous in Scots law with being outlawed.

As a declared fugitive and rebel Renwick was now liable to be arrested on sight, and handed over to the authorities. There were also Acts on the statute-book forbidding anyone to harbour or supply a rebel on pain of being charged with the same crimes as himself. However, even this was not enough to satisfy the Privy Council, who framed a further document, known as Letters of Intercommuning, directing still more severe penalties specifically at Renwick. On 20th September – the same day as Renwick was proclaimed a rebel – the document was issued by Royal Proclamation and ordered to be proclaimed throughout the kingdom. It was also publicly printed, to ensure the widest possible circulation. Letters of Intercommuning were the ultimate sanction against anyone declared outlawed by the state, and their terms were pitiless in the extreme. Characterising Renwick as "a seditious vagabond and pretended preacher" the document repeated at length the accusations against him in the Criminal Letters. It then went on: "To the effect the said Mr James Renwick may have no rest, supply, corresponding or intercommuning with any of our subjects, and that any who shall do so may be liable to penalty of law, we command and charge all and sundry our lieges and subjects that they, nor none of them presume nor take upon hand to reset, supply, or intercommune with the said Mr James Renwick, rebel foresaid, nor furnish him with meat, drink, house, harbour, victual, nor no other thing useful or comfortable to him, or to have intelligence with him by word, writ, or message, or any other manner of way whatsoever, under the pain to be repute and esteemed art and part with him in the crimes aforesaid, and pursued therefor with all rigour to the terror of others; and we hereby require all our sheriffs, stewarts, bailiffs of regalities and baillieries, and their deputes, and magistrates of royal burghs, and all or other our good subjects to apprehend and commit to prison the person of the said Mr James Renwick wherever they can find or apprehend him, according to justice."

Here was an attempt to cut off Renwick not only from the basic necessities of life, but from all human society. From this point on, anyone presuming even to speak to him, or in any way to acknowledge him, would be subject to the same penalties with himself. This meant, in effect, that all members of the Societies were placed under the same ban. The proclamation effectively outlawed them all, and exposed them to the arbitrary will of the Government. As if to confirm this, on 6th October the Privy Council re-issued a proclamation which had been originally issued in 1682, commanding all the king's subjects, of whatever sort, to give immediate notice of the presence of any rebels or fugitives, and to assist the local magistrates in bringing them to justice. This proclamation was ordered to be read in the parish churches of the most disaffected areas, so that none could plead ignorance.

Renwick, when the proclamation against him was issued, was in Galloway, in an area in the north known as the Glenkens. The Glenkens had been noted as a prominent centre of field-preaching in the 1670s, and there Renwick found many faithful friends ready to rally round him. In August and September 1684 he held a series of meetings in the wooded countryside around New Galloway, which afforded reasonable protection from pursuit. As was his wont when he spent some time in one place, he preached on the same texts on several occasions. One of these was Zechariah 2:8: "He that toucheth you, toucheth the apple of his eye"; another was Jeremiah 30:7: "It is even the time of Jacob's trouble; but he shall be saved out of it." In a series of messages on these texts Renwick strove to comfort his hearers with the knowledge that, despite all outward appearances, God still had a care for his Church, which was precious to him; and that he would in the end vindicate those, however small a remnant, who remained faithful to him throughout the fiery trial. His sermons were taken down in note form by hearers, and some are extant to this day. They form an interesting study both of his preaching style and of his ability to apply Scripture, in a forceful and relevant way, to his contemporary situation and to the circumstances of those who heard him.

To avoid detection, most of Renwick's meetings were held under cover of night. However, the royal proclamation had inevitably brought him into greater prominence, and he and his hearers were now in growing danger from spies and informers. While some of these were undoubtedly paid agents of Government, others were local people who hoped to ingratiate themselves with the authorities. These made it their business to keep watch on his meetings, whenever they could find them, and to report the names of those going and coming whom they knew. Renwick's continued presence, in a fairly compact part of the country, offered greater opportunities for such activity on the part of the unscrupulous. As a result, a number of his hearers were tracked down and arrested. A court held by the Duke of Queensberry at Kirkcudbright, on 10th October, dealt out harsh punishments. For merely hearing Renwick preach in the courtyard of a house, two young women, Mary and Elizabeth McClure, were sentenced to be transported to the plantations. A prominent local sympathiser, Lady Shaw of Holme, admitted to having heard Renwick "upon the Garpel burn" preach one of his sermons on Zechariah 2. She too was banished to the plantations.[1] Others were committed to prison. For Renwick's hearers, of whatever age or condition they might be, it was clear that attending on the purely preached Word of God, in Covenanted Scotland, was now a matter of immense personal sacrifice.

Meantime, the combined effects of the proclamations were not slow to show themselves. The pace of events quickened dramatically. For some time already, those who reckoned themselves at risk from the authorities had felt obliged to leave their homes and wander where they could for their own safety. Now, they were literally driven underground. Alexander Shields wrote a graphic account of the conditions to which the Societies were now reduced: "In prosecution of this cruel proclamation the wanderers were put to many hard shifts and perplexities, where to find hiding-holes, to hide themselves from the country people, as well as the soldiers; which they were forced to seek under the ground, by digging in the remotest hags of mosses they could find, when they could not have them with safety and secrecy above the face of the earth . . . at length, the persecution became so flagrant and furious; so many forces, foot, horse and dragoons, being poured into all the parts of the country where the wanderers were most numerous; and not only commissioned to hunt, hound, chase and pursue, and seek them out of all their dens and caves, but empowered to murder and make havoc of them, wherever they could meet with them; the country in the meantime giving either all ready concurrence, in obedience to the forementioned proclamation, in raising and pursuing the hue and cry after them, and refusing to reset, harbour, supply or correspond any manner of way with them; whereby many were taken and murdered, and the rest reduced to incredible straits, not only of hazard, but of hardships, of hunger and cold."

For the Societies, already under severe pressure, the turn of events was alarming in the extreme. A General Meeting on 15th October took urgent stock of the fast deteriorating situation. It was clear that the Societies were particularly endangered by the allegation in the recent proclamation that Renwick had taught the principle of political assassination. There was agreement that some kind of public statement was called for to refute this claim, and to vindicate the Societies from the aspersions it cast on them. However, opinions differed on how much further the statement should go. One party argued that, if matters were allowed to continue as they were, with the persecution raging unchecked, the Societies faced imminent extinction. An exceptional situation, it was claimed, demanded exceptional remedies; and it was time for the Societies to carry the battle, at least in some degree, to the enemy. Particular indignation was expressed at the activities of spies and informers, and it was urged that strong action be taken to frighten them into submission. However, some were not so sure. Renwick himself argued that to take an unduly militant stance could be counter-productive, and enrage the authorities still further. Others supported him. The issue was long and keenly debated, but in the end the more militant section carried the day. Renwick, accepting the will of the majority, agreed to prepare the draft of a public declaration and to submit it to a committee of the Societies on 28th October.

On the due date the document was finalised and approved, and ordered to be published on 8th November. Entitled *The Apologetic Declaration and Admonitory Vindication of the True Presbyterians of the Church of Scotland, Especially against Intelligencers and Informers*, it bore strong marks of Renwick's composition. It started by noting "the virulent persecution and ignominious calumnies" of those in positions of power, "to all of whom, nevertheless, that are reconcilable unto God we heartily wish eternal salvation". It went on to affirm the Societies' previous actions in disowning the king and declaring war against him, as expressed in the Sanquhar declaration. However, it continued: "That therein our mind may be the more clearly understood, and for preventing further mistakes anent our purposes, we do hereby jointly and unanimously testify and declare that we utterly detest and abhor that hellish principle of killing all who differ in judgement or persuasion from us, it having no bottom upon the Word of God, or right reason; so we look upon it as a duty binding upon us, to publish openly unto the world that we are firmly and really purposed not to injure or offend any whomsoever, but to pursue the ends of our covenants, in standing to the defence of our glorious work of reformation, and of our own lives."

The "apologetic" section completed, the more contentious "admonitory" part of the paper followed. "We do hereby declare unto all, that whosoever stretch forth their hands against us, while we are maintaining the cause and interest of Christ against his enemies, in defence of the Covenanted Reformation; by shedding our blood actually, either by authoritative commanding, or by obeying such commands; who lay search for us or who deliver up any of us to the spilling of our blood; stirring up enemies to the taking away of our lives; all such as in obedience to the enemies' commands raise the hue and cry after us; informing against us wickedly, compearing before the adversaries' courts to our extreme hazard and suffering; we say, all and every one of such shall be reputed by us enemies to God and the covenanted work of reformation, and punished as such, according to our power and the degree of their offence. . . . Let not any think (our God assisting us) we will be so slack-handed in time coming, to put matters in execution as heretofore we have been; seeing we are bound faithfully and valiantly to maintain our Covenants and the Cause of Christ; therefore let all these aforesaid persons be admonished of their hazard. And particularly all you intelligencers, who by your voluntary information endeavour to render us up to the enemies' hands, that our blood may be shed; we desire you to take warning of the hazard that you incur, by following such courses; for the sinless necessity of self-preservation, accompanied with holy zeal for Christ's reigning in our land, and suppressing of profanity, will move us not to let you pass unpunished. Call to your remembrance, all that is in peril is not lost, and all that is delayed is not forgiven. Therefore expect to be dealt with as you deal with us, so far as our power can reach; not because we are acted by a sinful spirit of revenge, for private and personal injuries; but mainly because, by our fall, reformation suffers damage, the power of godliness will thereby be brought to a very low ebb, the consciences of many more dreadfully surrendered, and profanity more established and propagated."

Unlike earlier and later declarations, the document was not published at a specific place but was affixed to a variety of market crosses and church doors across the country, without ceremony. The fact that the day selected was a Saturday – and that the deed was done at night – may well have been meant to ensure that it came all the sooner to the attention of the episcopal clergy, at whom it was largely directed. At all events, the document caused a sensation. By the moderate Presbyterians, it was regarded with horror. This was not so much because of its principles, with which some of them may even have felt inclined to agree; but because of the reprisals which it seemed certain to invite from the Government. The authors of the paper had of course styled themselves as "the true Presbyterians of the Church of Scotland" and so, it was argued, had drawn all of that name, by association, into the guilt of their action. Not only so, but any offensive action resulting from the paper would be charged upon the whole body of the Presbyterians, without distinction. The net result was to make the Societies even more odious in the eyes of the majority who did not share their principles.

But of course it was by the Privy Council that the paper was particularly resented. When they came to know of it, early the following week, they reacted with a fury which bordered on the irrational. Three young men brought in before them on 13th November felt the full weight of their wrath. One of them, John Semple, was alleged to have affixed the paper to a church door, and was tortured for several hours by the thumbscrew to make him reveal its authors. The next day, after further torture, he and his two companions – John Watt and Gabriel Thomson – were remitted to the Justiciary Court for trial. Sentenced to death in the late afternoon, they were taken immediately to the Gallowlee, between Leith and Edinburgh, and there, in the gathering gloom, were brutally executed. The old record recalls how, in their last moments, they sang the words of the 119th Psalm, at the 84th verse:

> How many are thy servant's days?
> When wilt thou execute
> Just judgement on these wicked men
> That do me persecute?

A new ferocity, indeed, was evident at this execution. Spectators were asked whether these men suffered justly; and, on refusing to answer positively, were instantly arrested. Friends who conveyed the dead to the Greyfriars churchyard for burial were threatened by soldiers, who seized the bodies and buried them ignominiously at the foot of the gallows.

Already, the Societies were being left in no doubt about the response to their paper. The situation was certainly not helped by two unfortunate incidents which took place towards the end of the year. One was the killing of Peter Peirson, the curate of Carsphairn, a notorious informer for the government, who was shot dead in his own house by a group of men who had been loosely connected with the Societies. The Societies were acutely embarrassed by this incident, and both they and Renwick quickly dissociated themselves from it and from those who perpetrated it. The second incident was the killing, on 20th November, of two troopers of the king's lifeguard, Thomas Kennoway and Duncan Stuart, in their lodgings at Swinabbey, near Livingston in West Lothian. Both had been harrying the local population, and Kennoway in particular had been a notorious persecutor over many years. There was nothing to link the killing to the Societies, and indeed those responsible were never traced. Predictably, however, these two deeds were seen as a direct consequence of the paper, and were made a pretext for measures altogether unprecedented in their severity. On 22nd November the Council passed an Act which was to set the tone for the blackest chapter of the entire persecution. It stands in their records thus: "The Lords of His Majesty's Privy Council do hereby ordain any person, who owns or will not disown the late treasonable declaration upon oath, whether they have arms or not, to be immediately put to death; this being always done in the presence of two witnesses, and the person or persons having commission from the Council for that effect." On 30th December a Proclamation was issued, in the name of the King, prescribing the death sentence for all who would own, or not disown, the declaration.

The effects of these measures were not slow to show themselves. On 18th December John Graham of Claverhouse, with a troop of dragoons, came upon six men at Auchencloy Hill, near New Galloway. On refusing to disown the declaration four were immediately shot: the remaining two were taken to Kirkcudbright where, after a mock form of trial, they were summarily executed. Five weeks later, on 23rd January 1685, a group of six men were surprised at prayer in a house in Glen Trool. All were shot. On 19th February another group of six men were surprised when meeting at Lochenkit Moor, north of Castle Douglas. Four were instantly shot, the remaining two being taken to Irongray, near Dumfries, and after a mock trial hanged on the spot. On 21st February at Kirkconnel Moor, near Kirkcudbright, another five men were surprised and shot. On 28th April, at Ingliston in Renwick's native parish of Glencairn, five men hiding in a cave were taken and shot.

These were merely the precursors of a reign of terror which was to rage unabated through the spring and early summer, and which was to blight this period in 1685 as the blackest chapter in the history of the persecution. In many parts of the west and south, summary executions became the order of the day. To be found meeting for fellowship or prayer, or going to or from a meeting in the fields, was to invite instant death. Scores were shot on the country roads and in the fields, sometimes after a mock form of trial, often without even any show of justice. Hundreds of others were banished to the plantations, many of them being first mutilated by having their ears cropped, or branded on the face with hot irons. In May, some two hundred prisoners were moved from Edinburgh and imprisoned in the grim fortress of Dunnottar, on the north-east coast, where they were confined for months in unspeakable conditions, and then banished to the plantations.

In the same month of May there occurred two of the most notorious events even of this terrible period. On the first of the month John Brown of Priesthill, a man noted far and wide for his Christian character, was brutally shot at his own door on the orders of Claverhouse, in front of his wife and young children. On the eleventh of the month two women, Margaret Lachlison, a widow of 63, and Margaret Wilson, a young girl of eighteen, were tied to stakes in the waters of the Bladnoch, at Wigtown, and left to drown in the incoming tide.[2] On that same eleventh of May, the blackest day in this blackest period, another five men were summarily shot in other parts of the west and south-west.

Renwick, for his part, was now living the life of an outlaw. Shields paints a graphic picture of the almost desperate circumstances to which he was now reduced: "The Council raised a hotter and harder, keener and more cruel persecution against him than can be instanced was ever prosecute against one man in our nation; nay than ever the most notorious murderer was pursued with; for having publicly proclaimed him a traitor and rebel, under the most odious characters, they sent forth the bloody soldiers, as ravening beasts of prey, to range, hunt, chase and pursue after him, through all the towns, villages, cottages, woods, moors, mosses and mountains of the country; who pillaged and plundered the houses where they heard he had been, or near to which he had preached; whereby he was reduced to many extreme difficulties and inconveniences, not daring to travel, yet finding no place of rest, but in the remotest recesses in the wilderness, exposed to the cold blasts of winter storms in the open fields, or in some shepherd's summer-shiels in the mountains, used in the summer, but lying waste in the winter; which yet were the best chambers he could find, where he made some fire of sticks, or heath, and got meat with great difficulty out of places at great distance, mostly from children, who durst not let their parents know of it. Here, he and they that were with him did sometimes remain several days and nights, not daring to look out, both for hazard of being seen, and for the boisterousness of the storm. He has often been compelled, wet and cold, hungry and weary, in great hazard, to run barefooted many miles together, having no time nor place to study, no library but the Bible, no closet but a moss-hag or mountain-glen, no place of assembling together but the most inaccessible places in the wilderness. . . . "

To many a man, such obstacles to preaching would have seemed insuperable. "Yet," Shields records, "such was his zeal for propagating and promoting the gospel, such was his diligence in preaching, baptising and catechising that, in the worst of times, few weeks passed without several public exercises, which to obtain access to, cost him incredible travail."

Renwick, indeed, was so far from being overcome by his circumstances that he rather gloried in them as coming from the hand of a covenant God. He wrote to Hamilton: "I may say this indeed, that the Lord suffers not my work, however insupportable to flesh and blood, to be burdensome to me; for though the world think my case most miserable, yet I think it is so happy that I know not a man this day upon the face of the earth, with whom I would exchange my lot. And when the world frowns most, I know it is the time wherein the Lord smiles most upon his own. Enemies think themselves satisfied that we are put to wander in dark and stormy nights through mosses and mountains; but if they knew how we are feasted, when others are sleeping, they would gnash their teeth for anger. Oh I cannot express, how sweet times I have had when the curtains of heaven have been drawn, when the quietness of all things, in the silent watches of the night, has brought to my mind the duty of admiring the deep, silent, and inexpressible ocean of joy and wonder, wherein the whole family of the higher house are everlastingly drowned, each star leading me out to wonder what he must be who is the Star of Jacob, the bright and morning star, who makes all his own to shine as stars of the firmament. And I may say this to his praise, that I have found so much of his kindness and supply in setting about his work in such hard circumstances, that though the prevailing of a body of death sometimes, and a desire to be with himself, make me long for dissolution; yet I think I could be content to dwell if it were a thousand years in this infirm and weakened body of clay, with continued toil and hazard, to carry his name to his people." In that supreme confidence, then, Renwick went on.

CHAPTER 10

A FALSE DAWN

APART from the intensity of the persecution, the year 1685 was notable for some important events in the national sphere which, at the time, gave some hopes that the long night of tyranny might soon be past, but which in the end showed these hopes to be misplaced. Renwick was to be closely concerned in some of these events, and, perhaps more importantly, in their consequences.

The catalyst for these events was the death, on 6th February, at the age of fifty-four, of King Charles II. His death brought to the throne a professed Roman Catholic, in the person of the King's brother, the Duke of York, who took the title of James II of England and VII of Scotland. Over the years, attempts by leading Protestants to block the Duke's succession had been constantly frustrated by the King, and now that he was on the throne many of them felt that the time for decisive action had come. The focus of this was in Holland, whither many leading Protestants had fled. These included the Duke of Monmouth, who had commanded the Government forces at Bothwell Bridge, but who had later fallen out of favour with the Court and was bitterly opposed to the Duke's succession. With Monmouth in Holland were a number of leading Presbyterians from Scotland. Chief of these was the Earl of Argyle, whose father had been one of the first victims of Charles II's government in 1661. The Earl by contrast had complied with the government, and indeed had done so to such an extent that he had been made a member of the Privy Council, on which he had served from 1664 to 1681. However, for reasons of his own he had scrupled to take the Test Act brought in by the 1681 Parliament, and although he had subsequently taken it with reservations, he was strongly suspected of disloyalty and was brought to trial. He was found guilty of treason, which of course carried a capital sentence, but before this could be pronounced he made his escape from Edinburgh Castle and fled to Holland. There, he became the focus of a group which included men such as Sir Patrick Hume of Polwarth and Sir John Cochrane of Ochiltree who had suffered harassment because of their Presbyterian sympathies and had gone to Holland to avoid further trouble. These however, like Argyle himself, had no sympathy with the cause as Renwick and the Societies had stated it but rather were men of the moderate Presbyterian persuasion who saw themselves basically as champions of Protestantism and saviours of their country from the hand of tyranny.

On 23rd April 1685 the first Parliament of the new reign met in Edinburgh. A letter from the king made it clear what he expected of the members. Their greatest interest, he wrote, rested in "our power and authority, which now we are resolved to maintain in its greatest lustre, to the end we may be the more enabled to defend and protect your religion as established by law, against fanatical contrivances, murderers and assassins, having no fear of God more than honour for us". He went on: "Nothing has been left unattempted by those wild and inhuman traitors for endeavouring to overturn your peace; and therefore we have good reason to hope that nothing will be wanting in you to secure yourselves and us from their outrages and violence in time coming, and to take care that such conspirators meet with their just deservings, so as others may thereby be deterred from courses so little agreeable to religion, or their duty and allegiance to us."

The fiction that the Societies espoused murderous principles clearly lay at the back of the king's letter. As has been seen, it was a fiction based on the Societies' Apologetical Declaration, which in fact had renounced, in the strongest terms, the principle of killing all those from whom they differed. But it clearly suited the authorities to give the fiction credence; and now that the king himself had done so they could pursue it with all the more conviction. The king's theme was enthusiastically taken up by his Commissioner, the Duke of Queensberry. In lurid terms he spoke of "that desperate, fanatical and irreclaimable party . . . wretches of such monstrous principles and practices as past ages never heard, nor those to come will hardly believe . . . it therefore concerns you both in honour and prudence no longer to dally with them but that the utmost severities be most effectually applied, and always taken, both to find out their favourers and retired and secret haunts". The Lord Chancellor, the Earl of Perth, used more venomous language still. "We have," he proclaimed, "a new sect sprung up amongst us from the dunghill, the very dregs of the people, who kill by pretended inspiration, and have nothing in their mouths but the Word of God, wresting that blessed conveyance of his holy will to us to justify a practice suggested to them by him who was a murderer from the beginning, whose idol is that accursed paper the Covenant. . . . These monsters bring a public reproach upon the nation, upon our religion, and are our great plague; let us for the sake of our allegiance, for his Majesty's honour, for our reputation abroad, for the vindication of our religion, and for our own peace and tranquility, make haste to get ourselves cured of it."

With such exhortations in their ears the Parliament lost no time in giving proof of their loyalty. Taking their cue from Perth's speech, they directed their attack first of all on the Covenants. On 6th May they unanimously passed an Act declaring it treasonable to profess the National Covenant and Solemn League and Covenant, to write in defence of them, or to own them as lawful or obligatory upon any subject in the realm. Here clearly was an attempt to strike at the root of Presbyterian dissent; an attempt, indeed, to bury once and for all the distinctive Reformation heritage which the Covenants had stood for. Two days later the Parliament declared it punishable by death to preach publicly either in the fields or at house-meetings, or even to be present at preachings in the fields, with heavy penalties for hearers in houses. They went on to ratify all the recent oppressive acts of the Privy Council, to the length of indemnifying officers of state and the army against the consequences of any crimes committed in the course of their duties. The significance of these measures lay not so much in their practical effects, since they could add little to the severity of the persecution in force already, but in the fact that the arbitrary actions of the Privy Council and the army were now being given the formal sanction of the highest Court in the land – that of the King in Parliament.

As if to anticipate the Parliament's decisions, the authorities introduced new measures of repression. At the end of April, yet more detachments of troops were sent to the western and southern shires. More military officers were empowered to hold courts, and given strict orders to enforce the laws against dissidents. To terrorise the local population, troops of undisciplined Highlanders were let loose on the most troublesome areas. In a letter about this time to Hamilton, Renwick dwelt on the unprecedented situation around him, though, as ever, not without some words of assurance: "The Lord is still increasing his people in number and spiritual strength, and many a sacrifice he is taking off their hands; for there are not many days wherein his truths are not sealed with blood, and that in all places, so that I think within a little there shall not be a moss or mountain in the west of Scotland which shall not be flowered with martyrs. Enemies have brought down the Highlanders upon us, and they with the forces do run through the country (Lord give direction and strength) and kill all whom they meet with, if they do not say whatsoever they bid them. We are fearing massacres; here is a massacre indeed. Oh that my head were waters, and mine eyes rivers of tears, that I might weep without intermission for the slain of the daughter of my people. Also they have given out by Act of Parliament and open proclamation, that all ministers and hearers who are found in the fields are to be killed presently; and, found in houses, the minister is to be killed, and the people fined. The devil now is come down in great wrath, because he knoweth his time to be but short."

But, in God's providence, the attention of the authorities was soon to be diverted elsewhere. Over in Holland, the plotters had been stirred to action. Argyle, it appears, had been planning some decisive step for a considerable time; indeed, from the evidence extracted from Earlston after his capture, it was clear that Argyle and some of those with him had been actively involved in the Rye House Plot in 1683 which had been discovered at the time that Renwick returned to Scotland. His three-and-a-half year exile had whetted the edge of his resentment against the government, and with the news of the Duke's accession to the throne he resolved that the time for decisive action had come. Plans were concerted with Monmouth, and it was agreed that Argyle should launch an invasion of Scotland while Monmouth would make a similar incursion into England.

At a Council of War in Amsterdam on 17th April the plans for the Scottish campaign were finalised. Argyle had hopes of considerable support, particularly among his own people in the Highlands, and his plans were made with every confidence of success. Steps were meanwhile taken to recruit support from other quarters. Overtures were made to the Scottish ministers in Rotterdam, inviting their concurrence, and this was speedily granted. A number of ministers agreed to join the expedition, ostensibly to act as chaplains. But among the parties whom Argyle had targeted to join his cause, he had one in particular in view. The Societies were potentially a major source of support, and in the west and south-west they were known to be particularly influential. Argyle was reasonably sure of the support he could expect from the Highlands, and if he could secure the west and south-west as well his cause would be very considerably strengthened. The support of the Societies was therefore seen as a priority. Such importance did Argyle attach to this that he sent one of his chief lieutenants, William Cleland, over to Scotland in advance of his own expedition. Cleland had done signal service at Drumclog and Bothwell Bridge, in giving him this commission Argyle no doubt had strong hopes that he would enlist the Societies' support to his cause.

Argyle, with some 300 men, duly set sail from Holland on 1st May, in favourable weather, and had a quick passage over to Scotland. After sailing round the north coast they made their landfall in the isle of Mull, in Argyle's own country on the west. About this time, they had a report from Cleland of his contacts with the Societies. "I hope," he wrote, "the malcontents are gained, and begin now to act. I have this order to write in their names, that if Mr Ker [Argyle's pseudonym] be for the work of Reformation, carried on from 1638 to 1648, they are for him." As it turned out, Cleland's confidence was misplaced, and his slighting reference to the Societies was an ample enough indication of the expediency which characterised his and Argyle's approach to them.

Leaving Mull, the expedition moved on to Campbeltown, in Kintyre, where on 20th May Argyle published a declaration. This rehearsed at length the evils and oppressions of the government, the tyranny under which the land was suffering, and the particular perils which it now faced from a professed Roman Catholic on the throne. In delineating these evils it went as far, if not further, than any declaration by the Societies or their predecessors. It spoke of "the cruel shedding of the best Protestant blood, the deluging of these lands with all villainous debaucheries and abominable licentiousness, to the very profligating of conscience, morality, and common honesty from among men"; "a most unrelenting persecution, and oppression of the generality of God's people, in their consciences, persons, and estates, with vexations and rigours almost incredible, the desolating of the churches, and changing of the ordinances of God, for setting up the frivolous and superstitious inventions of men"; "the cruel executing to the death of several hundreds within these twenty years, besides many hundreds more, that have either fallen in the fields, or been made to perish in their imprisonments or transportations, and that for the alone cause, or on the occasion of their conscientious nonconforming". It declared the aims of the expedition to be "the restoring and settling of the true, reformed, Protestant religion, in its power and purity; the suppression and perpetual exclusion of anti-Christian popery, with all its idolatrous superstitions and falsehoods, as also its most bitter root and offspring, prelacy, with its new and wicked head the supremacy, and all their abuses; and the restoring of all men to their just rights and liberties, the removing of all oppression, and establishing such righteous laws and methods of government, as may be most for securing of liberty and property, with the greatest ease and equality".

With these statements and intentions no-one could take serious issue. Nevertheless, for the Societies the Declaration was fatally flawed. As Renwick was later to say, it was "not concerted according to the ancient plea of the Scottish Covenanters". Indeed, at no point did it refer to the Covenants, nor to the Presbyterian government of the Church. It was essentially a broad-based Protestant manifesto, designed to have the widest possible appeal, and, in the Societies' view, calculated to attract elements which they saw as diametrically opposed to their testimony. The Societies had other reasons too for not giving Argyle their support. While many respected Argyle for his stand, it was remembered that, as a member of the Privy Council, he had lent his weight to many oppressive measures; and it was strongly rumoured that he had been instrumental in voting down a reprieve for Donald Cargill in 1681. Sir John Cochrane, one of his chief lieutenants, was widely reported as having provided the information which led the government troops under Bruce of Earlshall to Richard Cameron and his party at Airdsmoss in 1680. There were ministers in company with Argyle who had sought to blacken the Societies' name in Holland; and some of them, indeed, were said to have been involved in the abortive attempt to prevent Renwick's ordination.

However, and perhaps inevitably, the Societies found themselves unable to present a united front to Argyle. Among the ministers who had come over from Holland were George Barclay and Robert Langlands, both of whom had been prominent as field-preachers in the 1670s. Barclay in particular had been closely associated with Cameron and Cargill, and had frequently preached with them, though he had not joined with them after Bothwell.[1] Argyle was shrewd enough to know that Barclay might have some influence among certain sections of the Societies; and so, some time after his arrival, he sent him to the Carrick district in south-west Scotland, where Barclay was well-known and where he had preached regularly in the fields. Argyle's expectations proved well-founded, and Barclay was able to influence several of the Carrick societies against the line taken by Renwick and the leadership of the Societies. As a result, for the first time since their initial dispute with Russel, the unity of the Societies was put under strain. This was to show itself gradually at first, but soon was to become an increasing threat.

However, before any support could reach him from Carrick, Argyle's expedition reached its inevitable end. His hopes of support – even from his own people in the Highlands – proved illusory; by a woeful piece of mismanagement he lost all his stores and ammunition to the enemy; and to make matters still worse, his own counsels were riven by internal disputes. On 18th June, after an abortive move on the Lowlands, Argyle was captured near Dumbarton and brought to Edinburgh, where on the 30th of the same month he was executed. In England, matters were to fare no better with Monmouth: defeated at Sedgemoor on 6th July, he was captured three days later and executed on Tower Hill on the 15th. In both countries the government took fierce reprisals, and many who fell into their hands were treated with savage cruelty.

The defeat of Argyle's expedition brought the Societies, and particularly Renwick, into much odium with those who had supported it. They were accused of standing by while men fighting for the Protestant cause were losing their lives; of putting their own narrow dogma above the common interest; of sabotaging a golden opportunity to be rid of oppression and tyranny. These criticisms were of course quite unreasonable. The Societies were only a small presence in the land; they were not organised as a military force; and in practical terms there was little that they could have done to influence the result. The criticisms continued nevertheless, and forced the Societies on to the defensive. Renwick for his part responded with considerable patience. He saw himself as no enemy of Argyle; indeed he had publicly expressed respect for him. He admitted that, though thinking that Argyle would not prevail, he yet would play a part in God's design by sufficiently weakening the government to allow a successful attempt against it to be made at no distant date. But he was ready, as always, to bow to God's sovereign purpose. Others however were not so willing to do so, and continued to blame the leadership of the Societies.

It soon became evident that the Argyle affair had been the catalyst for a sense of dissatisfaction on the part of not a few of their members with the direction the Societies were taking. As the most prominent public figure in the Societies, and their only preacher, it was inevitable that Renwick should bear the brunt of the criticism. A feeling grew, among many previously loyal supporters, that in distancing the Societies from other non-conforming Presbyterians Renwick was leading them along too narrow a path. This discontent was at first focused in the Carrick area where Argyle's agents had been active, but it was soon to spread more widely. Questions began to be asked about Renwick's authority, his leadership, and the position of influence which he held. It was but a step from this to question his ministry, the validity of his ordination, and his right to preach. The result was that from this point onwards Renwick was to endure not only the persecution of a hostile government, and the obloquy of the conformists, but a stream of carping criticism from those whom he had once counted his friends. This was often to be a sore trial; but Renwick, as always, was to find the grace and strength to bear it.

CHAPTER 11

TRIAL AND CONTROVERSY

DESPITE the controversies which raged around him Renwick was determined not to be diverted from his main purpose. In the winter of 1684-85 he had continued to preach regularly, at times taking the use of parish churches when conditions were particularly difficult outdoors. One such occasion was on Sabbath 8th February 1685, when he preached at night in the church of Cambusnethan on the words in Zechariah 14:5, "And the Lord my God shall come, and all the saints with thee". This meeting, predictably, came to the notice of the authorities, but too late for them to take any effective action.

As the year progressed, and the authorities' attention was taken up by Argyle's expedition, so Renwick found that his opportunities for preaching increased. Abandoning his enforced practice of holding meetings by night, he held several meetings in the open fields, attended by numerous and eager audiences. One of these, at Darmead on 22nd May 1685, was reported to the Privy Council, but again by the time that word reached them it was too late for them to act. The report spoke of "a considerable meeting with that supposed preacher, a disturber of the peace of all honest men, Mr Renwick" and claimed that "there were above one hundred armed men who were exercised betwixt sun rising and eight o'clock in the morning, and thereafter sermon began and continued the rest of the day; at which meeting there were several persons made their repentance for their offences in taking the oath of allegiance, the oath of abjuration, the Test, and for hearing and communicating with indulged ministers, and so were by him there received into their society, and some were delayed until a new occasion, their offences being many". The circumstantial nature of these and other accounts suggests strongly that an informer had infiltrated the meeting. Renwick was well aware of this danger, and frequently warned his hearers against it. It was to counter this and similar dangers that he encouraged his hearers to come armed, and that he frequently used an armed bodyguard for his own protection. There is therefore no need to regard the account of the "hundred armed men" as other than accurate. Of course, the whole purpose of carrying arms was for self-defence. Renwick never approved the use of arms for any other purpose: indeed he strongly condemned the few instances where members of the Societies had used arms offensively. But when it came to defending the worship of God, and the lives of those who engaged in it according to God's Word, Renwick strongly believed that he had ample Scripture warrant for the use of arms. And, of course, he had the example of others, such as Richard Cameron, to confirm him in that opinion.

It was probably about this time that Renwick held a field-meeting which formed the basis of one of the very few accounts of his preaching to be given by a hearer. James Nisbet was a young man from Ayrshire who was an enthusiastic follower of the persecuted Gospel. His father, John Nisbet of Hardhill, was a veteran who had endured hardship and exile for the same Cause, and who was eventually to suffer a public death in the Grassmarket in Edinburgh. This appears to have been the first occasion on which James Nisbet had heard Renwick preach, and his delight at the occasion is evident. "I went," he says, "about sixteen miles to hear sermon preached by Mr James Renwick, a faithful servant of Christ Jesus, who was a young man endued with great piety, prudence and moderation. The meeting was held in a very large, desolate moor. He appeared to be accompanied with much of his Master's presence, and prefaced on the 7th Psalm and lectured on 2nd Chronicles 19th chapter, with a sad applicatory report that the rulers of our day were no such friends to religion as those at that time, but upon the contrary great enemies to it. He preached on Mark chapter 12 v. 34 in the forenoon. After explaining the words he gave thirteen marks of a hypocrite, with pertinent and suitable applications. In the afternoon he gave eleven marks of a sound believer, and made a large, full and free offer of Christ to all sorts of perishing sinners that would come and accept of him for their Lord and Saviour, and for their Lord and Lawgiver. His method was both clear, plain and well-digested, suiting the substance and simplicity of the Gospel. This was a great day of the Son of Man to many poor exercised souls, who this day got a Pisgah view of the Prince of Life, and of that pleasant land that lies beyond the banks of Jordan."

On 28th May 1685 Renwick was at Blackgannoch, in the hills near Sanquhar, where he attended a meeting of the Societies. At this meeting he produced a draft of a declaration, on which he had been working for some time, protesting against the accession of the Duke of York to the throne. The document was in reasonable and measured terms, and was in many ways typical of Renwick's style. It opened by rehearsing the cruelties and oppressions of the time, in which the new king had taken his full share; it quoted the various Acts of Parliament against Roman Catholics, showing how inconsistent it was "with the safety of the faith, conscience and Christian liberty of Christian people to choose a subject of Antichrist to be their supreme magistrate"; and it warned against the dangers of Romanism being "intruded again upon these Covenanted lands, if God's mercy and power meeting together in a wonderful way prevent it not". It protested, too, at the general erosion of civil liberties in the land ("the freest subject and best gentleman in the kingdom is obliged to give an oath before any single soldier or dragoon meeting them upon the way") and it maintained that the Parliament recently called by the new king was neither free nor lawful, nor was it competent for "exercising any power or jurisdiction, or proceeding in any parliamentary way".

Interestingly, the document struck a new note by appealing in challenging terms to the churches in England and Ireland, seeing "we are all bound in one Covenant and Solemn League together" to be more zealous in pursuing the ends of the Covenants, and to show themselves more mindful of their persecuted brethren in Scotland. "Remember how you have passed by, lightly looking upon our bleeding wounds, denying us help, though we have been like to give up the ghost; remember these things, and break off your sinful ways by repentance; abandon all lukewarmness and indifferency in the Lord's matters; give up with your own things; be tender of God's declarative glory, which is lying at the stake; quit yourselves like Christians and men; and stretch your hands to the helping, strengthening, encouraging, and comforting a poor, wasted, wronged, wounded, reproached, despised, and bleeding remnant, with whom you are in Covenant."

There was also an appeal to "all Protestant Reformed churches, kingdoms and commonwealths" seriously to consider "the low and dangerous state of the Gospel interest" through the resurgence of Romanism, and to be "bestirring yourselves, considering the distressed case whereinto we are brought, as a share of the true Protestant interest, and refreshing us with your help". In making these appeals Renwick was again giving clear evidence of the catholicity which had ever been a mark of the Reformed Church in Scotland. Holding to this principle as he did, it clearly grieved him that he and others who were standing in the vanguard against tyranny had not received the degree of brotherly help that they might have expected, particularly from those who were one with them in the bonds of the Covenants.

The declaration closed with a strong disavowal of the "murdering and assassinating principles" with which the Societies had been falsely charged following the Apologetical Declaration of the previous year; "all which principles and practices we do hereby declare before God, angels and men, that we abhor, renounce, and detest; as also all manner of robbing of any, whether open enemies or others, which we are most falsely aspersed with". It disowned, too, any actions not done by the common will of the Societies, nor with their approbation, such as "the unwarrantable manner of killing that curate of Carsphairn, it being gone about contrary to our declaration, without deliberation, common or competent consent, in a rash, and not in a Christian manner"; and, finally, it affirmed the Societies' intention "to continue in the profession and obedience of the true religion of Jesus Christ, according to his Word and our Covenants; to defend the same, and to resist all contrary errors, corruptions and innovations".

The declaration was duly approved by the General Meeting, and was ordered to be proclaimed at the cross of Sanquhar the same day. Accordingly, immediately the meeting ended, Renwick and some 200 men went to Sanquhar and posted copies of the declaration. The action was preceded by a prayer by Renwick and the singing of a psalm, and the men then melted again into the mountains. The second Sanquhar Declaration, as it was called, attracted much less attention than the first, and probably less than any other public statement of the Societies. The authorities were of course distracted by their continuing pursuit of Argyle, and the declaration itself, for all that it characterised the new king as a "murderer" and "idolater" was nevertheless generally moderate in its tone, and, in places, was not unlike Argyle's own declaration.

Robert Hamilton, indeed, to whom Renwick had sent it in draft, had thought it unduly weak, and not sufficiently expressive of the Societies' principles. He also seems to have suspected that the fairly broad terms of the declaration, and its emphasis on the common enemies, Romanism and tyranny, might be used by some on either side to explore the prospects of an alliance between the Societies and Argyle. Renwick was somewhat taken aback by this suggestion, and he felt that Hamilton had allowed his suspicions to prejudice his judgement. "I think," he wrote to him, "the commentaries of politics have made you look upon it after another sort than otherwise you would have done. For we require it to be taken alongst jointly with our other testimonies and actings, and so the door is no wider than it was; neither can any show anything in that declaration but what I think may easily be reconciled with our former proceedings. So, I think it a thing below you or me to trouble ourselves with the various expositions that persons, for their own ends, put upon it." Renwick finalised the declaration in his own way, and there is no evidence that he modified it to any degree to meet Hamilton's objections. In the event, the declaration attracted relatively little notice, and was never made the subject of any specific reprisals by the authorities.

By the time the second Sanquhar Declaration was posted, Argyle's expedition was nearing its end. The defeat of the expedition meant, of course, immediate danger for those ministers who had accompanied Argyle, and many of them were forced into hiding until they were able to return to Holland by what means they could. Foremost among these were George Barclay and Robert Langlands, who had earlier sought to persuade the Societies to join with Argyle. These two ministers now gave it to be known that they would welcome conference with Renwick and the Societies, in an effort to reach a mutual understanding, and, perhaps, to resume joint preaching in the fields. Renwick, on hearing this, and to demonstrate goodwill on his part, at once agreed to a meeting. This took place at an agreed rendezvous on 22nd July, and was resumed for a time on the 28th of the same month, by mutual agreement.

Attempting to seize the initiative, Barclay and Langlands began by proposing that both sides should sink their differences and make common cause of preaching the Gospel, as in the days before Bothwell. Renwick however could not in conscience agree to this. Unity, he maintained, could not be achieved but on the basis of truth; and before unity could be addressed the causes of division had to be dealt with. Asked what these were, he produced a list of points. The two ministers had not joined with Cargill and Cameron after Bothwell; they had left the country and deserted the work; they had joined with the corrupt Scottish congregation at Rotterdam; and they had spread slanders against the Societies among the Dutch churches.

Taken somewhat aback by these charges, Barclay and Langlands defended themselves with a good deal of warmth. They had stayed in Scotland, they claimed, for as long as the people were prepared to hear them, or rather for as long as the Societies had not prejudiced the people against them. They had said nothing against the Societies but what had been in the Societies' own declarations. Going on the offensive, they claimed that the Societies had arrogated to themselves an authoritative power in the state, and had claimed to be acting as the only true representatives of the Church of Scotland. They had isolated themselves from other Presbyterians and were to all intents and purposes a faction. Their first Call to ministers had adopted an exclusive position, debarring any from fellowship who did not share their own distinctive opinions; and they were persisting in this stance to the prejudice of the Presbyterian cause as a whole. They had shown an intolerant attitude by publishing, some months earlier, a formal Protestation against the church at Rotterdam, accusing it of corruption, and naming various ministers, including Barclay and Langlands themselves, as having joined with it and treacherously betrayed the cause. These allegations, they claimed, were so extreme that, if true, they did not deserve to live, far less to be ministers.

Renwick, in reply to this onslaught, tried to argue that the Societies did not now insist on the precise forms of words used in some of these papers; indeed the first Call to ministers had been withdrawn, and he accepted that parts of the Rotterdam Protestation were less felicitously worded than they might have been. The ministers, however, were in no mood for reasoned explanations. They went on to charge the Societies with inconsistency, claiming that in taking ordination from the church of Groningen Renwick had joined with a church more corrupt than the Church of Scotland ever had been. They instanced what they claimed were unscriptural practices of the Dutch church, including the observance of festival days, the use of three sprinklings in baptism, instrumental music in worship, and the subjection of the church to the civil magistrate. Renwick admitted that these indeed were imperfections, but he argued that a distinction had to be drawn between deficiencies in a church which had never been fully reformed, as the Dutch church never had been, and failings in the Church of Scotland, which represented backsliding from a previously reformed position. He had also, he recalled, testified against these things on the day of his ordination, and he knew that some of the Dutch ministers, such as William Brakel, were actively protesting against them. For his own part, he was willing to submit his actions to a competent judicatory of the Church of Scotland when her institutions had been restored. But again the ministers persisted. What right, they asked, had the Societies to look outside the Church of Scotland when seeking ordination? And what right had the Dutch church to ordain anyone as a minister of the Church of Scotland without the consent of that Church? Was that not equivalent to the consecration of the Scottish bishops by the Church of England, at the onset of episcopacy?

In this spirit of recrimination the meeting dragged to its inevitable end. An almost farcical note was struck when the Societies charged Barclay with hearing an indulged minister in the Scottish church at Rotterdam, notwithstanding that others in the congregation had walked out when he appeared in the pulpit. Barclay replied lamely that he had been sitting on the inside of a seat, and could not have left without causing considerable disturbance. Renwick responded that in that situation a withdrawal would have been even more effective than if he had been sitting at the door. Not so, said Barclay, for it would have given great offence. The only offence taken, countered Renwick, would have been on the part of those who sympathised with the indulged ministers themselves.

The next day, 29th July, was the date appointed for a General Meeting of the Societies. The two ministers were generously allowed to attend, and to give their own account of the conference. It was a liberty which was glaringly abused, for Langlands, in addressing the meeting, mounted a strong assault on the Societies and again attacked the basis of Renwick's ordination. Renwick, replying, again vindicated himself strongly from the charges, but before he had time to mount a proper defence there was an alarm of approaching troops and the meeting was forced to disperse. The parties were not to re-convene, either that day or afterwards.

The meeting had been a disaster. Far from bridging the gap between the Societies and the ministers, it had widened it. For the Societies, the consequences were serious. A sizeable minority, particularly in Carrick, had been inclined to favour Argyle, and remained critical of the stance taken by the leadership. The two ministers were not slow to capitalise on the situation. While Barclay returned relatively soon to Holland, Langlands, who had a persuasive tongue, stayed on for some time and went around the country, preaching a message of tolerance and understanding, and characterising the Societies as factious and divisive. He was helped by a young unordained minister, Adam Alcorn, who joined forces with him for a time.[1] In Carrick particularly, and also to some extent in the Livingston and Calder area of Lothian, they found a receptive audience. The result was the first serious breach in the ranks of the Societies, and the first organised reaction against Renwick and the leadership. From that time, recounts Alexander Shields, sizeable numbers turned against him. Among these were some younger men of particular ability, on whom he had set a high value. This was heavy to bear, and caused him greater grief than the outward persecution.

Langlands for his part pursued the assault relentlessly. On 20th October 1685 he wrote a lengthy letter to Gavin Wotherspoon, a senior member of the Societies and a close associate of Renwick. Wotherspoon had written privately to Langlands, for whom he had some respect, regretting the current divisions and expressing a desire after closer fellowship. Langlands reciprocated Wotherspoon's wishes, and assured him of his own credentials: "I should adventure on any toil or hazard," he told him, "to have the people of God in Scotland one in the truth, united and built together on the old foundation." However, while he shared Wotherspoon's aspirations, he made it clear that he laid the blame for disunity squarely at the door of the Societies. In his letter, which he caused to be circulated widely, he went on to denounce them strongly for what he saw as their exclusivism and their subversion of Presbyterian principles. To add weight to his arguments, he claimed the support of "persons whom you and others reverence", including Alexander Peden, the most prominent of the old field-preachers, who, he said, had written disassociating himself from the Societies' practices "with that sharpness that I believe would be unpleasant to many to hear".

Renwick, of course, got notice of Langlands' letter, and on 13th December he sent an equally full and public reply. The difference between the two letters is notable. While Langlands had written in a strident, hectoring style, Renwick's letter, by contrast, was a model of circumspection and patience. He struck a conciliatory note at the very outset, tempered, as always, with a note of realism: "It does not a little trouble me that you have and expressed so great mistakes of us . . . many are the wormwoods and bitter ingredients in our cup, and I think our sad and wide breaches are amongst the bitterest . . . for mine own part, union in the Lord would be a most rejoicing, pleasant and desirable thing; I say, that union that is bottomed upon the truth and cemented with love, for *any* kind of union would be but a conspiracy and not union. O for that soul-ravishing day when we shall have union rightly qualified! I think that would be the Church of Scotland's restoration."

Renwick went on to counter Langlands' criticisms point by point. Langlands had alleged that the Societies had "overturned Presbyterian government, even to the foundation, and had put in its room a popular confusion". He had maintained that the Societies had taken it upon themselves, and their individual members, to impose spiritual censures and to judge what were necessary causes of separation. Renwick strongly denied this. "Simple withdrawing," he wrote, "is not the inflicting of a censure, but only the believers testifying their sense that the censure should be inflicted by such as are competent"; and he pleaded that, in a "broken state of the church, where ecclesiastical judicatories for censures cannot be had" such action was justifiable, otherwise "all must go into a mixed confusion together, the faithful must become partakers of other men's sins, private and popular means of reclaiming offending brethren shall be stopped, and the testimonies of the faithful shall fall to the ground."

He went on to deal with a particular claim by Langlands that the Societies had taken it on themselves to dictate terms to ministers. The Societies, he wrote, "never in the least intended any restrictions on ministers, but only desire that they may declare unto them the mind of God faithfully, both anent the sins and duties of the day. This is no restriction, neither is it any imposition, neither is it a prescribing rules to ministers; for the Word of God has prescribed this rule. I hold that people are not to judge ministers, yet they are to have a judgement of their own duty how to carry towards ministers. I am against people's desiring anything of ministers but what is divinely bound upon them by the Word of God, and ecclesiastically by our national and solemn Covenants, and Acts of our General Assemblies; so this is not the people's imposition, restriction, or binding, but what is bound by the authority of God and the church."

Next, Renwick refuted a claim by Langlands that the Societies had arrogated to themselves the exercise of civil government. He drew a distinction, which Langlands had failed to make, between disowning a tyrannical ruler, as had been done in the Sanquhar Declaration, and assuming the right of magistracy. The disowning of a tyrant had been no more than "an act radical and natural"; and, he added, "we crave only that right that God and nature have given us". Renwick was at pains to deny that the Societies' public actions had carried any formal or judicial character, but had been founded upon "the law of nature, the fundamental laws of the kingdom, and our laudable constitutions". If the Societies had claimed to act representatively, they had had justification for doing so as the true representatives of a covenanted nation, which was bound by the oaths of the Covenants; they were only doing what the whole nation was under obligation to do. At the same time, he conceded that in this respect the declarations might have been "otherwise expressed, that so they might not have admitted of such various senses".

Finally, Renwick dealt with some personal charges in Langlands' letter. Langlands had alleged, pointedly, that Renwick had written to a friend in Ireland "that there is not a minister in Scotland, England, or Ireland, faithful, save one". Wrote Renwick: "I humbly and kindly desire, that you would consider upon what grounds you have said such a thing. For the charge I deny; and the expression, yes, such a thought, would savour so much of the basest of self that therefore I would abhor it. I shall say no more as to this, but God pardon the unfaithfulness of ministers; and let their deeds prove who has been faithful, and who not." Again, he denied having said, as Langlands alleged, that he was not a minister of the Church of Scotland. "That which I said was, that I am a minister in that place wherever I have a call from the people, and do embrace it." "And," he added, not without a hint of humour, "if your assertion will follow from this, truly I see not well; but I am short-sighted always."

In concluding his letter Renwick expressed the hope that Langlands would take nothing he had said "in ill part". "For," he added, "so far as I can see into mine own heart, it is neither self, nor prejudice, that has moved me unto it; but merely that truth may be cleared, and that the actings of the poor wounded suffering party may not be so sadly misrepresented, to the great detriment of the cause of Christ. I beg you would not give ear to busybodies and talebearers whispering in your ears; for such have had no small hand in widening our breaches. I wish they may have pardon of God for what they have done."

He ended with some stirring words of Christian longing and hope: "O that the Lord's elect were agreeing in truth! O that all these that shall agree in heaven were agreeing upon earth! I think if my blood could be a means to procure it, I could willingly offer it up, upon that account. But I speak as a fool. O that all the Lord's people were searching out their sins, taking with their guilt, mourning for, and forsaking their iniquities! This would be yet some branch of hope. But in the meantime, it does not a little quiet and comfort me that Christ has told that the government is upon his shoulders, and he knows how to erect a glorious fabric out of a mass of confusion. And, I believe, he will make the succeeding generation to reap a glorious fruit of the sad sufferings and contendings that have been in our day."

Renwick's letter may not have borne much fruit at the time, but it did have an interesting sequel. Many years later, Langlands, now a respected senior minister of the Church, was in company with Patrick Walker, the contemporary biographer of Cameron and Cargill, who had been a close friend of Renwick. Walker took the opportunity to remonstrate with him over his exchange with Renwick. Langlands, far from vindicating himself, was overcome with emotion. "He said," says Walker, "he was never so much ashamed of anything in his life"; "for," said he, "I dipped my pen in gall against him, but he dipped his in honey to me."[2]

It might have been expected that, after Argyle's defeat, the persecution of Renwick and the Societies would relax for a time; but far from doing so, it was resumed with renewed vigour. As a result, he was reduced to even greater straits, having now to face not only the outward persecution but the attacks of former friends. "Yet," says Alexander Shields, "all these things did not move him . . . but under all those afflictions he was confirmed more and more that the work was the Lord's, and by the grace and goodness of God he was still the more animated and enlarged in spirit and enabled in body, to increase his diligence in preaching, baptising and examining every week, once at least, which had such success that a great and effectual door was opened to the bringing in of many to Christ, and bringing out such multitudes, flocking after the persecuted Gospel ordinances in the open fields, that it was impossible for him to answer all the calls he received from all parts to preach to them."

In a letter to Hamilton in late October 1685, Renwick speaks of having lately "made a progress through Galloway, and found never such an open door for preaching the Gospel, the people coming far better out than they did before". He had, he wrote, "got eight field-meetings kept there without any disturbance, and six in Nithsdale, many coming out who were not wont to come, and none in any of these places staying away that came out formerly". And despite the activities of Langlands and the others, the position of the Societies remained encouraging. While many in Carrick were "jumbled" and the few in Livingston and Calder were "all in a reel" the main areas of the Societies' strength – Nithsdale, Annandale and Clydesdale – remained solidly loyal.

As he looked back on a tumultuous year, in a letter at the start of 1686, Renwick could take some comfort even in the midst of all his trials. "God has taken this last year many from us, by banishment, and by death on scaffolds, especially in the fields, where none, for the most part, were to see them die but the executioners; and yet God fills up their rooms again. Neither are these things permitted to damp such as are left. Some have, which is more sad, fallen off from us, and yet God is filling up their places also, and making others more steadfast; and notwithstanding both persecutions and reproaches, the Lord has opened doors for me in several places of Scotland, where there used to be no access before, and has multiplied my work so upon my hands that I have observed my work, I say, to be now in some shires threefold and in some fourfold more than it was. Oh that God would send forth labourers! Also, it is almost incredible to tell what zeal, what tenderness, what painfulness in duty, what circumspectness of walk, in many young ones of ten, eleven, twelve and fourteen years of age, in many places of Scotland, which I look upon as one of the visible and greatest tokens for good that we have."

And, as Renwick took courage from the younger generation, so he was strengthened by an encounter with one now nearing his end. There were few events around this time from which Renwick took more satisfaction than his reconciliation, in January 1686, with Alexander Peden, the veteran field-preacher, just before his death. Notwithstanding the Societies' earlier reservations about Peden, he and Renwick had been on terms of mutual respect; indeed Renwick had gone so far as to invite him, following Peden's return from Ireland in March 1685, to share the work of preaching with him. For his own reasons Peden had declined; but he had said, memorably and prophetically, to Renwick: "Go, sir, and be busy about the work God has put you to; for, think on it, neither you nor I will ever see the other side of it." Later, however, Peden had been carefully cultivated by Langlands, Barclay and the others, who saw in him an influential ally to their cause, and he had been somewhat too credulous in believing their adverse reports of Renwick. As a result, Peden had expressed himself very bitterly against him.

On his deathbed Peden had qualms of conscience about his treatment of Renwick, and he could not rest until he had sent for him. Renwick came at once, and was able to spend some time with Peden. What happened at this memorable interview is best told in the inimitable words of Patrick Walker, who had his account from eye-witnesses: "When he was a dying, he sent for Mr Renwick, who hasted to him, who found him lying in very low circumstances, overgrown with hair, and few to take care of him, as he never took much care of his body, seldom he unclothed himself, these years, or went to bed. When Mr James came in, he raised himself upon his bed, leaning upon his elbow with his head upon his hand, and said, "Sir, are ye the Mr James Renwick that there is so much noise about?'. He answered, 'Father, my name is James Renwick, but I have given the world no ground to make any noise about me; for I have espoused no new principle or practice, but what our Reformers and Covenanters maintained'. 'Well, sir,' said Mr Peden, 'turn about your back'; which he did in his condescending temper. Mr Peden said, 'I think your legs too small, and your shoulders too narrow, to take on the whole Church of Scotland upon your back: sit down, sir, and give me an account of your conversion, and of your call to the ministry, of your principles, and the grounds of your taking such singular courses, in withdrawing from all other ministers'; which Mr Renwick did in a distinct manner, of the Lord's way of dealing with him from his infancy, and of three mornings successive in some retired place in the King's Park, where he used to frequent before he went abroad, where he got very signal manifestations and confirmations of his call to the ministry, and got the same renewed in Holland a little before he came off: with a distinct short account of his grounds upon which he contended against tyranny and defections, and kept up an active testimony against all the evils of that day.

When ended, Mr Peden said, 'Ye have answered me to my soul's satisfaction, and I am very sorry that I should have believed any such ill reports of you, which have not only quenched my love to you, and marred my sympathy with you; but made me express myself so bitterly against you, for which I have sadly smarted. But, sir, ere you go you must pray for me, for I am old and going to leave the world'; which he did with more than ordinary enlargement: when ended, he took him by the hand, and drew him to him, and kissed him, and said, 'Sir, I find you a faithful servant to your Master; go on in a single dependence upon the Lord, and ye will win honestly through and cleanly off the stage, when many others that hold their head high will fall and lie in the mire, and make foul hands and garments': then prayed, that the Lord might 'spirit, strengthen, support and comfort him in all duties and difficulties'."

With the veteran's words to encourage him, Renwick committed himself to another year of service.

CHAPTER 12

THE CONTROVERSIES DEEPEN

THE year 1686 marked something of a turning-point in the persecution. The severities of the previous two years were relaxed, and some of the arbitrary measures of repression were modified. A new strategy was forming among those in power, which was eventually to issue in a policy reminiscent of the indulgences of a previous era. At the same time, the new king began to show his hand more openly in favour of his co-religionists. He made clear to the Parliament and Privy Council that he expected the laws against Roman Catholics to be relaxed, in order to remove what he considered to be discrimination against their civil rights and their ability to occupy public positions. However, to his irritation, the Parliament which met on 29th April 1686 proved unexpectedly resistant to his overtures; and in the face of this resistance he resorted to increasingly arbitrary measures. In the midst of these preoccupations the instruments of government in Scotland found themselves having their attention diverted from their pursuit of non-conforming Presbyterians. As a result, Renwick and the Societies experienced something of a temporary respite.

However, while Renwick now found himself less troubled by outward persecution, the troubles from within became more acute. So far, the attacks of the opposition had been directed in a fairly general way against the Societies and their leadership. However, given Renwick's prominent position, it was predictable that they would eventually focus on Renwick himself; and he may well have anticipated that this is the course that events would now take. If that were so, he did not have to wait long.

At the beginning of 1686, a paper was found to be circulating in Carrick which amounted to a direct assault on his standing and ministry. The author of this paper was a certain Robert Cathcart, a young man who had previously been an enthusiastic member of the Societies, and whose defection was thus all the more wounding. Cathcart was able and articulate; his paper was skilfully prepared and expressed, and its language was clearly designed to make the maximum impact. It began with the now familiar criticism of the Societies, though this was expressed in unusually bitter terms: "I think really they are men whom the Lord has given up in a great measure to the delusion of their own deceitful hearts, to believe lies, and to follow the dictates of an erring conscience; yes, and whom the Lord in his anger has plagued with judgements, for their errors are palpable and conspicuous to all who know their practice. With the Papists they would have their church infallible; they decline a minister, be he never so faithful, for the least alleged personal failing. With the independents they take upon themselves the power to depose, thereby delivering the power of the keys of discipline to be in the hands of the laity alone. I think they needed not to have troubled the church at Groningen with ordaining their rabbi Mr Renwick; they might as well have ordained him themselves, ordination being as much in their power as deposition."

The scornful reference to Renwick was followed up by a more explicit assault. "That article of the Covenant anent church discipline and government they have altogether violated and broken, sending over a youth, scarce read in the common heads of divinity, to Groningen, a most corrupt church, never yet come the length of prelacy in its reformation, to be ordained; and having declined the faithful ministers of the Church of Scotland, and set him up in their room, as Jeroboam the son of Nebat did, when he had made the idol calves and set them up at Dan and Bethel, he cried, Behold thy gods, O Israel! So did they of him, Behold thy representative, O Church of Scotland! I can call him nothing but a creature of their own making, and an idol whom they set up in the room of honest ministers of Scotland, whereby they have made the poor suffering remnant to sin. . . . Will they have ordinances of the Gospel to be dispensed by none in Scotland but Mr Renwick? Is there none sufficient for that office but he? Must the Gospel live and die with him? Suppose he were a minister of the Church of Scotland, must we be all tied to him? But a minister of the Church of Scotland he is not, neither can he be admitted to sit a member of a church judicatory in Scotland without breach of its ancient and well-ordered government, for the church at Groningen had no more power to ordain a minister of the Church of Scotland than the clergy of England had long ago to consecrate Sharp Archbishop of St Andrews." Cathcart summed up: "These men have done more harm to the church by their practice than the public enemy was able to do these 25 years by persecution. All the enemy did was a denial of them to preach, and a shedding some of their blood, but these men have dismembered the political body of the church; they have severed one member from another."[1]

In substance there was little in Cathcart's paper which had not already been ventilated by Barclay and Langlands, and the paper showed how well Cathcart had imbibed the teaching of his mentors. But the virulence of the paper, and the vigour with which it was expressed, caused a sensation, and it was widely circulated, not only in Carrick but much further afield. While the paper may have been the work of one individual, it clearly struck a chord with many who shared his opinions, and who were eager to give it currency and credibility. It soon of course came to the notice of the Societies, and of Renwick himself. Renwick did not immediately prepare a reply, since a General Meeting of the Societies was shortly to be held, and it would clearly be best to have the Meeting's authority for any action he might consider taking. In the event, he was to have that opportunity rather earlier than he expected, since representatives from Carrick, who had boycotted the previous two Meetings, decided this time to put in an appearance. What motivated them is not clear, and was a mystery even to Renwick himself. However, as a firm believer in conference and discussion, as against conflict and confrontation, he could well have welcomed the prospect of a reasoned debate with those who had now vented themselves so bitterly against him.

The Meeting, which was clearly a crisis point for the Societies, took place at Friarminion, a desolate spot in the hills above Sanquhar, on 28th January 1686. Representatives of most of the Societies were present. All had written commissions except those from Carrick, who claimed to have been verbally commissioned by those who sent them. After some demur their commissions were sustained, and they were allowed to sit as part of the meeting. Renwick, of course, well knew that his critics had been schooled by such men as Barclay, Langlands and Cathcart, and in an attempt to disarm them he made an opening statement in which he dealt with the grounds of objection. He explained the sense in which the Societies took their various declarations, making clear that they did not necessarily abide by all the expressions used, particularly those which might suggest an assumption of ecclesiastical or civil authority. Similarly, he defended the Societies' General Meetings as in no sense authoritative or judicial, but merely "meetings of Christians for promoting the work of

God in our station and capacity". He explained the sense in which the Societies regarded ministerial fellowship, emphasising that they did not see all differences as justifiable grounds for separation, and recognising the right of private judgement. Finally, he spoke at some length about his ordination, defending all the circumstances of it, and quoting from a report sent back by two delegates to the Dutch churches, which refuted claims that the churches in Holland were, in effect, subordinate to the civil magistrate.

Renwick then turned to challenge his critics. He asked them, pointedly, if they adhered to Cathcart's paper or had had a hand in spreading it, but received only an evasive reply. A similar answer met his question as to whether they adhered to the Declaration by Argyle. He then challenged them for associating with ministers, such as Langlands and Barclay, against whom the Societies had unresolved objections, and for doing so without the general consent of the Societies. The Carrick men contended that where, as they saw it, the general consent was unreasonably withheld, they were free to associate as they pleased. They laid their position on the line: "We are clear to call and hear all such ministers of the gospel as have faithfully owned, do own and adhere to the true received principles of the Church of Scotland, founded upon the written Word of God, and whatsoever declarations or testimonies, former or latter, particular or general, are agreeable thereto." They were then asked whether, having had their points heard, they were willing to rejoin the fellowship of the Societies. Again they evaded the question, and asked whether the Societies would join with them. Renwick, at this, decided to force the issue to a conclusion. He asked all the others present whether, in the light of the evasions, and the actions of the Carrick men in disregarding the will of the majority, they were willing any longer to associate with them in General Meetings and Societies. The answer was a convincing negative. The Carrick men protested that it was merely because they were "clear to call faithful ministers" that they were being cut off from fellowship. Renwick of course denied this; but when he and others tried to reason with them, the Carrick men refused to listen further, and walked out of the meeting.

Once again, an attempt to resolve issues by debate had been a disaster. The meeting had worsened the situation rather than improving it. When they returned home, the Carrick delegation held a meeting of sympathisers at which it was agreed to spread their causes of discontent more widely, and to make people of influence aware of their position. The disaffection spread south into Galloway and north into other parts of Ayrshire, and began to threaten the cohesion of the Societies in a part of the country where they had been at their strongest. It became evident to Renwick and the rest that some effort must be made to retrieve the situation before it spread out of control.

So it was that in March 1686, at a time of very tempestuous weather, Renwick with a few friends ventured to make an expedition into Carrick. It is not clear how Renwick had meant to address the situation, or whom he had intended to meet; but in the event his agenda dictated its own terms. His coming had clearly become known, for scarcely had he and his friends settled into their lodgings when they were visited by Robert Cathcart, and a number of others with him. Their attitude did not bode well for recon-ciliation. Truculently, Cathcart asked Renwick what he was doing there, and whether he intended to preach. Renwick replied that he had merely come to see Cathcart and the others; and, while he did not intend to preach, he had little doubt that if he decided to do so, he would have no lack of people to call him. Cathcart assured him that he knew the mind of the people, and that they wished neither to meet nor to converse with Renwick.

There followed yet another of the confrontational discussions with which Renwick was now well familiar. Though Cathcart maintained that he had not come to debate, but rather to protest against Renwick's presence, he nevertheless challenged him on a wide range of issues, pressing his points with increasing vehemence. Renwick maintained his composure throughout, and while dealing courteously with all the points put to him, nevertheless refused to compromise one inch of his position. Cathcart told him that he recognised him as a minister of the Gospel, but not as a minister of the Church of Scotland. Renwick maintained that the appropriation which he had to the Church of Scotland made him a minister of that Church, since he had been sent abroad by the Societies to be ordained, and called by them when he came home. Cathcart pressed him particularly on the manner of his ordination, accusing him of disowning the ministry of the Church of Scotland, and accepting ordination from a church with known corruptions in its practice. Renwick defended himself vigorously against this charge, maintaining that, at the time, there had been no ministers in Scotland who were faithfully discharging their public work, or who might not have sought to impose sinful restrictions on his ministry, as had been done in the case of Richard Cameron. The Dutch church, he pointed out, had already vindicated itself from the charge of subjection to the civil power, as he had made clear at the meeting in January. Cathcart pressed him on the point that the Dutch church used three sprinklings in baptism. Renwick held this to be a matter indifferent, provided there was no superstitious significance attached to it, as he was convinced there was not. He produced a book by an eminent divine which he offered to quote in his support, but Cathcart and his friends were dismissive of this.[2]

The rest of the discussion followed an all too familiar pattern. Widening the debate, Cathcart and his associates accused the Societies of exclusivism, and of being deviants from the received practice and principles of the Church of Scotland. Renwick strongly denied this charge, asserting that the Societies were merely "following the faithful that had gone before them, maintaining nothing but what was authorised by the Acts of the General Assembly". Cathcart asked him bluntly if he recognised the ministry and government of the Church of Scotland. Renwick strongly asserted that he did. How then, asked Cathcart, can you recognise the government and not the governors? Renwick maintained that there was an essential difference. "Though all the ministers in Scotland, yea in the world, were dead, the government stands in the Word of God." As for himself, he recognised only those governors of the church who put its government and discipline rightly into execution; but no others. He dismissed claims by the other side that the Societies had debarred them from fellowship because they had called those whom they regarded as faithful ministers. On the contrary, it was by associating with men unfaithful to their calling – some who had unjustly traduced the Societies and others who were disaffected towards the Covenants – that the Carrick men themselves had caused the separation.

Cathcart, now becoming increasingly agitated and vehement, called out that he was formally protesting against Renwick exercising any part of the ministerial function, or even engaging in private converse, in any part of Carrick or the neighbouring shire of Wigtown. Renwick, in an attempt to save the situation, took him by the hand and pleaded with him to stay and debate the issues soberly. Cathcart however was irreconcilable; and, accompanied by his friends, abruptly rose up and left the meeting. From a distance he shouted back at Renwick and the rest, hurling a series of accusations and reproaches which made it only too clear to Renwick that his attempt at reconciliation had utterly failed.

There was clearly to be no opening now for Renwick in Carrick, and there was no purpose in staying any longer. Later that same day, he and his friends took their leave. By now, they had an increasing presentiment of danger; and they even feared treachery on the part of Cathcart and his associates. Their fears appeared to be justified when, that very night, a party of troops came from Cumnock in search of a field-meeting where Renwick was reported to be planning to preach. Renwick himself had made no such plan, but the news was enough for him to realise the depth of the bitterness against him, and the futility of making any more efforts at reconciliation.

The campaign against Renwick and the Societies now gathered pace. Shortly after the meeting in Carrick, a sympathiser of the Societies was visiting some ministers and others imprisoned on the Bass Rock. With them he found a copy of a letter from the Carrick men whom Renwick had met in January, giving an account of the meeting and asking the ministers' advice. There was also a paper, entitled *An information against Mr Renwick's party, given in to ministers,* attacking the Societies on a wide range of fronts. On enquiry it emerged that the papers had been left by Alexander Gordon, who had been present at the meeting, and who was now playing a prominent part in the opposition to Renwick. Gordon, the informant discovered, had also left the papers with ministers imprisoned in Blackness Castle, near Queensferry, and probably with others. There was nothing on the face of the "information" paper to suggest that it had not been compiled by the Carrick men themselves, but the style and substance of it pointed directly to Robert Langlands, and it had clear echoes of his letter the previous October. The Societies, it charged, had arrogated to themselves the government of church and state; they had imposed restrictions on ministers and cast off the whole suffering ministry; they had imposed on the Dutch church, through the "lying misinformation" of Robert Hamilton, to ordain Renwick, whose first public work had been to denounce faithful ministers, even Robert MacWard, after his death; they had made "canons" laying down the qualifications of those fitted to be members of their meetings, forbidding association with those they regarded as unfaithful, even to the extent of servants joining in family worship with their masters, or children with their parents; and, not least, they had "cast off most part of the societies in the shires of Ayr and Galloway, chiefly upon these two heads, that they would not disown and condemn the declaration published by Argyle, and because they were clear to call and hear faithful suffering ministers".

This latest paper was duly reported at the Societies' General Meeting on 7th April, where it caused a good deal of consternation. It was one thing for such allegations to be circulated privately, among the Societies' own constituency, as Cathcart's paper had been, or Langlands' letter to Wotherspoon; it was quite another for them to be brought before influential ministers whose support the Societies were keen to cultivate. It was unanimously decided that a detailed response was necessary, for the Societies' own vindication. A Committee to draw this up was appointed, comprising five leading members of the Societies, including Renwick himself. Somewhat surprisingly, the task of producing the first draft was entrusted to William Boyd, Renwick's former fellow-student, who had returned from Holland in June 1684. Boyd had later been arrested by the authorities, and had spent some time in Dunnottar Castle, but he had contrived to escape and was now back with the Societies. In the event, Boyd's attempt at a draft Vindication did not gain general acceptance, and Renwick found himself obliged to rewrite virtually the whole document himself.

As if Renwick did not have enough to distract him, at around this time he was again drawn into confrontation with his former fellow-student, John Flint, whom the Societies had recalled from Holland after he had attached himself to the cause of James Russel. Flint had returned from Holland in July or August 1684, though not in deference to the Societies, and had promptly set himself up in opposition to Renwick. He acted as a fully-fledged minister, preaching to those who would hear him, and even conducting marriages. He was helped for a time by James Russel's brother Thomas, who had studied with him in Holland.[3] Flint sought to appeal to the more strict among Renwick's followers, particularly to some who had scruples about the Dutch church or who were attracted by the distinctives which Flint and his party sought to project, such as payment of tolls and customs and reform of the names of days and months. While he was never a real threat to Renwick, he did succeed in inducing some of Renwick's followers to leave him for a time. The Societies enquired of the Dutch church about Flint's credentials, and were told that he had received neither licence nor ordination from them, but merely a certificate confirming that he had completed his studies. On the strength of this they issued a public Protestation or Testimony against him, and were able to reclaim several who now acknowledged their error in hearing him. As a result, Flint's influence declined to the point where he was left with only a handful of followers.

At their General Meeting on 28th January 1686 the Societies had before them a request from Flint to meet him, which with some reluctance they granted. In the event the meeting did not take place until 28th May, when Renwick and some others met Flint briefly in Edinburgh. Flint complained of Renwick's behaviour towards him and Boyd at Groningen, and accused Robert Hamilton of giving false information to the Dutch church. Renwick and the others answered these allegations, and in turn challenged Flint with his behaviour since coming home. The meeting proved inconclusive, but while Flint showed no desire to be reconciled to the Societies he had now ceased to be any real threat to their unity. Renwick had the satisfaction of knowing that Flint had lost any potential for divisiveness which he once had, and that the caucus comprising Flint, James and

Thomas Russel and Patrick Grant was unlikely to trouble him and the Societies further. James Russel by now had fallen into disgrace in Holland through an irregular marriage; Flint and Thomas Russel, who had preached together for a time, had parted company; and Grant, though continuing a pamphlet war with the Societies for many years, was not to be a significant threat in Renwick's lifetime.[4]

In the meantime, the other traducers and cavillers were spreading their propaganda widely. After the meeting in Carrick Robert Cathcart wrote to various people of influence in Edinburgh, Ireland, and elsewhere, claiming that Renwick had recognised the validity of three sprinklings in baptism, and that when this was put in question he could say nothing, but merely "took out a book out of his pocket and said that would prove it". There were of course many who could and did testify that Renwick had at no time used the practice himself, and indeed held that it would be a reprehensible innovation were it introduced in the Scottish church; but in the differing circumstances in Holland he could not in fairness condemn it. However, the allegations caused Renwick no little trouble.

At the same time, Alexander Gordon and his accomplices were busy in their own way. They wrote to ministers who had gone to England and Ireland, sending them copies of their "information" and urging them to return home. They met with some encouragement from the ministers they had approached in the Bass and Blackness, who arranged for some young men from Edinburgh to go to preach to them. Gordon himself went over to Holland, where the "information" was spread among the Dutch churches.[5] He tried to enlist sympathy from the Scottish ministers in Rotterdam, though with limited success, but managed to prevail with George Barclay, whom he met in Amsterdam, to return to Scotland for a time.[6]

However, what Gordon no doubt saw as his most telling achievement was to bring back an account of a meeting with William Brakel, who had been so instrumental in Renwick's ordination, and a foremost supporter and favourer of the Societies. Brakel's view was now very different, and the report of it filled the Societies with dismay. No doubt, Brakel had been influenced by what he had heard from Gordon; but there can also be little doubt that his view had been coloured by a violent disagreement with Robert Hamilton, with whom he had earlier been on terms of close friendship.

The source of the disagreement was a call which Brakel had accepted to a church in Rotterdam, instigated largely at the behest of the civil authorities. Hamilton judged that, in accepting the call, Brakel had compromised the principle of spiritual independence, and, true to character, he had not hesitated to tell Brakel so in forthright terms. Brakel was highly offended, and made his displeasure very plain. His bitterness was very evident in the account now brought back from Holland: "I am certainly informed that Mr Hamilton gave me out in Scotland as being one that inclined to Erastianism and as one that had perfidiously relinquished my charge and do exercise my present charge only by virtue of a certain civil or politic call, but truly they are only fancies, and lies, reported only for that end that I might have no credit amongst you if any time I should make known to you his cheats, and lying reports, and show by what means he deceived me and that I might thereby be the less able to oppose him. . . . He stirs up a schism amongst you for his own advantage. . . . By his improvidence he has done much damage to the Church of Scotland: for a long time he did live very obscurely and in contempt; now he hopes by evil means to acquire to himself some power, now he nourishes divisions amongst you under pretext of piety; do not you follow him, who himself lies hidden and exposes you to all hazards."

But the most part of the account was given over to Brakel's view of Renwick and the Societies. "If I were with Mr Renwick, I would put him to call to mind the saying which at his parting I said to him, while he was requiring of me some memorable token, Be not righteous over much, neither make thyself over wise; why shouldest thou destroy thyself? Now you understand not this; but remember that this I said to you, that sometime it shall be useful. Now it is time to live according to that word. Oh what need has he now of that admonition! If I were present with them that do adhere to Mr Renwick, these that refuse to hear ministers, I would show them how great a sin schism is; and that the wrath of God is not far off from them who make and cherish separation. I with tears in the name of Jesus would beg that, leaving schism, they might live with their brethren in peace, love and unanimity. To decline union in every truth is nothing but pride and lordliness . . . if there be any that in his conscience thinks other ministers ought not to be heard, he errs in simplicity, and it is necessary that most quickly he leave that error."

Brakel reacted with particular vehemence to reports, diligently spread by Gordon and the rest, that the Societies had been giving their various declarations the virtual status of terms of communion. "As for the Sanquhar declaration, in so far as it denies the king's authority and declares a war against him, it is a mere madness . . . it is no Christian duty to debate about these and the like things, and for such causes to raise a schism. Oh how sad is it that so many do place godliness in maintaining the Sanquhar declaration, and in separating from them who in their judgement are not so zealous in these or other circumstances. I admonish them to cease from these and such like courses, if they be lovers of Christ and his cause and love not their own bodily and spiritual ruin. I pray therefore, do not make such feckless things grounds of schism; do not I pray stain piety with such a blot. Why do you sport with God, religion and the church? Leave things of the state to statesmen. Leave off such debates; God's anger is kindled against Scotland; do not kindle it more."

Brakel had particularly harsh words for the Protestation against the Scottish Church in Rotterdam, which he insisted had been compiled by Hamilton: "I warn you to forbear any such like toys. Place not piety in such things. It is enough that you have raised a schism by such cavils and brought a stain upon piety and that you have given occasion to the ungodly to reproach the name of God. Return unto the way, you that love godliness, be of one mind with all that fear the Lord, and if there be any that are obstinate, let them be gone."

Renwick, though Brakel's remarks about him had been candid enough, saw no need to take offence at them. He had been deeply indebted to Brakel for his ordination, and he continued to hold him in respect. As it happened, the Scripture which Brakel had quoted at him was one that he had often in his mind, for, he said, it often helped him to avoid extremes of opinion, practice, or self-conceit. Brakel's words against the Societies were more serious, but Renwick was content to leave these to be dealt with by the Vindication which had already been commissioned by the General Meeting. He did not want his critics at home to have the satisfaction of a hasty or ill-tempered response, either on his own behalf or that of the Societies, and in this he was undoubtedly right.

CHAPTER 13

TESTIFYING AMID TRIBULATION

THE machinations of his critics, and their constant harassment of him, continued to cause Renwick much pain. Particularly wounding were the attacks from those who had formerly been his associates, and with whom he had shared fellowship in the Gospel. Yet, even these trials did not deflect him from the work closest to his heart. The first months of 1686 were as busy as any in his ministry. On 6th May he wrote to Hamilton, apologising for being so long silent, and excusing himself on the ground that he had had so much to do. "I would," he wrote, "have written far sooner, but my work keeps me busy; so much of it lies in the remote corners of the land, as Galloway, Nithsdale, Annandale, etc. I have not been near Edinburgh since the 16th of October 1685, and I have travelled since through Clydesdale, Eskdale, some of the Forest[1], Annandale, some of Galloway, Kyle and Cunningham; and in all those places I examined the Societies as I passed through, several other persons coming to hear, and I found my work greater this last journey than ever before. Also in lower Cunningham, where there had never been any field-preachers, I got kindly acceptance, and great multitudes came to hear; and I have had several calls since from that countryside. Such like have I found through Renfrew. Moreover, the Lord has wrought a great change on the barony of Sanquhar, the parish of Kirkconnel, and these dark corners. Generally they come to hear the Gospel and are quitting many of the defections of the time. I may say, to the Lord's praise, that our meetings were never so numerous, and the work did never thrive more than since man opposed it so much."

Such an account of Renwick's preaching tours is rare in his correspondence, and he was generally reticent in writing of them, even to friends such as Hamilton. However, some fuller details do emerge from the accounts of those meetings which came to the attention of the authorities. Where this happened, some of the hearers were invariably tracked down and questioned, and their testimonies placed on record. Particularly memorable was a meeting at Stonehouse, in Lanarkshire, on 17th January, when, at a time of tempestuous weather, Renwick felt justified in taking the use of the parish church to preach, and to baptise some children. Graphic accounts survive, by people living in the neighbourhood, of their being aroused late at night by strangers asking for horses to take them over the swollen Avon Water, which lay between them and the church. Witnesses told of the church being "so throng (i.e. crowded) that the kirk walls were like to burst" and such was the volume of the psalm-singing that it could be heard a quarter of a mile away.

A particularly interesting testimony was given by a countryman who had been made to act as a guide and been taken by some of the worshippers into the church, "where he saw a man in the pulpit, a young man of the age of thirty years or thereby as he conceived, of a round face and fair hair, and that his text was in the 34th Psalm in those words 'O taste and see that God is good'". It is one of the few testimonies to Renwick's personal appearance. Shields records that he was "of a little stature, and of a comely youthful countenance"; and to James Nisbet there was "none so comely in features". But above all, it is a striking tribute to his appeal as a preacher, and to the hunger of his hearers for the Gospel, that on a wild January night several hundred people were prepared to assemble in a cold, desolate building to hear him, many of them having to travel long distances in darkness and danger.

Most of Renwick's meetings continued to be held under cover of night. At times, however, and particularly in summer, he ventured to preach in the fields in the hours of daylight. One such occasion was in Lauderdale, in Berwickshire, on Sabbath 18th July. Again, graphic accounts of this occasion survive, some of them by hearers who were captured by the authorities, others by local herdboys who had come upon the meeting and, for security's sake, had been kept there until the preaching had finished. One hearer, John Stewart, described how on the Saturday night two men from Edinburgh had come to his house and invited him to "hear a preaching and he would think his travel well worth it". The three of them had left next morning before sunrise, stopping for breakfast on the way, and until the minister arrived one of the other two, known simply as "William", had prayed, read Scripture and sung a psalm. Stewart went on to testify that there had been two sermons, both from the Song of Solomon; "that the minister came from Lothian by the Redstoneridge, but knows not whither he went after sermons; that he thought there was about six-score at the meeting, whereof two parts were women, twelve had horse, diverse of them swords, the minister a shabble, one a pair of pistols, and two of them carabines". John Blaikie, a herd-boy of eighteen, testified that "coming from his dinner on Sunday last to look after his flock he saw a multitude of people together who had scouts on tops of the hills", and that when he and his companions came near them "they would not suffer them to go from them again but made them stay all the time of sermon; that when he asked who preached he was told it was Mr James Renwick". Another, John Rankin, said that he too had been detained against his will; he confirmed that the preacher had been Renwick, and that his text had been "the first chapter of the Song of Solomon at the fourth verse".

Later in the summer the local courts in Dumfries were kept busy questioning people who had attended a night-time meeting kept by Renwick at Gawin Moor, some five miles north of Dumfries, on Sabbath 15th August. Estimates of those present ranged from three hundred to a thousand; they had had "15 or 16 torches"; Renwick had preached from Hebrews chapter 13, verses 13 and 14, and afterwards baptised several children; and there had been twenty to thirty armed men present. Another night-time meeting, at Dechmont Hill in the parish of Cambuslang on Sabbath 17th October, was reported to have attracted up to 1,500 people. This meeting was remarkable in that it was held only some five miles from Glasgow, and such were the crowds attending it that it seemed to one witness that the whole parish of Cambuslang was present. Renwick had begun preaching at ten o'clock at night and afterwards had baptised some sixteen children, and the congregation had all been dismissed before daylight. Estimates of the armed men present ranged from twenty to sixty.

These were of course only the meetings which came to the attention of the authorities, and there can be no doubt that Renwick preached much more extensively than the court records suggest. What does emerge from the rather scanty evidence is that the meetings were well-organised and well-disciplined, and that Renwick, far from operating on his own, was the centre of a highly efficient organisation which not only protected him from harm, but also largely arranged and managed his preaching programme. What is also clear from these records is that Renwick's ministry at this time extended over wide areas of central and southern Scotland and that the influence of his preaching was far greater than his opponents would have it believed. According to them, Renwick was but the leader of an insignificant handful, steadily losing any little influence he had. The reality was that, under sustained persecution from outside and the attacks of erstwhile friends from within, he could still number his congregations in many hundreds.

In the summer of 1686, just after his field-meeting in Lauderdale, Renwick spent some time in the north of England. He had been there at least once before – briefly in the spring of 1685 – but on this occasion he stayed for some three to four weeks. His visit allowed him time for a brief respite from the pressures which afflicted him in Scotland. His stay in England was in no sense a holiday, however, as he preached regularly each Sabbath, and also occasionally through the week. He still had to take careful precautions for his safety, and though most of his Sabbath services were held openly without disturbance he deemed it prudent to hold all his weekday meetings at night. Many of his hearers were Baptists, or Anabaptists as they were then known, who, though differing in practice from the Presbyterians of Scotland, nevertheless admired the testimony of the persecuted ministers and indeed had contributed to their support.

All went well until Renwick, with perhaps more honesty than policy, ventured to preach one day on the theme of infant baptism, vindicating his and the Scottish Church's position from Scripture, and supporting his arguments with quotations from eminent divines. His hearers listened politely, but afterwards made clear to him their resentment at what he had done. They had, they reminded him, been ready to support the suffering church in the past, and any other Scottish ministers who had visited them had avoided such controversial subjects in their preaching. Renwick was disappointed, but unrepentant. As he saw it, his work was to declare the whole counsel of God; and if he was to be beholden to his hearers at the cost of faithfulness to his calling, he had no doubt what his priority should be. He suggested to his hearers that their hospitality to Scottish ministers had been damaging both to the ministers and to themselves; for it had hindered the ministers from fully delivering their consciences, and had made their hearers feel that they had put the ministers under obligation not to preach anything that would offend them. This was altogether too frank for his hearers' liking.

Later, when he was leaving, one of them told him that they had intended making a collection for him; but, he added drily, he supposed Renwick would not accept it. Renwick said that he had not gone among them for that purpose, and the matter was not further pursued. Later, he wrote somewhat ruefully to Hamilton: "They who before had seemed to have much love and affection would not afterwards carry themselves civil. . . . I say that they that deal freely with them will not get long their countenance." There is no evidence that he visited England again.

Alongside these efforts, no trouble was spared to blacken the name of the Societies, and Renwick in particular. His very readiness to debate with opponents, and to try to seek accommodations, became a tool for them to disparage him. He was depicted as weak, easily led, and beholden to the more extreme elements among his followers. He had come, it was said, merely "at a throw of the dice", a contemptuous allusion to the method of his selection by the Societies. Progressively, the attacks on him grew more vicious. A paper was drawn up, and sent over to Holland, describing him as "but a poor, unlearned, empty, blown up, proud thing" who had now been deserted by everyone except "about a hundred silly, poor bodies that were running through with him and robbing the country".

Sadly, these new attacks prevailed with some whom Renwick and the Societies had previously counted their friends. Among them was Jacob Koelman, a Dutch minister and associate of William Brakel, who had formerly shown the Societies much kindness, and in 1679 had taken part in the ordination of Richard Cameron. In a letter of 30th September 1686 Robert Hamilton reported with dismay that Koelman too had now turned the Societies' enemy. In Hamilton's own presence he said he had "very distinct information from sure hands, that the report of a witnessing party in Scotland was all lies; that there were indeed about a hundred bodies there, led by Renwick a poor blown up illiterate person, who but very lately had any profession of religion; that he preached publicly but once in twenty days, or a month; that the people that followed him were for killing all that were not of their own judgement; that their suffering was their sin, bringing themselves in hazard; and that the ministers had told him that if ever there were a General Assembly or States of their mind, they would make Renwick and Hamilton, and all that have been active in misleading these poor bodies, suffer for it in the highest degree; that they are a dreadful party, who will sometimes go into a gentleman's house and take whatever makes for them, and when done will run away, whereby the poor family is both spoiled by them, and laid open to the enemies' persecution; and that Renwick would come to a place for one night and preach, and then presently runs away; and thus occasions the silly people to be murdered and plundered".

It was sufficiently wounding that Renwick's enemies should vent such calumnies against him; but that former friends should be so credulous, and so ready to believe the worst of him, caused Renwick much grief. He received at about the same time a letter from Koelman, couched certainly in more measured terms than his tirade to Hamilton, but nevertheless implying that Renwick was following separatist courses and that he should seriously consider uniting with his brethren rather than maligning them.

Renwick responded courteously but firmly. "I know," he wrote, "you are informed in many falsities, and you do credulously believe and sedulously spread the same. This from the hand of famous, learned and godly Koelman is most wounding to me." He told him: "I am as much for a right qualified union as any; but the union which is had without truth and holiness I can call no other thing but a conspiracy. . . . I cannot unite, where I must thereby harden the hearts and strengthen the hands of such as are engaged in and carrying on a course of defection and backsliding from the Lord, and so partake of their sins. I cannot unite, where I cannot expect the propagating of the words of Christ's patience, deposited to us at this time to contend and suffer for. I desire to mind what is given in command to Jeremiah, Let them return unto thee, but return not thou unto them. I must not divide from the Head, to unite with any professed members." But even in these uncompromising words, Renwick was careful to make a qualification. He was speaking, he told Koelman, in a "broken and declining state" of the Church; and it was in that context that he wanted his words to be interpreted.

The exchange with Koelman only served to confirm the words of Alexander Shields: "The keenest, most cruel and most constant persecution, most prevailing with his opposites, and most piercing to him, was the persecution of tongues; and of their tongues especially, who sometimes said the same thing, and were embarked in the same lot with himself; giving him occasion to complain with David, Mine own familiar friend, in whom I trusted, which did eat of my bread, has lifted up his heel against me. . . . So incessant were they with their whisperings that, to his greatest grief, they so far insinuated themselves into his most endeared familiars, as to incense them also against him; and not only induce them to entertain, but to engage them also to express invectives against him." But, as always, Renwick was able to ascribe even these bitter trials to the will of the Lord. Writing to Hamilton about this time he noted: "The Lord has seen that our furnace, by the inquisition and torture of the common enemies, has not been searching enough, therefore he must prepare another kind of furnace to try us better. Blessed are they who shall come forth as gold. God will arise, and dispel these present mists and confusions, and let it be seen what great need there has been of all that comes to pass."

His former friends, to maintain the momentum of their attacks, invented increasingly outrageous accusations against him. They put it about that he was secretly in league with the Government; that he was plotting to deliver up those ministers who differed from him; even that he was a paid agent of Rome sent over to subvert the Church of Scotland. As time went on, this new persecution became sharper still. The basest of charges against him were hawked around the country. He was made the butt of the scorner, and lampooned in cheap rhyme. In the face of all this evil, Renwick maintained his integrity. He was well aware of what his adversaries were doing to him; he confided to Hamilton in August 1686 that he was being subjected to "as gross slanders as can be invented". But he would not, he insisted, answer railing for railing. He maintained he was less concerned about any offence done to himself than about the damage his traducers were doing to themselves; and events were to prove him right.

As they were to find, it was but a step from slandering Renwick to descending into a general looseness of life and conduct. Alexander Gordon, his leading detractor, was to become notorious for drunkenness and eventually died after a drunken brawl; and John Dick, Gordon's close associate, was later to be employed as a trooper in the Government's service. Others became enmeshed in complicity of various kinds with the authorities, and forsook even the appearance of a public witness. As a result, not a few whom they had imposed upon came to revise their opinions, and to rue their credulity. Renwick emerged from the trial with enhanced standing in the eyes of many. In October 1686 he could write to Hamilton: "Notwithstanding of all breakings, my business multiplies still upon my hand, and people are more earnest now than ever I knew them after the Gospel." For Renwick, continued faithfulness was bringing its own reward.

There still of course remained other trials to be confronted. In a letter of 23rd October to Hamilton, Renwick desired to know his mind "anent a particular which is like to break us more than any thing that the ministers can do". He was referring to the question, agitated by some, of whether it was right for young people or servants who supported the testimony of the Societies to join in family worship with parents or masters who complied with the authorities. The matter had been first raised at a General Meeting in January 1685, and had led to inconclusive debate. Renwick was deeply troubled at the potential of this issue for dividing the Societies. He well understood the plight of some who found it grievous to their consciences to join in worship with parents or masters who, for example, called down God's vengeance on the Societies, or prayed for the success of their persecutors. At the same time he was conscious of the scandal to which the Societies exposed themselves if they were seen to be encouraging divisions in families, or the break-up of natural loyalties. He therefore proceeded with great caution. He recognised that there was no solution to the problem which could be applied indiscriminately, without recognition of all the circumstances. He therefore gave what private advice he could to enquirers, and sought to prevent the matter coming before the Societies for any formal determination. That, predictably, did not prevent the Societies from being portrayed as disturbers of family unity, a charge which their opponents did their utmost to exploit. Indeed, in their paper of early 1686, Alexander Gordon and his friends had instanced a case of an individual debarred from the Societies' meetings because he had joined in family worship with his father, who heard the indulged ministers. The matter continued to trouble the Societies, but Renwick's judicious approach avoided a more serious breach.

The closing weeks of 1686 were a busy time for Renwick. Around mid-November he ventured to visit Galloway. He had stayed away from the area since his earlier confrontation with Cathcart, but he now clearly felt that it was time for him to test the loyalty of the people again. He was careful not to intrude into Wigtown, which Cathcart regarded as part of his "parish" and where he had debarred Renwick from preaching, but thought that he could reasonably go into the adjoining area of central Galloway where he had preached several times before, and where he had been able to count on the support of friends loyal to him. However, as he later recorded: "I met with no small opposition . . . a great many were vexed, and did their utmost to oppose it." Indeed, Renwick was to find that the disaffection which had started in Carrick had by no means spent its force, but had spread its influence through the surrounding country. Scarcely had he arrived in Galloway when he was confronted with a written Protestation, "in the name of all the Societies between the Dee and Cree" objecting to his "intrusion" into their bounds until his ordination had been approved by "some competent number of the faithful ministers of the Church of Scotland". Any such intrusion, the paper went on, would be regarded as "horrid and abominable usurpation" which would be "not only divisive, but destructive to the poor suffering remnant of this church".

The paper, unlike those previously brought against Renwick, was confused and inarticulate, and had clearly not been written by any of the ministers against whom Renwick had been contending. Nevertheless, he found it sufficiently disturbing that such a paper should have emanated from a district which he had once counted loyal, even before many others. He was disturbed too by the fact that, apart from the strictures against himself, the paper classed as "debatable matters" a number of issues which he had thought were no longer in debate, such as hearing the curates, paying the Cess, and swearing the Oath of Abjuration. That such matters should even be thought of as "debatable" appalled him; and he determined to controvert the paper at the first opportunity.

A few days later, when he held a well-attended meeting in the fields, he read the paper before his audience, pleading with its supporters to renounce it, and urging others to disassociate themselves from it. He also framed a reply, in the form of an open letter, in which he exposed the paper's inconsistencies and errors. What, he argued, was the point of asking for matters to be determined that had long ago been decided in principle by the General Assemblies of the Church? Why were the protesters bringing into debate matters that had been resolved by the Church in her best days? Were they not thereby challenging Reformation principles? And who did they reckon could now comprise a "faithful General Assembly"? As to his own position, Renwick was utterly unyielding. His ordination, he affirmed, had been "valid and lawful" and he was prepared to give satisfaction on that point to any truly faithful minister, or indeed to anyone with a genuine concern. Renwick vigorously defended himself against the charge of "intrusion". He had never intruded on any faithful minister's labours; nor had he embarked on his work until he had been persuaded and convinced of the need. "I think," he wrote, "I may say before God, that it was pity toward the scattering sheep of Christ in this land, who were fainting and swooning through the famine of public ordinances, that moved me to subject myself, in such a weak condition, to so great a work, and to undergo so many perils and wanderings. It is most likely, if labourers had been faithful and laborious, I had laboured none to this very day."

Renwick suspected, and probably rightly, that the paper against him had not had its true origin in Galloway, but among those with whom he had earlier contended in Carrick. He therefore closed his reply with some words of heartfelt appeal which reflected how much this latest onslaught had grieved him. "Notwithstanding of all that you have done against me, I have love to you, and desire to behave myself as a friend. I may say I am filled with a great measure of sorrow and amazement when I consider your present course and carriage, and compare it with your former. Many of you and I have wandered in the silent watches of the night together, been in perils together, fled from the sword of the common adversary together; and I appeal to yourselves, if you have not found sometimes something of the power of God in our solemnities together. You have suffered much at the hand of the enemy, even to the shedding of the blood of many of you, which I hope was acceptable to God, and is a part of the seed of the church. You professed with us the same thing that we own and profess this day; you were the most forward for action, and we gloried in you, and boasted of you, and I think this has been our sin, and a part of the cause of your judgement." He closed with some words of solemn warning: "Consider how you have sadly wronged the interest of Christ; have made the enemy to blaspheme; made conscientious sufferers to stumble and fall; have hardened the hearts and strengthened the hands of those who are engaged in a course of defection, so that they do not turn from the evil of their ways; have done so much to deprive posterity of the truths which ought to be transmitted to them; and finally, how you have thereby sinned against your own souls. Now, I beseech you, consider your ways."

Renwick continued to believe that the authors of the Protestation were not fully representative of the people in Galloway; and so he persevered with his preaching tour. As he progressed, he was more and more confirmed in this view; and later he was able to record: "I had great access to preach the Gospel, the Lord wonderfully restraining enemies, and drawing out very many to hear, and moving them to give great outward encouragement." He was able to hold thirteen meetings in the fields, four of them in the hours of daylight, and had nine meetings with the local Societies. Looking back on his visit he concluded: "I hope, through the Lord's blessing, that that small piece of labour shall not want its fruit."

Leaving Galloway, Renwick moved on to the area around Dumfries, where he visited John Welsh's old parish of Irongray. There he met with still more opposition, this time from a prominent local elder who protested formally at his presence. Renwick however stood his ground, and asserted his right to be there on the call of the people. By this time he was becoming inured to criticism, and felt able to be more assertive in vindicating his position. His adversary was put to shame. Later Renwick recalled the episode with a touch of dry humour: "He was so drunk, either with wine, or with the fury of the Lord, or with both, that he could hear nothing, and he answered with nothing but with clamour and crying (O the depths of Satan!) that I had destroyed the church, and that the ministers had a libel drawn up against me. Whereupon I declared that none of these things did terrify me, and that this was the work of the Lord, and that I was resolved in his strength to go on in it, while my breath governed my joints, and I enjoined silence upon him." Renwick had learned valuable lessons in the hard school of experience.

Despite all the internal pressures on Renwick, the year 1686 had been characterised by a marked slackening in the outward persecution. Indeed, Renwick himself could reflect in a letter to Hamilton that "the enemies this year have not been so hotly pursuing after us as they were". But the year was not to end without evidence of the ongoing reality. On 2nd December, at a meeting in Edinburgh, the Privy Council decided to issue a proclamation against him. The timing of this was significant. Renwick's recent preaching activity had of course brought him once more into prominence, but his visit to Galloway had been particularly resented by some who had earlier shown their readiness to stop at nothing in their opposition to him. The issuing of the proclamation so soon after his visit may well, therefore, have been more than a mere coincidence.

The proclamation was duly published under the royal authority on 9th December. It was by far the most virulent of all the proclamations issued against him, and its intemperate style and language were notable. "Forasmuch," it ran, "as one Mr James Renwick, a flagitious and scandalous person, has presumed and taken upon hand, these several years bygone, to convocate together numbers of our unwary and ignorant commons to house and field conventicles (which our law so justly terms the nurseries of sedition and rendezvous of rebellion) in some of the western shires of this our ancient kingdom, and has frequently preached at these rebellious meetings his seditious and traitorous principles and opinions, intending thereby to debauch some of the ignorant people from their bounden duty, and obedience they owe us as their rightful sovereign lord and monarch; and we out of our royal care and tenderness to our people, being desirous to deliver all our loving subjects from the malign influence of such a wretched imposture, have therefore with advice of our Privy Council (as is usual in such cases) not only thought fit to declare the said Mr James Renwick an open and notorious rebel and traitor against us and our royal government; but likewise hereby authorise and require all our loving subjects to treat him as such; and also prohibit and discharge all our subjects, man or woman, that none of them offer or presume to harbour, reset, supply, correspond with, hide or conceal the person of the said Mr James Renwick, rebel foresaid, under the pain of incurring the severest punishments prescribed by the Acts of Parliament and proclamations of our Privy Council, made against resetters of rebels; but that they do their utmost endeavour to pursue him as the worst of traitors. . . . And for the better encouragement of such as shall apprehend, and bring in the person of the said Mr James Renwick, traitor foresaid, dead or alive, he or they shall have the reward of one hundred pound sterling money, to be instantly paid to him by the Commissioners of our Treasury; and we ordain these presents to be published at the Mercat Cross of Edinburgh and Mercat Crosses of the head burghs of the several shires of this kingdom on the south side of the water of Tay, and other places needful, by the sheriffs in the said respective shires, that none pretend ignorance."

Renwick had of course already been denounced a traitor and fugitive, so that in practical terms this Proclamation made no basic change in his standing with the government. But the virulence of the proclamation, and particularly the incitement of the hundred pounds reward – a huge sum in those days – clearly placed him in increasing danger. It was a risk which, as he well knew, also extended to those who had any contacts with him. A sad illustration of this was provided less than two weeks later, in a signal act of bloodshed. On 20th December David Steel, of Skellyhill near Lesmahagow, was brutally shot by Government troopers, in the presence of his wife, before his own door. Steel was only 33 years of age, but he had become a leading member of the Societies and was held in such respect that he had presided at several of their General Meetings. He had been a close and dear friend of Renwick, and a staunch supporter in all the troubles he had had to face. To this day, the ancient tombstone in Lesmahagow churchyard proclaims him as "true Steel". His death was a sharp reminder that the persecution, however it may have abated for a time, was still being carried forward unrelentingly.

CHAPTER 14

THE INFORMATORY VINDICATION

ENWICK'S critics were wont to say that he would not join or work with any other ministers, since he judged no minister faithful but himself. It was a charge which he was ever eager to refute. In a letter to Hamilton on 23rd October 1686 he wrote: "I am with many under the suspicion that I desire no help, though the persons were never so right; whereas the Lord is my witness, it would be my greatest rejoicing this day, to have some ministers to concur with me, for it would be a great advantage to the work, and a great ease to me." He added: "O that the Lord would send forth labourers!" It was a prayer that was often on his lips.

In a remarkable way, Renwick's prayer was already in process of being answered. The very day before he wrote to Hamilton, there had escaped out of prison in Edinburgh a young man who was to become his close friend and fellow-worker, and who later was to leave to posterity a valuable record of Renwick's life and ministry. Alexander Shields was born near Earlston, in Berwickshire, in or around 1660. He showed early promise as a student, and graduated at Edinburgh University at the age of fifteen. Thereafter he was employed as a private tutor before going over to Holland, where he studied for some years at Utrecht. After returning briefly to Scotland he went again to London, acting for a time as secretary and assistant to the great John Owen, and then, at the behest of Scottish ministers in the metropolis, accepting licence at their hands for the ministry. He does not appear to have held a settled charge, but preached privately for a time in houses.

It was on one such occasion, on 11th January 1685, that he was arrested by the authorities for holding an irregular meeting. After being detained for some time he was sent back to Scotland, where he endured lengthy interrogations by the Privy Council and Justiciary. Shields could not have returned to Scotland at a worse time; the persecution was at its height, and the Oath of Abjuration, disowning the Societies' Apologetical Declaration of November 1684, was being ruthlessly pressed. Shields defended himself bravely, but was given clearly to understand that, unless he took the oath, he would be tried for high treason, with every prospect of being sent to the scaffold. In the face of this pressure he yielded, and on 26th March 1685 he took and subscribed the oath before the Justiciary. It was a decision he came bitterly to regret, and he was injudicious enough to record his feelings in a letter which was intercepted by the authorities. It was all the worse for Shields that the letter was addressed to a certain "John Forbes" at Rotterdam, whom, when under threat of torture, Shields confessed to be John Balfour of Kinloch, the leading figure in the killing of Archbishop Sharp. As a result Shields was in extreme danger of his life, and after further pressure he subscribed the terms of the oath a second time on 6th August. He was then sent prisoner to the Bass Rock, where he remained for some fourteen months. Early in October 1686 he and some other prisoners were returned to the Edinburgh Tolbooth, from which he contrived to escape on 22nd October.[1]

Shields appears to have been acquainted with Renwick for some time, and may possibly have met him when the two were studying in Holland some years earlier. At all events Renwick kept in touch with Shields during his imprisonment, and he commended him on at least two occasions in his letters to Hamilton. Renwick was at this time working on the Vindication with which he had been entrusted by the Societies, and such was his appreciation of Shields' abilities that he sent him a draft of the document for comment while Shields was a prisoner on the Bass. It was a gesture that Shields deeply appreciated, and he clearly felt himself indebted to Renwick for his confidence in him despite his compromises with the authorities. It was therefore scarcely surprising that, on making his escape from prison, Shields' first instinct was to seek out Renwick. This took him some time, as Renwick was travelling constantly in Galloway, but Shields finally caught up with him at a field-meeting in the wood of Earlston on 5th December. The following day Renwick explained to him that while he himself was reasonably satisfied with his repentance for what he had done, he could not be engaged for preaching work without the agreement of the General Meeting. To this, Shields readily assented.

The General Meeting was held at Wanlockhead on 22nd December. Shields attended, and was closely questioned on his adherence to the Societies' principles, and on the circumstances of his compromise with the authorities. By this time, Renwick had drafted most of the text of the Vindication, and this was largely used as a basis for the questioning. Special emphasis was laid on the reasons stated in justification of the Societies' stance of withdrawing from other ministers. Shields affirmed his acceptance of the Societies' principles at every point. He then went on to confess his guilt for what he had done, expressing himself with such contrition and grief as moved the whole meeting. Wrote Renwick later: "He spoke largely to all these particulars, discovering such heinous and manifold sin therein, that, I think, none could have done it unless they had known the terrors of the Lord. He showed also the aggravation thereof, desiring every one to look upon his sin with the aggravating circumstances that he can see in it. And he expressed so much sense and ingenuousness that none, I think, could require more of him; and I know not who would not have been satisfied as to the foresaids, who had heard him express himself so fully, so plainly, so freely, and with so much sense, grief, and self-condemning." The result was that "the Societies for themselves, and I, with the concurrence of some elders then present, did call him to officiate in preaching the Word to the suffering remnant of this Church".

Shields and Renwick duly preached together the following Sabbath, 26th December, when Shields took as his text the words in 2 Corinthians 5:11: "Knowing therefore the terror of the Lord, we persuade men." They were words which were of course deeply applicable to himself, and he did not hesitate to make application of them before the meeting. Renwick was more than ever impressed: "He particularly asserted every part of our present testimony, both as to non-compliance with enemies, non-concurrence with defective parties, and disowning the pretended authority of James VII, and also doctrinally confessed his own particular defections, and cried out that 'knowing the terror of the Lord' in these things he persuaded men." Shields again accompanied Renwick at a public fast-day's preaching some days later, when Renwick enumerated no fewer than forty-one causes of fasting and humiliation. Shields fully associated himself with these, and again made application of many of them to himself. "So," concluded Renwick, "I find Mr Alexander to be one with us in our present testimony. I look upon him as having the zeal of God in his spirit, and the poor remnant have much of his heart; and I think the Lord is with him, and that he cannot be challenged as deficient in the application of his doctrine. For mine own part, I have been refreshed with hearing him, and have been animated to zeal by his preaching and discourse."

Renwick was a shrewd judge of men, and his recent experiences had certainly not disposed him to accepting new arrivals readily. But in Shields he appears to have known instinctively that, as he put it, he had a man of the "right stamp"; and his confidence in him was not misplaced. For the short time that remained of Renwick's life, Shields was to prove a true and loyal friend. He took part in many of the enterprises in which Renwick was engaged, and his keen intellect proved invaluable at a time when the Societies were giving a more public testimony of their work and witness. Indeed, a bond had long been developing between the two which now grew and strengthened. Differing certainly in temperament, they yet provided a mutual support for each other.

Renwick had a further cause of satisfaction from the meeting on 22nd December. Earlier in the year, the Societies had heard favourable reports of a minister in Ireland, David Houston, who was said to have witnessed against the state supremacy and to have spoken warmly of the Societies' testimony. They were sufficiently interested to appoint two men to go over and consult with him. When the two returned they reported that they had met Houston and were very impressed with him, and that he was willing to come over to Scotland; they had also, however, heard allegations against him which they felt merited further inquiry. The Societies then appointed another of their number, James Boyle, a close confidant of Renwick, to go over to Ireland again and to meet with Houston and his accusers. Boyle fulfilled his task diligently, even in some cases bringing Houston and his accusers face to face. He found nothing to substantiate the allegations, and brought Houston and a friend back with him to meet the Societies. Houston was duly interviewed at the General Meeting on 22nd December. He answered patiently all the questions put to him, and satisfied the Societies both on his adherence to their testimony and his innocence of the allegations against him. As a result he was called by the Societies to preach among them, though not, as yet, as a settled minister. Renwick believed that that further step could not be long withheld, "for he preaches very zealously and faithfully wherever he goes . . . for mine own part I thought he seemed to have a right state of the cause, and a right impression of the case of the Church, and to be tender-hearted and zealous in the frame of his spirit, particularly for the royalties of Christ, and against the idol of the Lord's jealousy, the ecclesiastic supremacy and civil tyranny". Houston, over the following months, was to vindicate Renwick's good opinion of him. While not rivalling Renwick's preaching gifts, or Shields' intellectual abilities, he yet gave the Societies faithful support at a time when they sorely needed it.

Renwick, meanwhile, was still busied with finalising the Vindication. He had had to assume this task single-handed since the rejection of Boyd's original draft, and it had been taking up an increasing amount of his time. He was so busy with his preaching work that he was unable to give it the attention he wished, and had to ask the Societies for a delay. He was eventually able to produce a draft, but found it no easy matter to satisfy the Societies. A succession of General Meetings called for still further revisions, and to complicate matters further Renwick was instructed to seek comments from Hamilton and the two students then in Holland – Lining and Boyd – as well as from local societies at home. When Lining and Boyd saw the draft, they represented strongly that the various grounds for withdrawing from ministers, which were elaborated in the document, should be understood as applying only in the present unsettled condition of the Church, and not in a settled or constituted state. Renwick had himself expressed this qualification in his various dealings with Langlands and the others, and he was content to insert it at various places in the text.

The business of considering the responses of course delayed the work even further, and by the start of 1687, eight months after the original commissioning of the document, it was still not in a near final state. But the accession of Shields gave the whole matter an impetus, and with his help Renwick was at last able to see the work through to completion. A special General Meeting was held over the three days 4th, 5th and 6th March 1687, at which the remaining revisions were worked through, and the document finally agreed for publication. Shields was commissioned to find a printer, and a sum of £120 Scots was voted for expenses. Since it would of course have been impossible to have the document printed in Scotland, Shields took it to London, hoping perhaps that his contacts there would be able to help him. But this proved equally impossible, and eventually he was obliged to take the document over to Holland. There he succeeded in getting it printed, and copies were in the Societies' hands before the end of the year. The Societies resolved that it be sold for "eight pence per book, and seven pence unstitched".

The document was entitled *An Informatory Vindication of a Poor, wasted, misrepresented remnant, of the Suffering, Anti-Popish, Anti-prelatic, Anti-erastian, Anti-sectarian, true Presbyterian Church of Christ in Scotland, united together in a General Correspondence, by Way of Reply to various Accusations, in Letters, Informations, and Conferences, given forth against them.* It bore the date 1687, and was a closely-printed booklet of 142 pages. It was almost entirely the work of Renwick, and its pages offer a valuable insight into his views on the most controverted issues of the time. Well-structured and closely argued, it became, in a very real way, his testimonial. Though the matters dealt with were contentious, the argument is sustained throughout in a reasoned, measured way, with no attempt at declamation or invective. In that respect, it differs markedly from the earlier Protestation against the Scottish Church at Rotterdam, or Renwick's testimony of 1683, both of which were heavily influenced by Robert Hamilton.

The Vindication consisted of four main sections – an opening section giving the historical background to the Societies, from the glorious days of the Second Reformation to the contendings of the latest times; a second section setting out their present testimony, particularly with respect to civil authority and the ministry of the church; a third, the fullest, answering in detail the various accusations made against them, under seven heads; and a fourth reproducing the text of their declarations. Of these, clearly the second and third sections were the most important. In giving an account of the Societies' testimony, the Vindication was at pains to point out that this was being done with no narrow purpose behind it. Certainly, it was designed to inform those at home; but it also had in view "that all the Christian reformed world, who will impartially weigh matters in the balance of the sanctuary, without affection or prejudice, may see with their own eyes, and attain unto a better understanding concerning us". Here again the Societies were following very plainly in the tradition of the Scottish Reformed Church. That Church had never been insular or parochial in its view, but on the contrary had seen itself as part of the reformed Church of Christ worldwide. Its sympathies had ever been with the Church universal.

The Vindication went on to state what the Societies professed to own and disown. In the former category were of course the Scriptures, the Covenants, and all the principles of the Second Reformation, with the contendings since; in the latter, everything directly or indirectly contrary to the Word of God, including "Popery, Quakerism, Libertinism, Antinomianism, Socinianism" together with "errors upon the left hand, as prelacy and Erastianism", and also, interestingly, "errors upon the right hand, such as Anabaptism, Independency, and Millennarianism". It then went on to testify at some length against compliances with the evils of the time, including the indulgences, cess-paying, taking of bonds and oaths, and all the other abuses against which the Societies had witnessed over the years. A particular testimony was given against "that promiscuous association in the late expedition 1685" which had been "contradictory unto the Covenanted Reformation of the Church of Scotland".

But Renwick well knew that the Societies had come under particular criticism for their attitude to magistracy – particularly the disowning of the king – and their discountenancing of ministers who did not share their opinions. The Vindication set itself to address these issues. It acknowledged at the outset that magistracy was "a holy and Divine institution for the good of human society" and that, if right magistrates could be got, walking in the fear of God, "we will own, embrace, obey, and defend them to the utmost of our power". But it did not hesitate to assert that where the office was consistently abused, the magistrate had forfeited his right to govern. This was a critical section of the document, and Renwick had taken obvious pains to state the Societies' position unambiguously. "Though we do not say that every tyrannical act or action doth make a tyrant, yet we hold that habitual, obstinate and declared opposition to, and overturning of, religion, laws, and liberties, and making void all contracts with the subjects, or when he usurps a power without any compact, or giving any security for religion and liberties, or when he is such as the laws of the land make incapable of government; these sufficiently invalidate his right and relation of magistracy; and warrant subjects, especially in covenanted lands, to revolt from under, and disown allegiance unto such a power." Renwick was here following directly in the steps of Knox and Buchanan, of Rutherford in his *Lex Rex*, and latterly of Cargill and Cameron. Of course, the mass of the people may have become so degenerate that they were unwilling to disown the tyrant; and in that situation "the more faithful and better part of that land, in the time of national and universal apostasy, and complete and habitual tyranny, adhering closely to the fundamental constitutions and laudable practices of that covenanted land, may reject and refuse the magistratical relation between the tyrant and them". This was however to be gone about with caution: "Yet they may not lawfully arrogate to themselves that authority which the tyrant has forfaulted, or claim to themselves the authority of judges; though, radically they have the authority of the law, by their natural right and fundamental power, but they cannot act judicially, in either civil or criminal courts; only in the interim they may lawfully do that which may most conduce to the securing of themselves, religion and liberty."

Having dealt with the magistrate's relation to the subject, the Vindication now turned to his relation to the church. This was stated in Renwick's best style, and indeed is a classic statement of an issue which has long been at the heart of Presbyterianism. "We allow the magistrate a power over the outward things of the church, viz what belongs to the bodies of church officers and members, but not over the inward things of the church, such as doctrine, worship, discipline and government. We own he may, and ought to preserve both tables of the law, and punish by corporal and temporal punishment, whether church officers or members, as openly dishonour God by gross offences, either against the first or second table;

*This wild-cherry or gean tree is said to mark the traditional site of
Renwick's birthplace at Moniaive.*

The memorial to Renwick at Moniaive.

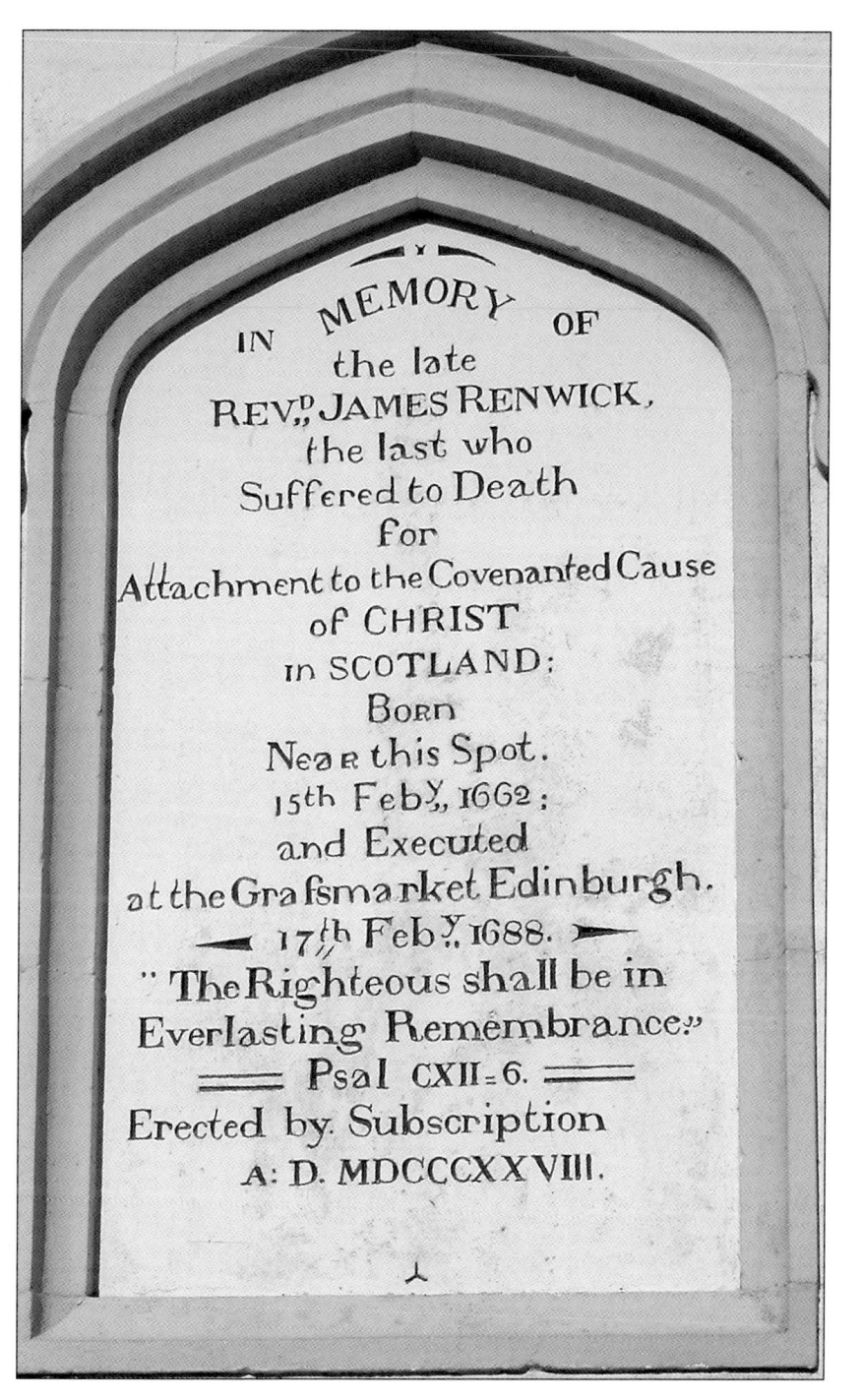

The inscription on the Renwick memorial at Moniaive.

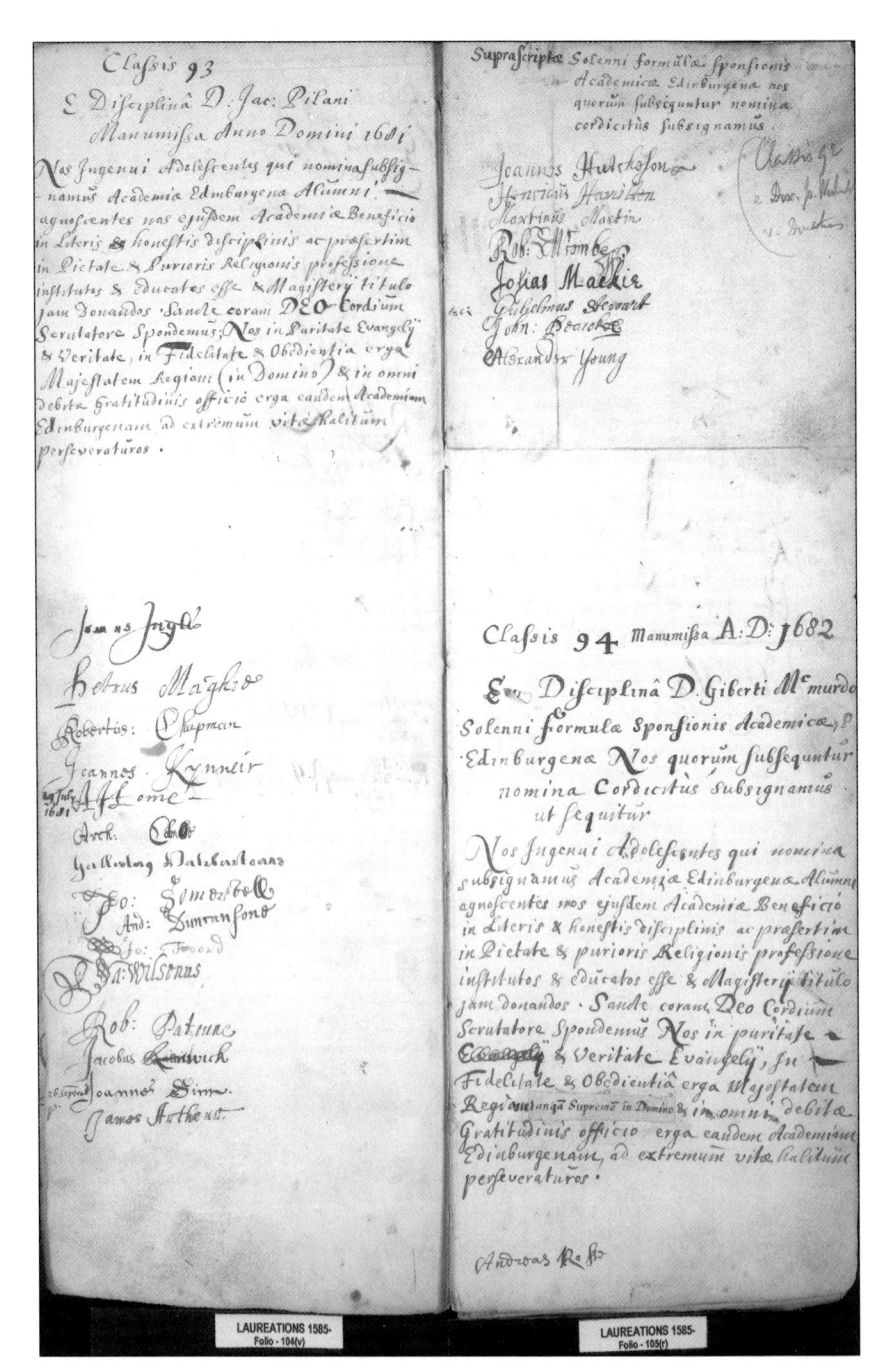

Photograph of page from Edinburgh University Graduation Register with Renwick's signature (in its Latinised form, Jacobus Renwick) as one of the graduates in James Pillans' class of 1681.

Above and overleaf: Photograph of two-page letter dated September 6th 1682, written from Edinburgh to Robert Hamilton. This letter is printed in W H Carslaw's The Life and Letters of James Renwick, *1893, pp. 12-15.*

himself to be the abenger hereof also. As I pleased to show mr Blackall, that some
friends here and I, have our forbears presented to him, and that when friends meets of this
yee will write to him in particular from them in generall, and show him
the last day of
the last monthe, was nominate by some friends haveing met in this place, a day
of thanksgiving for the noble testimony the Lord had holpen him to give; and
his enableing him so signally to stand out & not to quite any of his masters; & the
relation of the whole businesse (which yee wrote) being in the entry of ye day
read in their hearing, that it might probe a mean to frame them for that duty;
And that they are not emitters of what he desires of them, they being it greatly
their duty, and to joyes in the Lord upon his account. And that yee and friends
with yow, & friends here, may be one in the Lord, & one in all our dutys, I thought
it fit to intimate here, that (as wee recken) the last thursday of this instant, &
the 2 thursday of October are denominat days of publick fasting by ye remnant
here, and that the next generall meeting of our friends is to be on the 3 day
of November. And as to what was done the last meeting, we referre yow to the
confused account thereof in your brothers letter. Yee shall receive all our mar-
tyres testimonies that are unprinted, but there are written in it the rest, two particular testimonies, or rather letters of James Skeen, which he never intended to
publick testimonies; So if yee think it fit (it being congruous of reason) they need not be
printed, or at lest, not as such: The one whereof is directed to all professors in
the shyre of Aberdeen; the other, To all & Every professors at South; Receive
also some Sermons of mr Wallwoods in a little book; but let the Sermons and
also the testimonies be well noticed, for not haveing correct Coppys, though I
wrote them, I cannot answer for the correctnesse of them. We have sent
yow also a letter with a paper written by mr Donalds own hand in answer
thereunto, but it is unperfected, he being taken away before he got time to
finish it: But as for that book which is in Glasgow it is not as yet come
to our hands, but when corrected, it is promised, and when gotten it shall be
sent wt all the (so called) Acts of parliat. So leaveing yow and all
his people upon the Lord, for Counsell and Direction, I am
Sir
Yours to my full power
to serve yow in the Lord
James Renwick

Receive moreover according to your desire
Running upon the Romans.

Above: The only known photograph (taken around 1880) of the Groningen Academy (or Broerenkerk) where James Renwick was ordained in 1683. The building was demolished in 1893. Below: Diagram of Academy buildings.

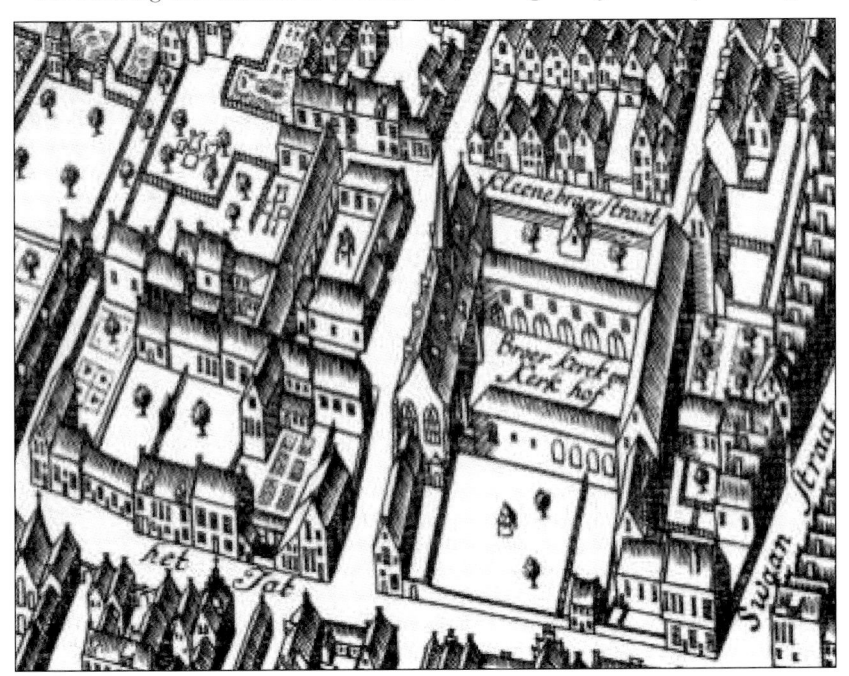

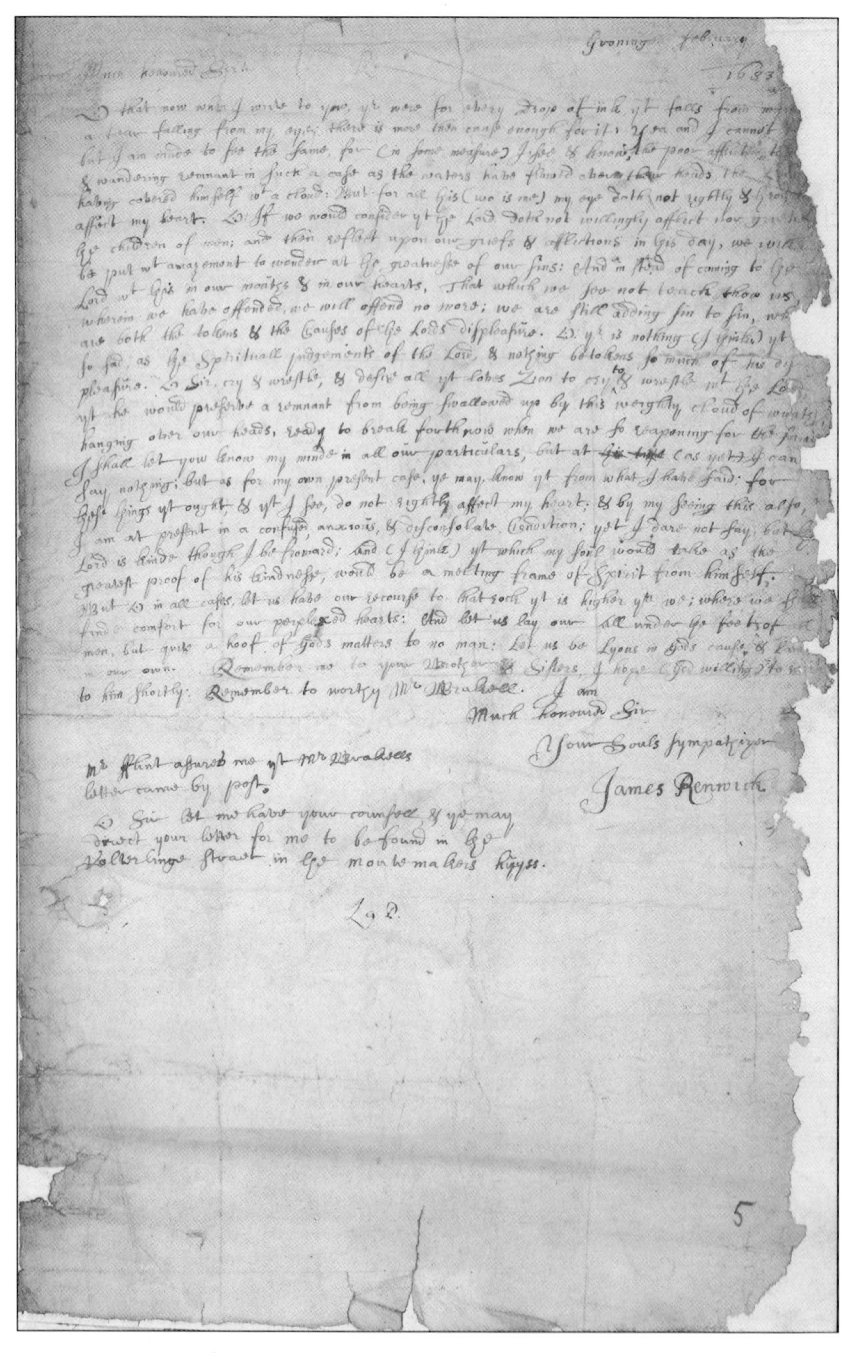

Photograph of letter dated February [6th] 1683,
written from Gröningen to Robert Hamilton. This letter is printed, with a facsimile,
in Carslaw (pp. 34-35). A few words at the right-hand margin are missing.

To The Generall Meeting.

Aprile 9   1685

Much respected, and beloved in ye Lord!

I have been (in some sort) exercised anent this protestation, both before, and since I spoke of it unto some of you; and I am still more and more perswaded, that the Lord is calling us unto it, upon severall Considerations, some whereof the paper it self bears: Therefor (as the Lord hath assisted me) I have written down my minde of it, and sent it unto you to consider and cognosce upon: It may possibly want rightly, yea no small necessitie for, and I hope there will be no different sentiments amongst you, anent any thing contained in it, if it be not anent the Vindicative part of it: But for mine own part, I see as many need of that, as of any other thing, considering how we are falsely reproached, and what the Vindication of the cause calleth us unto: And as for the miscarriages in the manner of that business, the telling of the Curat of Carspyairn, considering that we have there will other things a Cause of Lamentation before the Lord, I thought it needfull to be particular in mentioning of the same, not for our Adversaries behoof (of whose behoof, in that matter we are not to regard) but for the behoof of many well-wishing and well-meaning people, who are laid on with false reports, &c. But if these who for better use I do, see it not needfull to be so particular as I have been, let that part of it, be changed; with judgement and discretion, not to marre the returning of the style. However my minde is, that we ought to be particular. And as for the manner of publishing the paper, considering the afixed upon Kyrks doors, neither is that manner so solemne and formall, for there is most needful, that it should be published upon the day of the sitting down of the pretended parliat, which if it cannot be done, let it be done so soon after, as possible, if ye agree upon ye affair: Therefor friends, with all expedition, would meet and cognosce upon it, and if possible one meeting, being delegat for that effort, might both cognosce upon it, and publish it: And as to ye place, I leave that to your own arbitrement, where it may be most safe and convenient, but I think, that ye Sanqr would be best, considering that the master of it, is Commissioner to ye pretended partiat, and also few friends can stay, being thereabout, to eat; save accidentally thereby. Now commending you all unto the Lord, for Lords Wisdome and direction, and to the advantage of his work. And withall, The day of the publication of the paper, ye would appoint a day of solemn prayer unto the Lord, by all our Societies, for that effort.

I am

Your reall Servant in the
matters of Christ
James Renwick

Scanned copy of letter dated April 9th 1685 to the General Meeting
of the Societies, sending a draft of what became the Second Sanquhar Declaration.
Unpublished.

Page 6

1689

Dear friend in the Lord,

I have no cause of complaining of my lot, there is a great necessity for it, and the Lord hath seen it for his glory, and he maketh me joyful in it. But there is one thing that doth a little trouble me, and yet when I look upon it again, I think there is not much cause of trouble in it. The matter is this: when I was apprehended and searched, there was found with me a little memorandum, containing the names of some persons to whom I had sent and from whom I had borrowed some books; as also a direction of letters to some doctors of divinity, or ministers abroad. Upon this I was interrogated in the Tolbooth by a committee, who said they had orders to torture me if I were not ingenuous. So as to the directions to the doctors or ministers abroad, I told that there was a purpose of writing letters unto them, but none were written. And being asked about the scope and design of the letters, I told it was to represent our sufferings and to procure their sympathy. It was asked with whom I kept correspondence abroad, I told, with Robert Hamilton, who I thought could do no injuries. And as to the names of the other persons, which were written short, I judged there was no hazard in explaining their names who were in the same hazard already. So I told that R:G: was Robert Gairdner; and being asked if he was in Scotland, I thinking that his positive answer would not let him be hid, I said, I supposed he was; but told no definite place. That [M:S:] was Michael Shields, but told no place of abode. That [Ja: A Wil] and [Ar: Wil] was James & Archibald Wilsons; and being asked about the place of their abode, I answered only, in Clydesdale. That [C:A] was Colin Allison, but spoke of no place of abode. That [P:F: R:] was Peter Flaming, for I thought he was went yesterday; and being asked about his occupation and abode, I told he trafficked with in the border of England. [Peter Clerk] his name was written full, and being asked particularly about him, I told he was a man of the country of New-milns, Galstoun, or Glendale, I know not ungently. [Ja: Costoun], his name was less full, and being asked about his abode, I told he lived in the new town of Galloway or thereabouts... that [M:] was... but spoke of no place of abode. I was most pressed to tell who [M:M: at Gl:] was, with whom a hat was left. And I answered, that I was not free to bring any other person into trouble, whatsoever they might do with me... that the business could not bring any into trouble... against folk for such... from torture, which...

Above and opposite: Scanned copy of two-page letter date 6th February 1688 to a friend, from prison in Edinburgh after his capture. Printed in Carslaw, pp. 254-56.

would in nowayes explain the Meane, unless they would not trouble the person. They said, they would endeavour to prevent all trouble of that kinde. Therefore I thinking that the persone's name was already among enemies in the place, and supposing there were some other of that Name, and also considering that trouble upon that account could hardly be expected; they questing that [M.M.] was [illegible] I told the Deborah alone, that [M.M.] was Mistress Millar. Her name was not set down in writ, by their Clerk, as he left word, and he hath no witnesses upon it. So I think it not probable that she can incurr any injurie; for I was not more particular. However I shall say no more as to this, but only advise persons in my circumstances, either not to write such memorandums, or not to keep them upon terms which I did inadvertently and inconsiderately. You may communicat this to whom you think fitt, especially to the persons concerned; but see that you take alongst with you all the circumstances. I studyed to save my self from lying, to preserve them from trouble, and to obeie the threatened torture. I was pressed much to tell my haunts and abodes these severall years by past; and I told that I have resorted sometimes to John Lockup his house, where the officers came upon me. But further I would give them no notice. So I passed. Now if there be any thing in this that may be offensive to friends, I shew there forgivenness for it, for if I had apprehended any sin in all this, or that any persone would be [illegible] I would then and now also rather undergoe all the threatened tortur. The keeper of the Tolbooth have frequently told me of many that were in the keeps, and some persons in Pentland, and other places who I will not protest, told me of bathsome a child to one Scot her husband, but I endeavoured to beat them out of it. As for my pocket book, which contained only two last sermons at [illegible] with the time and place. Young such sermons I have no further to write at this time, for I resolve to write some after this, which I should have more publick than this. I desire it none may be troubled upon my behalfe, but rather rejoyce with him, who with hope and joy is waiting for his marriage and coronation houre. I am

Your friend and servant in the Lord
James Renwick.

Above: The desolation of Auchengilloch, with the monument marking the preaching spot.
Below: A closer view of the Auchengilloch monument.

Above: Darmead memorial.
*Overleaf: A close-up view of the memorial, bearing the names of Cameron,
Cargill and Renwick. Below: Plaque, Darmead.*

IN MEMORY
of
CAMERON
CARGILL
RENWICK
And
Their Brethren
who worshipped
on this spot
in the time
of the last
Persecution

They jeoparded
their lives
unto the death
in the high
places of
the field

Above: The ruins of Friarminion, a frequent refuge of Renwick and meeting-place of the Societies.
Below: Plaque appearing on a commemorative wall built near Friarminion.

THIS COMMEMORATIVE WALL
WAS ERECTED BY

KIRKCONNEL PARISH
HERITAGE SOCIETY

IN RECOGNITION OF

THE HISTORY OF COVENANTING
ACTIVITIES WITHIN KIRKCONNEL PARISH

Near here at Friarminnon at least one Conventicle or Clandestine
Field Preaching took place, led by Alexander Peden (1626 – 1686),
a great Covenanting leader and orator. After his burial,
the Authorities disinterred his corpse and sought to hang it on the
Cumnock Gallows. Being unsuccessful, they buried the remains
in unhallowed ground at the base of the gibbet

Above: The Covenanters' Memorial in the Greyfriars Churchyard, Edinburgh. The inscription makes two references to Renwick. Below: The lower part of the inscription on the Covenanters' Memorial.

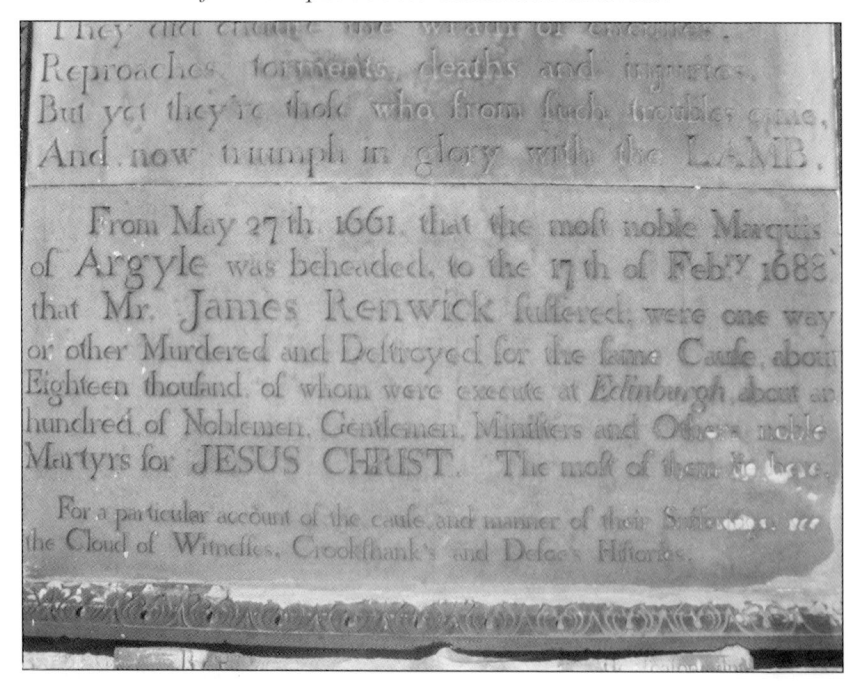

They did endure the wrath of enemies.
Reproaches, torments, deaths and injuries.
But yet they're those who from such troubles came,
And now triumph in glory with the LAMB.

From May 27th 1661, that the most noble Marquis of Argyle was beheaded, to the 17th of Feb'y 1688 that Mr. James Renwick suffered, were one way or other Murdered and Destroyed for the same Cause, about Eighteen thousand, of whom were execute at *Edinburgh* about an hundred of Noblemen, Gentlemen, Ministers and Others noble Martyrs for JESUS CHRIST. The most of them lie here.

For a particular account of the cause and manner of their Sufferings, see the Cloud of Witnesses, Crookshank's and Defoe's Histories.

but this he may not do every way, but after his own manner, not intrinsically, but extrinsically, not under the consideration of a scandal, but of a crime; we grant he may order such things as are for the wellbeing and subsistence of the church, and for that end may convocate synods in some cases of the church, beside their ordinary meetings, and may be present there in external order; but not preside in their synodical debates and resolutions; he may add his civil sanction to synodical results, but we deny him any power to restrain church officers in dispensing of Christ's ordinances, or forbid them to do what Christ has given them in commandment; we own that as he ought to take care of the maintenance of the ministry, schools, and poor, so imperatively he may command church officers to do their duties; yet we deny him an elicitive power, either to do himself what is incumbent to church officers, or to depute others to administer ordinances in his name, or by any ministerial power received from him; finally, we allow him a cumulative power, whereby in his own way he assists, strengthens and ratifies what church officers do by virtue of their office; but we deny unto him a privative power, which detracts any way from the church's authority. For he is a nursing father, and not a step-father."

Renwick concluded this section by rehearsing the unparalleled events of the previous reign, which he saw as an unanswerable argument for the action the Societies had taken in disowning the king. To succeeding generations these events have become well known; but here was the first published recital of them, by a contemporary, and one well equipped to recount them in all their stark horror. Renwick had unimpeachable authority for all that he claimed, and he described relentlessly the unspeakable evils the regime had done: " . . . chasing, catching and killing upon the fields, many, without sentence passed upon them, or time previously to deliberate upon death; and without taking notice of anything to be laid against them; drowning women, some of very young, and some of exceeding old age; imprisoning, laying in irons, exquisite torturings, by boots, thumbikins, and firematches; cutting pieces out of the ears; banishing and selling as slaves old and young, men and women, in great numbers; bloodily butchering upon scaffolds, hanging some of all sexes and ages; heading, mangling, dismembering alive, quartering dead bodies; oppressing many others in their estates, forefaulting their possessions, robbing, pillaging their goods, casting men, women and children out of their habitations, interdicting any to reset them under the pains of being treated after the same manner; and all this for their adherence unto the Covenanted work of Reformation." And so, he concluded, "we have disowned, and yet adhere to our revolt from under the yoke of tyranny of Charles the Second, and declare that his whole government was a complete and habitual tyranny, and no more magistracy than robbery is a rightful possession. And in like manner we disown the usurpation of James Duke of York, succeeding and persisting in the same footsteps of tyranny, treachery and cruelty."

Having dealt with the magistracy, the Vindication moved on to deal with the Societies' attitude to the ministry. Here the charge had been one of exclusivism and isolationism; of refusal to countenance any Christian ministers, however worthy, who did not espouse the Societies' distinctive views. Of all the charges against them, this was the one to which the Societies were most sensitive; and so the Vindication responded to it at greatest length. The ministry, it affirmed, was the ordinance of God, and all faithful pastors were to be highly honoured for their work's sake. Schism, or unwarranted separation from true and faithful ministers, was "a very heinous, hateful and hurtful sin". Yet, particularly in the present broken state of the Church, it might be duty to withdraw from ministers "chargeable with defection". The Church of Scotland had been blessed with a high degree of reformation, and the land as a whole had come under solemn covenant to God to maintain and defend the true religion. This made it impossible to overlook failings in the public witness of ministers which might be tolerated in a less advanced Church. In these circumstances "when a backsliding or defection is embraced, avowed, or obstinately defended, in such things as have been reformed, we judge it lawful, reasonable and necessary to leave that part of the Church which has made such defection, and to adhere unto the other part of the Church, whether more or fewer, who are standing steadfastly to the defence of the Reformation, until the defections of the backsliding party be confessed, mourned over and forsaken. This is no separation from the Church of Scotland, but only a departing and going forth from her sins, backslidings and defections, as we are commanded by the Lord." Such a "separation", the Vindication maintained, was not "active", but merely "negative and passive". "We deny and altogether disown a separation from communion with this Church in her doctrine, worship, discipline and government, as she was in her best and purest days; for we only oppose the transgressions and defections of this Church, and endeavour to separate from these." The Societies had merely chosen to "stand still", to remain where they were, or where their faithful forefathers had stood, until the abuses and defections of the time had been remedied and removed. And since there were no competent Church courts to which they could bring complaints, "people may do what is competent to them, by withdrawing from such ministers even without the presbyterial sentence. For though no-one have the power of the keys but church officers, yet people have a discretive power over their own practice, anticipating that power when it cannot be in Christ's method exerted."

Having stated the principles, the Vindication went on to specify the circumstances in which withdrawal from ministers was seen to be justified. Withdrawal could not be defended merely on grounds of personal weaknesses, vagaries of temperament, or the like, or because of differences of judgement in secondary matters which did not concern the public testimony. But systematic abuse of the ministerial office, in whatever form, made withdrawal imperative. This extended not only to those who were personally scandalous, but to those who had no true call to the ministry, such as "all Popish priests, that have their mission from Antichrist" and "all prelatic curates, that have theirs from the Episcopal hierarchy, which is also Anti-Christian". It embraced also those Presbyterian ministers who "have subjected their ministry to the disposal of strange lords, by laying it aside in obedience to their mandates, by accepting a new grant, licence and warrant from the usurpers of their master's crown, and become servants of men, and subjects to another head than Christ". This was of course mainly directed at those who had accepted the Indulgence, "the mother of all our divisions". However, the exclusion applied to all who upheld the royal authority in any form, since this carried with it the blasphemous claim of supremacy over the Church. This covered any ministers who paid dues or taxes, or who complied in other ways such as taking oaths or bonds. Ministers who were guilty by association must also be avoided – those who, while not complying openly themselves, nevertheless encouraged others to do so, or defended those who did. In this category were those who pleaded for union with the indulged. Similarly, there could be no fellowship with ministers who were sinfully silent, either by refusing to preach at all, or by not denouncing the evils of the times. And finally, the Societies could not countenance those ministers who caused division, or made it their business unjustly to malign brethren. This was an obvious reference to men such as Barclay and Langlands with whom the Societies had been so troubled.

There is some evidence, not surprisingly, that this was the most difficult part of the document to compile, and Renwick was well aware of the sensitivity of what he had written. In particular, he was keen to avoid any hint of censoriousness which a catalogue of this sort might suggest. But this was no arbitrary list. The grounds for exclusion of each group were stated at length, and in carefully reasoned terms. In every instance justification was claimed from Scripture and the standards of the Church, or the Acts of General Assembly. The overall message was clear. The

Societies abhorred schism and division as much as anyone; they had no wish to break fellowship with other Christians, particularly those whose position approximated to their own; but where the Word of God and the standards of the Church made their path of duty clear, they were obliged to follow. In no other sense did they claim to justify their position. And they were careful to make clear that, in each case, the grounds stated for withdrawing were to be seen in the context of the unsettled condition in which the Church was now placed. The phrase "in this broken and declining state of the Church" was used repeatedly to ensure that this important qualification was not misunderstood.

Having put their case negatively, it was now time to make clear who those ministers were with whom the Societies would be free to join. They were, in short, any who were free of the grounds for withdrawing already stated. If they had been guilty of these in any way, they would be expected to make a public confession; "and we hope that no minister, whether free of these things or sensible of the guilt of them, will think this an imposition". Additionally, "they must discharge what they have in commission from Christ faithfully; therefore they must take up the right state of the Lord's cause against both right and left hand opposites, and maintain the present testimony, and condemn and preach down the present defections, and propagate the received principles of the Church of Scotland, according to the Word of God, the constitutions of our Church, and the oath of our holy Covenants. There is nothing here required but that which is bound upon them by the authority of God in the Scriptures, and the ecclesiastic authority of our Church in the Acts of our General Assemblies. And therefore, however we be reproached as that we have cast off all the ministers of the Church of Scotland and will hear none of them, yet here we declare, that if any minister will come forth, or wherever we can find any minister so qualified, discharging their commission faithfully, we will call them, hear them, own, countenance and embrace them, obey, and submit ourselves to them in the Lord, and defend and maintain them, to the uttermost of our power. And we desire that this may be taken as a serious and solemn invitation from us to all faithful ministers tender of their Master's honour, and zealous for his kingdom's propagation, to come forth and take part in the day's work and testimony, and take trial of our earnestness herein." These conditions may have seemed to some to be impossible; but by the time the Vindication was published the Societies had of course admitted Shields and Houston, and they could point to these as evidence of the genuineness of their offer.

Apart from the magistracy and the ministry, the Vindication dealt with a number of other issues on which the Societies had come under attack.

Langlands and others had alleged, for example, that their General Meetings claimed to exercise civil and ecclesiastical authority, and to issue binding rules and resolutions. This was stoutly denied. While the findings of the General meetings were "of a binding force upon all them who are consenters" they were "by no ways obtruded as extending over the whole kingdom, because coming from us; though we think there lies upon them also a moral obligation to perform such necessary duties". The Vindication particularly refuted the notion that the Societies, as such, had any power of church discipline or ecclesiastical authority over their members. Such power could only be exercised by church officers, duly appointed under Christ. The Vindication stated unambiguously the classic Presbyterian position: "Under no consideration whatsoever we judge it warrantable to assert that radically and originally the power of church government is seated in the people, and from them derived unto the pastors and elders, as it is in civil government, which comes from God the supreme Lord and King of all the world, and is radically seated in the people, and from them derived unto and conferred upon their magistrates and civil governors; whereas ecclesiastic government comes from Christ the mediator and king of his own church, and by him is immediately conferred upon the rulers and officers of his house, with whom he has promised his presence unto the end of the world."

Other parts of the Vindication dealt with the Societies' public declarations; their first call to ministers, in 1683; and the Protestation against the Scottish Church at Rotterdam. These sections were more or less defensive in tone. In the case of the declarations, Renwick found himself obliged to admit that some mistakes had been made. Not every statement, especially in the latter declarations, could reasonably be pressed. The Lanark Declaration in particular contained expressions which were "very exceptionable", particularly in assuming an apparent right to magistracy. The first call to ministers had been "in some things unsound" and was no longer to be professed. The Rotterdam Protestation had contained "unsuitable expressions" and had not been handled after the "due method". But in all these cases Renwick defended the general intention of the Societies. Not only so, but he argued that even some of the expressions themselves were defensible if properly understood. This applied, for example, to the designation "Representatives of the true Presbyterian Church and covenanted nation of Scotland" which the Societies had used in some of their declarations. The term "representatives", Renwick explained, did not mean "those who ordinarily are understood by this word, viz persons formally invested with authority and delegation from these whom they represent, but only a poor people appearing most publicly for pursuing the ends of our Covenants, some way representing the body that should have done it, in that they did it in their stead, though they could not have their concurrence. It denotes the more faithful and better part of the church and kingdom, representing others who should deserve the same signature, who in the time of complete tyranny and national apostasy are endeavouring closely to adhere unto the degrees of reformation in the best times of that church and state, acting jointly according to the Word of God, the church constitutions, and fundamental laws of the land." These were bold words, for they set the Vindication at odds with some earlier pronouncements of the Societies themselves, notably the Lanark declaration of 1682, which had clearly implied a representative power on the part of its authors. At the hands of some, and particularly his old adversary Patrick Grant, Renwick was to come under strong attack for what Grant saw as an abandonment of an essential principle of the Societies, and one which, Grant argued, Renwick himself had once espoused.[2]

The one remaining matter in the Vindication was Renwick's own ordination by the Church in Holland. As he well knew, the Societies had come under severe criticism for this as an intrusion on the jurisdiction of the Church of Scotland. While it was a matter that concerned him personally, it had nevertheless been a decision of the Societies acting in a corporate capacity, and he therefore felt justified in dealing with it, albeit briefly, in the Vindication. His main defence was that, since there was no faithful or sympathetic church court in Scotland to whom the Societies could apply, they had had no alternative to seeking the aid of a foreign church. This was part of the duty of fellowship which branches of the church universal owed to each other. Just as "the Church of Scotland could never monopolise to herself the sole power of ordination of all that would officiate in her service in a broken state of the Church", so "we knew assuredly that the reformed churches of Christ abroad had a power to licence and ordain ministers either to the church universal, or in particular cases to particular churches, upon the request of a people, cumulatively not privatively; that is, for to help and confirm these churches in their own power; but not to deprive them of their rights, or to usurp authority over them; not as an act of authority over, but as an act of charity to them". In ordaining him, the Dutch church had not assumed any authority to the detriment of the Church of Scotland. Not only so, but it had accepted wholeheartedly the principles of the Church of Scotland's testimony, and carried out the ordination on the basis of that Church's confessional standards and practice.

The Vindication closed with an earnest appeal to "our brethren, into whose hands this shall come". It pleaded for a fair understanding of the

Societies' position, for no wilful distortions of their testimony, and for any objections to be fairly stated. In a spirit of charity it promised amendment of anything in the Societies' practice that could be shown to be contrary to Scripture or to the testimony of the Church. "In the meantime," it concluded, "we commit the cause unto the Lord, and desire to wait until he shall arise and give testimony for his truths. For, as we are firmly persuaded in our consciences before God that this is his cause, and the Covenanted Reformation which we are owning and suffering for; so we are hopeful that he shall, in his own appointed time, make himself known unto the world owning the same, how low soever it be now; and that as he has been pleased, even in these times of hot and heavy persecution, to raise up and signally to spirit not a few honoured worthies valiantly to contend, faithfully to witness, and patiently to suffer for the same cause, even to resisting unto blood, so we hope the same testimony shall be continued to the Reformation, until he shall make the blood which has been shed sealing the same appear above ground to be the seed of the Church, and cause his people to reap the fruit of this present fiery furnace."

At this distance in time, it is difficult to assess what impact the Vindication had on the society of Renwick's day. So far as his critics in the church were concerned, it probably did not achieve any significant changing of minds. That in any case was not Renwick's design. To the generality of the people it no doubt had a curiosity value, as emanating from "those wild people who disowned the king" as the Societies were generally known. The Vindication was of course called forth in self-defence, as an answer to the misrepresentations to which the Societies had been subjected. But, at least so far as Renwick was concerned, self-defence was not the only motive behind it. As its conclusion makes clear, its author had an eye to the future. Increasingly as his life neared its close, Renwick was conscious of the need to leave to posterity a record of how the true church of God in Scotland had conducted itself at a time of unprecedented persecution. There is evidence that he saw this as a responsibility, not merely to the church in Scotland, but to the wider universal church of which the Church of Scotland was a part. The record of God's faithfulness, and of his people's perseverance against such extreme odds, could be a source of strength to the persecuted church in all ages and circumstances. There are good grounds for supposing that Renwick would have wished to see that as the continuing relevance of the Vindication today.[3]

CHAPTER 15

THE WOEFUL TOLERATION

IN his work on the Vindication Renwick had had occasion to deal at length with the question of ministerial communion. It was a subject which was never to be far from his thoughts. Even as he wrote, events were taking place which were to drive an even deeper wedge between him and the other ministers. These events had their source in the king's failed attempt, the previous April, to persuade his Scottish Parliament to relax the penal laws against Roman Catholics. The king had nursed his resentment ever since; and on 21st August 1686 he sent a letter to his Privy Council in which he made his displeasure plain. "It was not any doubt we had of our power," he wrote, "that made us bring in our designs to our parliament, but to give our loyal subjects a new opportunity of showing their duty to us, their justice towards the innocent, and their charity towards their neighbours, in which we promised ourselves their hearty and dutiful concurrence." That concurrence, however, had not been forthcoming; and the Parliament, which so long had been compliant to the sovereign's demands, now found itself out of favour. It was dissolved on 8th October 1686 and was not to meet again in the king's reign.

The king's letter to the Council carried an ominous hint of his future plans. "We have," he wrote, "also thought fit to let you know, that as we have performed our part in supporting those of the Protestant religion, so we resolve to protect our catholic subjects against all the insults of their enemies, and severity of the laws made against them." Nothing further was said on this at present, but as a foretaste of his intentions the king went on to allow Roman Catholics the liberty to practise their religion in houses, and to be free from any prosecution for this, civil or criminal, "in all time coming". For good measure he added: "And to the end the catholic worship may with the more decency and security be exercised at Edinburgh, we have thought fit to establish our chapel within our palace of Holyroodhouse, and to appoint a number of chaplains and others, whom we authorise and require you to have in your most special protection and care."

To give Roman Catholics freedom to practise their religion was one thing; but it was a far greater step to set aside the long-standing penal statutes which forbade them to occupy positions of trust and influence in the state. Indeed, the king himself had recognised the force of this when he had sought to achieve his aim through Parliament. He was not, however, to be daunted. If he could not attain his object by Parliamentary means, he would do so by his own prerogative. Like his brother, his father and his grandfather, James claimed a sovereign and absolute authority in church and state. This had however been used sparingly, and even the draconian measures of his brother's time had either been ratified first by an obsequious Parliament or been promulgated through the king's executive tool in Scotland, the Privy Council. So determined was James to achieve his ends that he decided to bypass both these channels. However, even he, heavy handed as he was, could see that the use of the royal prerogative solely to benefit Roman Catholics would alarm the majority of his subjects, and probably be counter-productive to his purpose. His main object, therefore, must be suitably disguised; or at least presented in such a way as to prevent undue attention being directed to it.

On 12th February 1687 James wrote to the Privy Council directing them to publish a proclamation in his name. Unlike the usual practice, the proclamation was not to be drawn up by the Council on the king's instructions; the text of it was sent with the king's letter, to be published as it stood. The document was skilfully drafted to accomplish the strategy the king had in view. Taking as its premise "the many and great inconveniences which have happened to that our ancient kingdom of Scotland of late years, through the different persuasions in the Christian religion, and the great heats and animosities amongst the several professors thereof", it went on to state the king's desire "to unite the hearts and affections of our subjects, to God in religion, to us in loyalty, and to their neighbours in Christian love and charity". The king had therefore "thought fit to grant, and by our sovereign authority, prerogative royal, and absolute power, which all our subjects are to obey without reserve, do hereby give and grant our royal toleration to the several professors of the Christian religion afternamed". First on the list were "the moderate

Presbyterians" who were allowed "to meet in future in private houses and there to hear all such ministers as either have or are willing to accept of our indulgence, and that there be not any thing said or done contrary to the well and peace of our reign, seditious or treasonable, nor are they to presume to build meeting-houses, or to use outhouses or barns, but only to exercise in their private houses". Next came Quakers, who were allowed "to meet and exercise in their form in any place or places appointed for their worship". And finally, came Roman Catholics, who though mentioned last, had by far the bulk of the proclamation devoted to them. James, again by his "sovereign authority, prerogative royal and absolute power" decreed to "suspend, stop, and disable all laws or acts of parliament, customs or constitutions, made or executed against any of our Roman Catholic subjects, in any time past, to all intents and purposes, making void all prohibitions therein mentioned, pains or penalties therein ordained to be inflicted, so that they shall, in all things, be as free, in all respects, as any of our Protestant subjects whatsoever, not only to exercise their religion, but to enjoy all offices, benefices and others, which we shall think fit to bestow upon them in all time coming". The proclamation went on to indemnify Roman Catholics against any penalties for past offences, either for practising their religion or holding offices contrary to the law; and, almost as an afterthought, awarded a similar indemnity to keepers of Protestant house-meetings and to Quakers.

There was one class, however, which was directly and specifically excluded from the king's favours. "It is our royal will and pleasure that field-conventicles, and such as preach or exercise at them, or who shall any wise assist or connive at them, shall be prosecuted according to the utmost severity of our laws made against them, seeing, from these rendezvouses of rebellion, so much disorder hath proceeded, and so much disturbance to the government, and for which, after this our royal indulgence for tender consciences, there is no excuse left."

The king's proclamation was published in Edinburgh on 20th February, and aroused no little controversy. Even to the "moderate Presbyterians", as it termed them, it was obvious that the promised toleration was no more than a device to distract attention from the king's favours to the Roman Catholics; and for that reason many of them saw it as tainted. There were however other reasons why the majority of ministers held off from accepting it. A hint of even greater clemency was in the air; and this was given substance when, on 4th April, the king issued a general toleration in England granting liberty to all non-conformists there, without specification, to worship either privately or publicly, and revoking all the penal laws against them. Though the king barefacedly stated at the start of his proclamation that "we cannot but heartily wish that all the people of our dominions were members of the Catholic Church" yet this liberty was generally welcomed and was at once embraced by many of the English dissenters. A mood was therefore created in Scotland in favour of a more expansive toleration which the "moderate Presbyterians" would find it easier to accept. In the meantime, anticipating this, a number of Presbyterian ministers who had hitherto remained silent now ventured to preach privately in families, while not formally accepting the toleration.

The expected "greater liberty" was announced by royal proclamation on 28th June. This time, there was no mention of the Roman Catholics. The toleration was presented as a simple act of goodwill on the part of the king. As in England, it granted all non-conformists liberty of worship, privately or publicly, and revoked all the penal laws against them. Meetings were permitted not only in private houses but in "chapels, or places purposely hired or built for that use". The only conditions were that "nothing be preached or taught among them, which may any ways tend to alienate the hearts of our people from us or our government, and that their meetings be peaceably, openly and publicly held, and all persons freely admitted to them, and that they do signify and make known to some one or more of the next privy councillors, sheriffs, stewarts, bailies, justices of the peace, or magistrates of burghs royal, what place or places they set apart for these uses, with the names of the preachers". These were similar to the conditions imposed in England, which the dissenters there had had no difficulty in accepting.

The response to the proclamation in Scotland was enthusiastic and immediate. To many of the ministers it appeared to be an answer to prayer. Steps were urgently taken for some form of united action, and a general meeting of ministers was held in Edinburgh at which it was agreed that the toleration should be accepted without reserve. On 21st July a letter of humble thanks was sent to the king, who was so gratified that he ordered it immediately to be printed by the royal printer. The address spoke of "the deep sense we have of your Majesty's gracious and surprising favour in putting a stop to our long sad sufferings for nonconformity" and assured the king that "as we bless the great God, who has put this in your royal heart, do withal find ourselves bound in duty to offer our most humble and hearty thanks to your sacred Majesty, the favour bestowed being to us, and all the people of our persuasion, valuable above all our earthly comforts". The address was signed not only by the ministers present at the meeting, but "in the name of the rest of the brethren of our persuasion, at their desire". Given this lead, the great majority of Presbyterian ministers fell into line. Men who had not ventured to preach now came forward again; some who had withdrawn to England, Ireland, or countries overseas, returned home; meeting-houses were built across the country, church courts reinstated, elders appointed, students licensed, and ministers ordained. To many, it appeared that the Church's day of deliverance had finally come. But it was of course a false dawn. Amid the prevailing euphoria, it was easy to forget that episcopacy was still established by law; that there was a Roman Catholic on the throne; and that Presbyterianism, even in a controlled form, was being tolerated only because this suited the king's plans to undo – even to reverse – the work of the Protestant Reformation in his Scottish realm.

As before, there had been one very specific exclusion from the king's favours to the non-conformists. "Provided always," ran the proclamation, "that their meetings be in houses, or places provided for the purpose, and not in the open fields, for which now after this our royal grace and favour shown there is not the least shadow of excuse left; which meetings in fields we do hereby strictly prohibit and forbid, against all which we do leave our laws and Acts of Parliament in full force and vigour; and do further command all our judges, magistrates, and officers of our forces, to prosecute such as shall be guilty of the said field conventicles or assemblies, with the utmost rigour, as they would avoid our highest displeasure." The king of course knew very well that such an approach would commend itself to the "moderate Presbyterians" whom he was seeking to conciliate. The meeting of ministers fully justified his expectations: their humble letter of thanks besought him "that those who promote any disloyal principles and practices (as we do disown them) may be looked upon as none of ours, whatsoever name they may assume to themselves". The climate of toleration clearly left no room for those who dared to call themselves Presbyterians while at the same time refusing allegiance to a Roman Catholic monarch who claimed "sovereign authority" and "absolute power" in church and in state.

To this excluded group it now fell to expose the evils of the much-vaunted toleration. The Societies well knew that the king's fulminations were directed at them; and now that the bulk of the ministers had accepted the toleration, their position would be even less secure than before. Renwick, who kept well in touch with events, made his position clear in a letter of 15th July to Hamilton, less than two weeks after the toleration was published in Edinburgh. While admitting that "the enemies are restrained from the execution of their rage in the former measure" he yet believed that "they are consulting and plotting the utter ruin and razing of the interests and followers of Christ". He went on: "If this were believed, people would not so readily be hoodwinked with their pretences of favour; but after so much sad experience, none who will not wilfully blind themselves need to be beguiled. There is a liberty now issued forth from the arrogant, absolute, and uncontrollable power of the intruder and usurper upon the prerogative of the great God, bounded with the restriction that his government may not be spoken against, and nothing said that may alienate the hearts of the people from him; prescribing the place of preaching, inhibiting the worship of God in the fields, commanding the severe execution of all the iniquitous laws against all such meetings, and requiring ministers to give up their names to some one or other of the civil powers; which restricted and strangely qualified liberty to Presbyterians is conveyed through the ceasing and disenabling of all our penal laws and statutes enacted against Papists, and the toleration of all heresies and sects."

To Renwick the toleration was an incalculable evil, deceiving as it did so many, and with the potential to deceive more; but more important still, intruding into and usurping the control over the affairs of the Church which Christ alone had the power to exercise. This of course went to the heart of the cause for which Renwick and others with him had been contending all the long years of the persecution; and it seemed to him that all these evils had now been crystallised into the one issue of the toleration. He determined to oppose it, and to witness against it, by every means in his power. In his sermons from this point on, even to the very end of his life, it was his almost constant theme. So serious was his view of it that he decided that a permanent testimony against it should be given in written form; and in the months that remained to him this was to take up a significant part of his time.

Renwick of course well knew that such a witness would render him even more unpopular with the majority of the ministers; and in this he was undoubtedly right. Even before the wider toleration was published, some of the ministers who had resumed preaching, or returned from exile elsewhere, had started to speak out against him. As time went on, and the toleration became an established fact, the trickle of abuse became a torrent. Renwick was particularly grieved that some of his chief detractors should be men who had been field-preachers since the very earliest days, and whom he had otherwise learnt to respect. In his letter to Hamilton he named specifically Gabriel Semple and Samuel Arnot, both former ministers in Galloway, who had suffered persecution for field-preaching in the 1660s. Arnot he singled out as having displayed "no small biasedness, credulity and impertinence, to say no worse". And of these men in general he had to say, with obvious sorrow of heart: "They do generally show themselves more than formerly to be of the contrary part, and set against this poor witnessing and suffering handful. They fail not to cry out against us; they charge us with false and gross transgressions. They press people every way to discourage and discountenance us; they carry as if their great design were to crush and ruin us; they spare no pains in preaching, converse and writing to effectuate this." He added: "O to live near God, that we may endure the storm!"

Matters would have been sufficiently difficult for Renwick had he had the support and presence of likeminded colleagues, but for much of this time he had to bear the obloquy alone. Alexander Shields had gone to Holland in March to print the Vindication, and although this had been accomplished by July he stayed on for some time to oversee the publication of a more substantial work of his own, *A Hind Let Loose,* which developed in greater detail the issues for which the Societies were contending. With him Shields had taken his brother Michael, who had acted as Clerk to the Societies since Renwick relinquished the task in 1683. In his absence Renwick was again pressed into service as Clerk, and the extent of his work is shown by the fact that many of the Societies' surviving papers from this period are in his handwriting. This additional task came on top of a continuing very busy preaching schedule, which took him to many parts of the country. The Societies had decided that, rather than show themselves intimidated by the increasing penalties against field-meetings, they should, as a public testimony, hold these more extensively; and in any event they felt that the more they confined themselves to houses the greater risk they ran of being apprehended.

So it was that Renwick found himself busier than at any time in his life, and the pressures on him began to build. On 15th July he wrote to Hamilton: "I have so much upon my hand that I cannot get it all done. For some weeks together, I scarcely get one night's rest, or any two days in one place; and, where I am, there I am so taken up, either with preaching, examination, or conference, that I almost can get no other thing done." In another letter he apologised for being so long in writing, pleading almost plaintively: "I cannot help it, having always such throng of weighty business, continual travel through many a vast wilderness, and sometimes bad accommodation; so that it is a rare thing for me to get a spare hour." He still however had the help of Houston, of whom he wrote in warm terms: "As for Mr David Houston, he carries very straight. I think him both learned and zealous. He has authority with him, which some way dashes those who oppose themselves. He discovers the mystery of the working of the spirit of Antichrist more fully and clearly than ever I have heard it." However, Renwick was soon to be deprived of even this helper also.

After his reception by the Societies Houston had preached for a time in the western shires, where one of his meetings, near Kilmarnock on 16th January, was reported to the authorities and brought his hearers into no little trouble.[1] In the late spring he went over briefly to Ireland, and though he returned to Scotland for a time, he went back to Ireland again on what turned out to be a more permanent basis in the summer. Renwick felt the absence of Houston keenly. Writing towards the end of the year he had to admit: "As for Mr David Houston, he went long ago into Ireland and is not yet returned, whereby we have suffered no small loss. I am certain some strange thing has happened him. The report is that he has been sore sick." There is a suggestion that Houston's erratic behaviour had been caused by some mental problem which may have been exacerbated by the hardships of his itinerant preaching. At all events, his contribution to the work of the Societies was effectively over.[2]

As the year advanced, and Renwick continued to witness against the toleration, so the campaign against him became more vehement. By none was this carried on with greater zeal than by those ministers who had had their ministry disrupted by the persecution and who had now chosen to resume it on the king's terms. To them Renwick was a standing rebuke; a voice which challenged their conscience and made them uncomfortable in the security they had sought for themselves. Renwick for his part did not spare them. In sermon after sermon he testified against the evil of the toleration and the dishonour which those accepting it had done to Christ as the only Head of the Church. As a result, the feeling against him grew apace. The ministers and their supporters, anxious to keep in favour with the government, went out of their way to denigrate him, and to vilify his character. They made it their rule to preach against him, to warn their hearers to shun any contact with him or his followers, and indeed to deliver them up to the authorities if they found opportunity. Eventually their resentment carried them beyond all bounds of sense or reason. The abuse of the previous year was mild in comparison with what was now cast at him. He was branded a Jesuit, one who secretly frequented mass; a white devil, carrying the devil's flag up and down the country; a fraudster; a cheat; an immoral person; one who had done greater harm to the Church of Scotland than all the twenty-seven years of the persecution. In face of all this vilification Renwick was given grace to hold on his way. Alexander Shields puts it graphically: "Under all these discouragements, as a mark at which all were shooting their arrows, the butt of the wicked's malice, the subject of all talk, the scorn of the profane, he continued still at his work in his wonted manner; his inward man increasing more and more when now his outward man was much decaying; and his zeal for fulfilling his ministry, and finishing his testimony, growing still the more, the less outward peace and accommodation he could find in the world."

As Shields clearly hints, the pressures on Renwick were inevitably beginning to tell. Almost continuously for four years he had endured privations and hardships which would have sapped the strength of any man; and his health, undermined by constant labour and travel, began to show signs of giving way. At about this time he wrote: "My business was never so weighty, so multiplied, and so ill to be guided, to my apprehension, as it has been this year; and my body was never so frail. Excessive travel, night wanderings, unseasonable sleep and diet, and frequent preaching in all seasons of weather, especially in the night, have so debilitated me, that I am often incapable for any work. I find myself greatly weakened inwardly, so that I sometimes fall into fits of swooning and fainting. I take seldom any meat or drink but it fights with my stomach; and for strong drink, I can take almost none of it. When I use means for my recovery, I find it some ways effectual; but my desire to the work, and the necessity and importunity of people, prompts me to do more than my natural strength will well allow, and to undertake such toilsome business as casts my body presently down again." Alexander Shields records that sometimes Renwick was so debilitated that he could neither travel on foot nor sit on horseback, but had to be carried by friends to and from the place of preaching, often in great pain. Yet never a word of murmuring escaped his lips. "I may say," he wrote, "under all my frailties, I find great peace and sweetness in reflecting upon the occasion thereof. It is a part of my glory and joy to bear such infirmities, contracted through my poor and small labour, in my Master's vineyard."

Despite his continuing weakness, Renwick pressed on with his preaching ministry. In the late summer and autumn of 1687 he undertook a programme of preaching as intensive as any in his whole career, visiting some areas where he had not been before, and, despite all the propaganda against him, meeting with considerable encouragement. In September he held a large field-meeting at Stonehouse, in Lanarkshire, when he preached from the Song of Solomon 4:16, "Awake, O north wind; and come, thou south" – a sermon which, in part, has been preserved. Another meeting in the same month near Paisley was one of the largest he had ever held, and caused particular irritation to the authorities. At the instance of the Archbishop of Glasgow the Privy Council on 5th October issued yet another proclamation noting that field-meetings continued to be held, that they were being frequented by "great numbers of persons of all sorts, many in arms" and declaring that preachers and hearers "shall be prosecuted with the utmost rigour and severity that our laws will allow". This was followed on 18th October by a further proclamation against Renwick personally, this time linking him with Shields and Houston, and offering a reward of 100 pounds sterling for each of them. Shields, who by this time had rejoined Renwick, suggests in his biography that this proclamation was prompted by reports that some beneficiaries of the Toleration, fearing the loss of their liberty, had threatened to betray Renwick to the authorities; and the proclamation – which otherwise did not differ much from the previous one – may have been designed to remind them of the incentive of the reward. Shields also records that at this time the persecution against Renwick was "very furious" and that in the period from June to November "there were fifteen most desperate searches, particularly for him, both of foot and horse; in which they were very outrageous, breaking into cellars, and breaking down the ceilings of houses in their search for him".

Renwick, then, was having to endure something of the same conditions as he had experienced in earlier years, with the added hazard of betrayal by professed Presbyterians. However, so far was he from being daunted by these dangers that he embarked at this period on a new phase of his work and ministry. For some time, the Societies had been considering how best they could consolidate their position at the local level. The effect of the Toleration had given these plans an impetus, and a decision had been made to appoint ruling elders elected by particular Societies. From a reference in one of Renwick's letters it appears that Houston had started this work prior to his final return to Ireland, and Renwick himself seems to have taken it up from late summer onwards. In October 1687 he admitted ruling elders on two consecutive Sabbaths – on the 9th at Tinto Hill, in Clydesdale, and on the 16th at Darmead. Thomas Lining, who was back in Scotland for a short time from his studies in Holland, attended the Tinto Hill meeting and recorded his impressions. "There was," he wrote, "as much gravity, order and solemnity, as at the admission of any elders these forty years." Some notes of the second meeting have been preserved. These are interesting not only as a defence of what Renwick was doing in his particular circumstances but, more generally, as an exposition of the classic Presbyterian position on the ruling eldership, and they can still be read with profit today.

"The ruling elder," Renwick noted, "is so called not because the power of ruling and governing the Church belongs to him alone; for that belongs also to the teaching and preaching elders, or to the doctors and pastors; but because to rule and govern is the principal and chief part of his charge and employment; it is the highest act of his office; it is not competent for him to teach, that belongs to the doctor; nor to preach, that belongs to the minister or pastor; but his office is comprised within the compass of ruling and governing the Church." And as the office of ruling elder was of Divine institution – a point Renwick was at pains to prove from Scripture – so "we ought to constitute him, for without him government and discipline cannot be rightly exercised". The office, it was true, had been largely neglected in the history of the Church, but there was clear evidence that ruling elders had been present in the Jewish synagogue, and in the Christian church of the early centuries. Experience had also shown that in times of particular difficulty in the Church "the admitting of qualified men to this trust and charge has been followed with no small blessing, and success and progress in a reformation; which we pray God may be the consequence of this our action".

Renwick of course knew that his actions would draw down upon him even more criticism and opposition. Was this not further evidence of the Societies' schismatic character, consolidating their isolationism, and creating, in effect, a church within a church? In any case, were ruling elders not meant to be appointed to particular parishes, not to the church as a whole? How was this consistent with the principles and practice of the Church? Renwick had thought out all these questions – and several more – and had his answers ready. Yes, ruling elders were normally appointed to particular parishes. But this was not a normal situation; the Church was in a broken, not a constituted, state, and there was a "moral impossibility" of adhering to the normal practice. In any event if the ministers were not at present tied to particular parishes, neither need the ruling elders be. As a rule however they would be expected to live in the areas which had elected them "so far as the troubles of the time may allow". And as for schismatic behaviour, the suggestion was utterly misconceived. "There is nothing like schism in it; for though we have not the concurrence of these ministers and elders who are departed out of the way, with whom we cannot join in other parts of their office, yet this work is agreed upon by the faithful ministers and elders who own the testimony of the day. There is here no new thing; there is here no innovation; there is here no setting up a church within a church, but an adding to the number of her officers, that the old church, to say so, may not die among our hands."

In a highly significant section Renwick advised on how ruling elders should exercise their duties in administering church discipline. He was well aware of the sensitivity of this subject, and its potential for divisiveness and misunderstanding; and he strove to achieve a balanced approach based firmly upon Scripture. He gave a series of short, specific injunctions, remarkable for their conciseness and pungency: "You must exercise your power over all persons indifferently and impartially, over the rich as well as the poor, the high as well as the low, your kinsfolk as well as others." "You must exercise your power towards all sorts of scandals and offences; the Acts of our Church appoint that, whatsoever it be that might spot a Christian congregation ought not to escape either admonition or censure." "If the offence be private, and known to but few, then follow the order prescribed to you by Christ in Matthew 18. If the offence be public and open, then is the offender, without previous admonitions, to be delated to the Session." "You must not upon every rumour or suspicion bring men to be questioned publicly, but you are first to make diligent and prudent enquiry about the truth of the matter and to see if it can be proven by witnesses." "You must take heed that fear or favour, or gifts or bribes, make you not wink at the faults of any; and that passion or malice or private quarrels make you not censure the miscarriage of any." "You must not use the censures of the Church as a bodily punishment, or penance to satisfy for sin; but as a spiritual medicine, for humbling and gaining of the soul." "You must carry yourselves with tenderness, compassion and moderation towards the offender, that you may commend yourselves to every man's conscience." "When the signs and evidences of unfeigned repentance do appear in these who have offended, you must show yourselves ready and willing to receive them, with all tenderness and compassion, and to forgive and comfort them, and confirm your love towards them." At a time when there was no approved directory for church discipline, Renwick had compiled an admirable digest of the principles guiding the subject. It was to be another twenty years before the Church of Scotland, now meeting in free General Assembly, drew up a formal disciplinary code; and the Form of Process, as it was called, incorporated many of the guidelines which Renwick had here laid down.

As the winter drew on, Renwick showed no sign of slackening his preaching work. The return of Shields and his brother had relieved some of the pressures on him, and he appeared to regain some of his former strength. It was as if in those days he had a presentiment that his time was fast running out, and that what he had to do, he must do with all his might. Interestingly, he now began to focus on the east and south-east of the country, where he had not often preached, even gravitating towards Edinburgh, despite the obvious dangers which this held for him. In November he incensed the authorities by holding a large field-meeting at the Braid Hills, within two miles of the capital, attracting a multitude of hearers. His text here was the noted verse from which Richard Cameron had preached his last sermon: "Be still and know that I am God" (Psalm 46:10).

A field-meeting held by Renwick in December 1687 provided James Nisbet with another opportunity to give an eye-witness account of his preaching. Again, Nisbet's enthusiasm and sense of privilege of the occasion pervades his narrative at every point. This is all the more remarkable considering the circumstances in which the meeting took place. The venue was a desolate moorland, at one of the bleakest times of the year. Rain fell incessantly throughout, and the hearers, exposed to the merciless conditions, were forced to huddle together for comfort as best they could. There was however no hint of abandoning or curtailing the meeting. Nisbet takes up the story: "Towards the latter end of this year I had the happy occasion to hear that great man of God, Mr James Renwick, preach on Song 3:9-10, where he treated sweetly on the Covenant of Redemption agreed between God the Father and God the Son in favours of the elect, and also on the Covenant of Grace established with believers in Christ. O that was a great and sweet day of the Gospel, for he handled and pressed the privileges of the Covenant of Grace with seraphic-like enlargement, to the great edification of the hearers. Sweet and charming were the offers that he made of Christ to all sorts of sinners. There were three instances that I observed of God's kind and watchful providence exercised towards us, first, although it was a day of rain from morning till night, and we as wet as if we had been drenched in water, yet not one fell sick so far as I could learn; and though there was a tent fixed for him yet he would not go into it, but stood without in the rain and preached, which had great influence on the people to patience when they saw his sympathy with them; and though he was the only man that kept closest to his text and had the best method for the judgment and memory of any that ever I heard, yet now when he perceived the people creeping close together because of the rain, he digressed a little and cried with a pleasant melting voice:

"'My dear friends, be not disturbed because of the rain, for to have a Covenant interest in Christ the true Solomon and in the benefits of his blessed purchase is well worth the enduring of all temporal elementary storms that can fall on us, and this Solomon who is here pointed at endured a far other kind of storm for his people, even a storm of unmixed wrath; and O what would the poor damned reprobates in hell give for this day's offer of sweet and lovely Jesus Christ to be their Redeemer, and O how welcome would our suffering friends in prison and banishment make of this day's offer of Christ!' 'And,' he added, 'I for my own part, as the Lord will help me, shall bear my equal share of this rain in sympathy with you.' And then he returned to his sweet subject again. Words fail me to express my own frame and the frame of many others that day; only this, we would have been glad to have endured any kind of death to have been at the uninterrupted enjoyment of that glorious Redeemer who was so lively and clearly offered to us.

"A second instance of kind Providence is, about the middle of the day there was a party of the enemy passed by within a quarter of a mile of us, yet they saw us not, for as they were riding by us there was a great cloud of mist passed along the side of the mountain where we were sitting; the mist came from the east, and the enemy were going west; and it kept pace with them all the way. Neither did we see any more mist all that day, which made it the more remarkable to us.

"And a third instance of kind Providence is that we understood by our scouts when we dismissed at night that the enemy were lying in all the ways that we were to go; yet the Lord brought us all safe to the several places where we were designed, and not one of us was taken, neither fell sick or faint by the way, although our number was considerably great. O behold a wonder-working God! O what shall I render unto the Lord for all his benefits, for here he was remarkably present with us by inward consolation and outward preservation. O my soul, bless thou the Lord! Amen."

CHAPTER 16

A FEARLESS WITNESS

THE end of the year 1687 found Renwick exceptionally busy. Even now, internal problems in the Societies continued to trouble him. He was particularly exercised about William Boyd, who after the rejection of his draft Vindication had returned to Holland, ostensibly for further study. Several in the Societies continued to harbour doubts about Boyd, believing that he secretly aspired to union with those who had been associated with Argyle, and was not so committed to the Societies' contendings as he ought to have been. Boyd sought to satisfy them by submitting a statement in which he professed full agreement with the Societies' position. On the strength of this he was somewhat grudgingly given a further testimonial to the Dutch churches. However, his behaviour after returning to Holland tended to confirm the Societies' misgivings. He particularly displeased them by applying for, and receiving, licence from the Presbytery of Groningen without their consent; contrary, they claimed, to an undertaking he had given on his departure. When he returned again to Scotland towards the end of 1687 he was taken seriously to task for his conduct. The question of the Toleration was raised, and Boyd frankly confessed that he did not see his way clear to preach against hearing those ministers who had accepted it. This caused some animated debate. Finally, in a desperate attempt to preserve unity, it was decided that though Boyd would not be given a formal call as a minister, individual societies could call and hear him at their discretion. Renwick felt unable to endorse this conclusion, though for unity's sake he did not oppose it, and he made clear that, for his own part, he would not feel able to preach with Boyd.

He was left in considerable distress over the affair, and after the meeting spoke personally to Boyd in an attempt to impress on him the seriousness of the situation he was causing. From the sequel, it appears that his words were not without result.[1] At the same time Renwick was able to draw some comfort from the fact that Thomas Lining, who had recently been back in Scotland for a time, had received a renewed vote of confidence from the Societies and had now returned to Holland to complete his studies.[2]

Renwick had meantime continued working, latterly with Shields, on the Societies' written testimony against the Toleration, which he had had in hand since July. At the same time, though it was now mid-winter, he was continuing actively with his preaching work. The testimony, which had been delayed longer than Renwick would have wished, was ready by late December, and he now sought an opportunity to make it public. After careful reflection he decided that this could best be done by going himself to Edinburgh and delivering it to the ministers there. He was well aware of the dangers into which this could bring him, and he had no illusions about the risks he was running. But his consciousness of the evil of the Toleration was such that considerations of his personal safety had to give way; and the more he reflected on it, the more he became convinced that a testimony in the capital of the kingdom, among the ministers of greatest influence, was what was demanded of him. Increasingly, too, the feeling that he might not have much longer to make such a testimony pressed in upon him; and so he came to see this as an opportunity not only for testifying against the Toleration, but for leaving some permanent record of his testimony to the whole covenanted reformation and all that he had sought to contend for.

Renwick at the time appears to have been in the eastern borders, and his route to Edinburgh lay through Tweeddale and the Lothians. He sent notice forward of his intention to hold a night-time conference of Society members near Peebles – which he had not visited before – and he arrived there in the last week of December. It was a move which brought him into very imminent danger. On the night chosen for the meeting the town authorities happened to be watching the exits from the town for suspected thieves, and the people making their way to the meeting were stopped and challenged. Renwick himself at one point found himself almost within touching distance of the officers, and evaded them very narrowly. The meeting perforce had to be abandoned, and four of those on their way to it were taken. Renwick made good his escape, and continued on his way to Edinburgh, where he arrived early in the New Year.

The ministers in Edinburgh who had accepted the Toleration had by now formed themselves into a self-styled Presbytery, with a senior minister,

Hugh Kennedy, as Moderator.[3] Renwick, on arriving in Edinburgh, attempted to find out when this body was next due to meet; but, on failing to do so, resolved to deliver the document to Kennedy himself. On 17th January 1688 he duly called on him and presented the testimony. Kennedy did not know who his visitor was, and Renwick did not identify himself. Kennedy however received him courteously, and promised that he would consider the document with his brethren. Predictably, Renwick heard nothing further of it, but he was satisfied that he had at least delivered his conscience.

The document later gained the publicity Renwick desired for it, being printed and published at Shields' direction, and with his preface. It was given the title, *The Testimony of Some Persecuted Presbyterian Ministers of the Gospel, unto the Covenanted Reformation of the Church of Scotland, and to the Present Expediency of Continuing to Preach the Gospel in the Fields, and against the present Antichristian Toleration in its Nature and Design*. It was closely and cogently argued, and bore the marks of careful preparation and study. Though Shields had a major hand in it, it also shows clear evidence of Renwick's style, and has some strong echoes of the Vindication. This is particularly prominent in the section dealing with the question of fellowship with those ministers who had accepted the Toleration.

The writers of the Testimony declared at the outset their credentials for making their protest against the Toleration. Any challenge to the true Reformed religion had been expressly protested against since Knox's days, and as heirs of the Reformation they had a duty to maintain that witness. "Considering the weight and worth, profit and price of those truths now committed to us to testify and suffer for, our indisputable duty as ministers and members of this church, the indispensable obligation of our holy Covenants; we cannot, must not, dare not forbear to offer our mite of a testimony."

The fundamental objection to the Toleration was of course that it had been granted by one who not only had usurped the authority of Christ as Head of the Church but was himself professing a false religion. Both Renwick and Shields were well aware that the Confession of Faith laid down that "infidelity, or difference in religion, does not make void the magistrate's just and legal authority, nor free the people from the due obedience to him"; and they knew, too, that this section of the Confession had frequently been quoted against members of the Societies, even when on trial for their lives. They sought therefore to address this point robustly: "We cheerfully subscribe to that article of our Confession of Faith; yet this we assert, that a Prince, who not only is of another religion, but an avowed enemy to, and overturner of the religion established by law, and intending and endeavouring to introduce a heretical, false, blasphemous and idolatrous religion, can claim no just and legal authority; but in this case the people may very lawfully decline his pretended usurped authority. For though infidelity or difference in religion does not make void authority, where it is lawfully invested with consent of the people, and without encroachment on their religious and legal liberties; yet it may incapacitate a person and lawfully seclude him from authority over a Christian people having the Reformed religion established by law and confirmed by solemn and national Covenants, both according to the laws of the land, which do incapacitate a Papist of all authority, supreme or subordinate; and by the oath of Coronation, which obliges all kings at the reception of their princely authority to make their faithful promise to maintain the true religion of Christ Jesus." Here too the authors had Knox as their guide, and they did not hesitate to quote his words directly: "No manifest idolater, nor notorious transgressor of God's holy precepts, ought to be promoted to any public regimen, honour or dignity, in any realm, province or city, that has subjected themselves to Christ Jesus and his blessed Evangel." The principle expressed in these words, as events were to show, was one for which Renwick was prepared to make the ultimate sacrifice.

In a lengthy section, apparently written by Renwick, the document exposed the evil of toleration as a principle and its inconsistency with the historic testimony of the Church. The irony of course was that now it was the Reformed religion itself that was being "tolerated" and this made the offence doubly heinous. "Toleration is always of evil, for that which is good cannot be tolerated under the notion of good, but countenanced and encouraged as good. Therefore it reflects upon our religion when a toleration is accepted which implies such a reproach; seeing it is not ratified as a right, nor encouraged as a religion, but tolerated under the notion of an evil to be suffered." Those who had accepted it were thus guilty not only of recognising the corrupt authority from which it came, but of casting a slur upon that very religion they were claiming to profess. Here, Renwick invoked James Durham and Samuel Rutherford to support his contention that fellowship with such ministers could not be justified. Durham had argued that ministers who had made defection from the truth had thereby forfeited their right to be regarded as ministers while they continued in their error; and to have fellowship with them was to encourage them in their sin. Rutherford had maintained that where the greater part of a church made defection, it was that part who were the separatists, not the lesser part who conserved the truth. Renwick therefore concluded: "We plead not here for schism or sinful separation; only we apply to this present case the constant doctrine of Presbyterians. Since in the toleration itself, addressing for it, and accepting of it, there is such a manifest scandal, there must also be a manifold offence in countenancing those that are so tolerated; it strengthens others to incorporate with them, and weakens the hands of these that witness against it." But he added characteristically: "We think it matter of mourning, not because we are excluded from the benefit of it, but that so many are included in the guilt of it, and exposed to the curse of it. Our duty to themselves, our greatest office of love we owe to them in order to their conviction, does oblige us to withdraw from them to shame them out of their sin; and not suffer it upon them, especially because they are brethren." Renwick, despite all that was being said against him, still regarded these ministers as brethren in Christ; men who were mistaken, certainly, but with whom he could share fellowship in the Gospel once they were reclaimed from their sin. Here was no exclusiveness for the sake of it; no personal bitterness, and no party rancour.

The final section of the document was concerned with a vindication of the Covenants and a vigorous defence of the field-meetings. The Covenants enshrined the principles of the Scottish Reformation, which were the essential framework within which the testimony had to be continued. And field-meetings were the most effective means of maintaining that testimony. Not that there was any virtue in preaching in the fields as such: for "we grant that under the Evangelical dispensation there is no place more sacred than another". But what was at stake was the freedom to preach the Gospel; and there was no better way of asserting that freedom than by meeting in the most public way possible. "The nature and end of meeting for Gospel ordinances is for a public testimony for Christ, against all sin, and every dishonour done to the Son of God; the preached Gospel being not only the testimony of Christ, but a testimony for Christ; wherever then the gospel is preached, it must be a testimony, and it cannot be a testimony except it be as public as can be." And, since free preaching within doors could not be had, field-preaching was the only option. God had given ample evidence of his blessing on meetings in the fields. To abandon them now would be to be seen to capitulate to the adversary. They must be continued as a public testimony. "Keeping of field-meetings now is not only most convenient for testifying, but a very significant testimony in itself. It is a testimony for the headship, honour, and princely prerogative of Jesus, which has been and is the great word of his patience in Scotland, since in these meetings there is a particular declaration of our holding our ministry and the exercise thereof from Christ alone, without any dependence on, subordination to, or licence from his usurping enemies, and that we may and will preach in public, without authority from them."

Renwick swiftly suited his actions to his words. On Wednesday 18th January, the very day after presenting the Testimony, he held another meeting on the Braid Hills, to the renewed indignation of the authorities, this time preaching from Hebrews 10:38, "The just shall live by faith". Perhaps then judging it prudent to withdraw from Edinburgh for a time he crossed over to Fife, where again he had not been much accustomed to preach, and there held several meetings, all apparently at night, over a period of some ten days. Notes of his preaching on three of these occasions have been preserved. From these records, it is difficult not to detect an increasing sense of weariness on Renwick's part with the pressures of the world, and an increasing longing to depart.

On the first occasion, on Sabbath 22nd January, he had as his text the words in Revelation 12:1, "And there appeared a great wonder in heaven; a woman clothed with the sun, and the moon under her feet, and upon her head a crown of twelve stars". He used these words to speak of the glories of the Church (the woman) as the bride of Christ, and the privileges of her members in being clothed with Christ's righteousness (the sun), overcoming the things of the world (the moon) and being maintained by his faithful messengers (the twelve stars). As the bride of Christ, the Church had the privilege of his protection; his provision, both natural and spiritual; his correction; his answers to prayer; and a right and title to the kingdom of heaven. The righteousness of Christ was for those conscious of their unworthiness, and of their inability to attain any merit of their own. It was "glorious, durable, and costly" and yet "cheap and easy to be obtained". "Take and receive it, and it is your own; open the doors of your hearts, open the two leaves thereof, the assent of your judgement and understanding, and the consent of your will. Get on this clothing of the Sun, the righteousness of Christ, on you, and it will not only be glorious, but a durable and strong clothing, proof against everything that may assault it." However, he insisted, Christ must be embraced "wholly". "Many would take him as a priest, to save them from their sins, but they cannot endure to receive him as a prophet, to teach and lead them aright in his way, and as a king, to reign in and over them; this crosses too much their nature." He must be embraced exclusively: "he must be your alone Saviour, without any competitor"; and also "willingly, knowingly, deliberately, and seriously". Then as was so often his wont, Renwick offered some "marks" of those who had "put on" Christ. They were those who were seeking to mortify sin in themselves; to render themselves without reservation to him; and to walk in the way of holiness which

Christ had commanded. They were those who had got above the allurements of the world, and could no longer find satisfaction in the things of time and sense. "Come," he exhorted his hearers, "come and leave the pleasures of the world; be more spiritually-minded than to be entangled with them; get them beneath your feet. Death is approaching, which will part you and them; and therefore set not your hearts on them, but look upon yourselves as pilgrims and strangers, as all your fathers were." He came to deal, finally, with the ministry of the Church. Faithful ministers – the "stars" of his text – were "adorned with a noble crown and with great glory" and a church possessing these was indeed in a blessed and a happy state. Conversely, however, unfaithful ministers were a plague to the Church, and "a great part of our misery in this land". This led him to speak once again of the Toleration, which continued to lie heavy on his heart. And, as he sought to impress his hearers of the evils of it, so, once more, he did not hesitate to urge them not to countenance the ministry of those who had accepted it.

Two days later, on Tuesday 24th January, he preached again in Fife from the words in Psalm 45, verse 10, "Hearken, O daughter, and consider, and incline thine ear; forget also thine own people, and thy father's house". He set the tone at the start: "We should be much exercised and taken up about heavenly things, meditating upon Christ, and upon heaven. Oh we should long and pray for that day when we shall see Christ riding in that stately posture, showing himself to be most mighty, overcoming his people more to his service, subduing their sins and corruptions, and breaking his enemies in pieces, who will not bow to him; his riding in this glorious posture may serve to comfort his people under all discouragements, and in the midst of distresses, for he has not only a sword to defend them, but a sceptre to rule and guide them." And, he went on, this care on the part of Christ should be reflected in the mutual care and sympathy of his people: "We should sympathise with one another; we ought to bear burden with all his afflicted members." This led him to challenge his hearers in Fife for their too ready compliance with the authorities and their lack of concern for the afflicted Church. "You in this countryside, where has your sympathy with his afflicted people appeared? For you have been at ease and in quiet, while many in the west have been sore persecuted; some to wandering, tossing, and hiding; others to bonds, imprisonment, banishment and death for his truths. Oh lie not at ease, but be concerned with his cause, and sympathise with his people." Sympathy, too, extended to rebuking fellow-believers when they went astray. "This is a great duty, though unpleasant to nature, and that which many do not like; it is the greatest act of love we can show to our brother, not to suffer sin upon him, but to rebuke him." And, if the brother proved heedless of "all our admonitions, exhortations and reproofs" then, according to the Scripture rule, "we should withdraw from him"; though even this was "an act of love to him" and should be done "with great tenderness". And so, in that spirit, Renwick did not scruple to counsel his hearers against hearing those ministers who had accepted the Toleration. "My friends, as you would keep yourselves free of the sin and snares of it, and of the judgements wherewith it will be pursued, keep yourselves free of countenancing these ministers who have accepted the same; for they have changed the holding of their ministry, and have its dependency upon the courts of men."

These warnings, as was usual with Renwick, were however set in the context of an earnest proclamation of the Gospel. His text allowed him to expand on what was always his favourite theme, and to confront his hearers with the claims of Christ as Saviour. "Oh frequent his ordinances appointed by himself, make use of the means he will approve of, and he will be found of you, and your soul shall be satisfied as with marrow and with fatness. . . . Though you have slighted him formerly, yet now is he willing to accept of you. Oh consider seriously upon it, for it is a matter of great concernment; of no less than that which concerns the eternal welfare of your immortal souls. . . . You must leave your idols, your corruptions, your predominant lusts, these old companions who were greater, higher and stronger than the rest; if you would leave these and come to Christ, you shall get much more than you left; you shall have your state changed from a state of misery to a state of happiness; from death to life; from darkness to light; you shall get more than tongue can express. If I had the tongue of angels and men, I could not get expressions to hold forth what you shall get, what a life you shall have. Oh therefore come and embrace Christ; leave all your own things, and close with him."

His final sermon in Fife, on Friday 27th January, was based on the words in Luke chapter 12, verse 32: "Fear not little flock; for it is your Father's good pleasure to give you the kingdom." As he had closed his previous sermon with a description of the blessedness of the Christian in this world, so he continued the theme here, but with emphasis on the glory to follow. "Let your thoughts be often in heaven, and your conversation much with heaven. O my friends, believers should be of so noble spirits, that seeing they are all kings, and have a crown and a kingdom to look to, they should disdain to be taken up excessively with time-things, and to be encumbered with that which is so perishing; but be heavenly-minded. Labour to be more and more denied to the things of the world; Oh labour to be clothed with the righteousness of Christ, and to get the vain and changeable world under your feet." And, once again, he gave some "marks", or characteristics, of the true people of God – the "little flock" of his text. "These who are the children of God, it will be their aim and endeavour to yield universal obedience to all their father's commands; not baulking any, because unpleasant to their nature; or obeying some, and slighting the rest. They will honour their father; they will greatly reverence him and fear before him; it will be their great desire to glorify him, and to have him exalted. Christ will be lovely in their eyes, and altogether desirable to their souls. These who are the children of God subject their spirit unto their father, cheerfully acquiescing in what he carves out to be their lot; and with patience and submission to embrace it, though hard to flesh and blood, without murmuring at his way of dealing with them, or their hearts rising against his sovereignty, or quarrelling with his way of procedure with them. They should not fear death; for if they looked rightly upon it, they would welcome it, when it comes, as a desirable messenger; for it is a chariot to carry them out of this miserable world unto their father's kingdom, where they shall enjoy their beloved fully and freely." It would have been surprising if the more discerning of his hearers that night had not detected a sense of identity on Renwick's part with those he was describing in these words.

Re-crossing the Forth, Renwick preached on the night of the following Sabbath – 29th January – at Bo'ness, a small seaport town in West Lothian, which at that time had a flourishing trade with Holland. Bo'ness and its neighbourhood had long been noted as a centre of disaffection from the government, and Renwick would have had no difficulty in finding a haven with loyal friends. His text here was Isaiah 53, verse 1: "Who hath believed our report, and to whom is the arm of the Lord revealed?" From the record of this sermon, fragmentary though it is, it is evident that Renwick was becoming increasingly burdened with a sense of the general unresponsiveness to the Gospel message and the lethargy and indifference of hearers. This applied both at the personal and at the public level. It was indifference to the Gospel which was at the root of so many compromises with the authorities – paying of cess, taking of oaths and bonds – and now, most obviously, acceptance of the Toleration. Much of his sermon, or at least the part of it which survives, was taken up with warnings against the Toleration and its consequences. Renwick had a mixed audience, and he knew that not a few of them saw nothing wrong in hearing ministers who had accepted the royal favour. He felt burdened to address the issue directly, come what might.

To ensure his hearers' attention he adopted a somewhat novel approach, posing and then answering the questions he knew were in their minds. "They are good men," he pictured some as saying, "who have accepted this toleration; why may not we then hear them?" "I grant," said Renwick, "that many of them are godly and gracious men; but their accepting of this antichristian liberty is no part of their godliness. They must not be countenanced in their sin, though they were never so godly, for their being so, makes their sin the more heinous." And again: "It is a great mercy to have liberty to preach the gospel; and having such a liberty; should we not make use of it?" Renwick agreed that the accepters did indeed have more liberty, but the gospel itself was in bondage. The king's proclamation had enjoined ministers not to preach anything which would alienate the people from the government. By accepting a liberty on such terms, the ministers had not only recognised the power of the king to grant it; they had accepted a man-made restriction on the ministry they professed to hold from Christ. The liberty, furthermore, had had as its object the restoration of an idolatrous religion; and those who accepted it had co-operated with that objective. "In consideration of these things, you may see it is sinful to accept of or countenance such a sinful liberty."

Renwick had three more objections to deal with before he was done. "What shall we do then? Better that we hear those who have accepted this liberty, than hear none." No, said Renwick, nothing could justify this. The believer's duty in such a situation was to mourn the loss of faithful ministers, and to pray that either the accepters would be convinced of their sin, or "that the Lord would raise up faithful ministers, whom you might hear, and whom he would countenance". Then again: "What is wrong with enjoying the liberty, defective as it is; is it not better than nothing at all?" Again, Renwick was unyielding. "A man may do with his own what he pleases, but he may not do so in the matters of God. He must not come and go in the matters of God. In these we should hold fast, and let nothing go." Finally, "could not the ministry of such men be edifying to the hearers?". Renwick commented feelingly: "It is a matter of sorrow and regret that so few are edified, even by these who desire to be found faithful to the master in this day of trial and temptation." He granted that those who came "in the sincerity of their soul", not recognising the evil of the Toleration, nor knowing anything of it, could in God's providence be edified; others, however, could "expect but little benefit" for "there is not a promise in all the Scripture that God will countenance and bless such a wicked course".

A sense of sadness, almost of weariness, had pervaded Renwick's sermon throughout; and, as he concluded, this became all the more marked. His final words were sobering in the extreme. It is rather remarkable that these should have had echoes of the first sermon he preached, at the start of his ministry in November 1683, and which in turn had echoed Donald Cargill's last sermon in July 1681, from the text "Come my people, enter into your chambers . . . " in Isaiah 26.20. It is remarkable too that in these closing words he should also have identified himself, as Cargill had done, with the prophet Jeremiah, preaching the message which God had entrusted to him, but to a people who wilfully would not hear. "All you who have not been preparing for wrath, by entering into your chambers, and shutting the doors about you, by fleeing into Christ the city of refuge, you have not believed this report. It is a matter of sorrow and grief to faithful ministers, when the report of what they preach is not believed. This was the matter of the prophet's sorrow here; and it was Jeremiah's grief, Jeremiah 13.17, 'But if ye will not hear it, my soul shall weep in secret places for your pride'. It is a sure token of sad wrath and desolation approaching, when preaching has little, or no other effect, than to make the hearts of people more fat, their ears heavy, and to shut their eyes, that they neither see, hear, nor understand, for then may we look for dreadful desolations. Oh, this is the great sin of Scotland, that the report of the gospel has not been believed by the generality of the people, that that which the faithful ministers of Christ have had in commission from him to tell them, has not been credited as it should. And what does this say, but that desolation and wrath is approaching? And happy are they, who are preparing for the same."

He had completed his commission; and his public ministry was ended.

CHAPTER 17

A Prisoner for Christ

On completing his preaching tour, Renwick was once again on his way. In the late afternoon or early evening of Tuesday 31st January he arrived back in Edinburgh, where he took up his quarters at a house on the Castlehill, in the shadow of Edinburgh Castle. Two friends either accompanied him or were already there, and all three apparently intended to leave early next morning. The house was owned by John Lockup, a local merchant, and a long-standing friend of Renwick. Lockup traded in goods from England, and was suspected by the authorities of handling goods which had evaded customs duty. As a result, his house was regularly watched. He was also known to be a sympathiser with Renwick, though it seems that the authorities were unaware of how deep his allegiance went. Lockup was in fact a prominent member of the Societies, and he had been a participant in their General Meetings at least as far back as 1682.[1]

Renwick had stayed at Lockup's house several times before without mishap, and indeed may have done so when in Edinburgh earlier in the month. But the circumstances now were different. He was known to have been recently in the city; and his preaching at the Braids had not only riled the authorities, but made them more vigilant. It certainly appears puzzling why Renwick, with a price of 100 pounds on his head, should not only have returned at this time to Edinburgh, but should have chosen to stay at a house where he was so obviously in danger. Alexander Shields, who is otherwise never critical of him, admits that he "wanted at this time his wonted circumspection"; but he traces it all – as

Renwick certainly would have done – to the Divine purpose.[2] Interestingly, Renwick had written to Shields during his earlier stay in the city, when he may or may not have stayed at Lockup's house: "I have not desired any to keep silent anent my being here, nor reproved any for coming into my quarters, whatever the hazard might be. I left that to the providence of God, and people to their own discretion, and I find it not the worst way."

Events now unfolded with a seeming inevitability. The house on the Castlehill was being kept under surveillance; and not long after Renwick's arrival a senior excise officer, John Justice, received a report that a stranger had been seen entering the house in the course of the evening. Justice decided to reconnoitre the house himself; and, listening outside, distinctly heard someone at prayer within. He suspected immediately it might be Renwick; and, acting on this suspicion, put his officers on notice to raid the house the following morning. Later that night, Justice was in company when there was talk of David Houston having being apprehended in Ireland. Justice boastfully said that "he would have another of them before long" and later is reported to have scornfully drunk Renwick's health, with the boast that "he would have him by seven next morning".

At seven the next day, Wednesday 1st February, Justice and his party duly raided the house on the Castlehill. Renwick and his two friends were already astir, and apparently ready to go on their way. On hearing the commotion at the door Renwick went to investigate. Justice, catching sight of him, exclaimed "My life for it, this is Renwick" and immediately shouted for assistance to take "the dog Renwick" to the guard. Renwick and the two others rushed to the back door of the house, which gave onto a courtyard, but found their way blocked by others of Justice's men. Renwick, who carried a pistol with him for self-defence, fired it over their heads; and in the resulting confusion, with the assailants retreating to either side of the court, he and his two friends made good their escape. Unfortunately for Renwick, when he was passing the officers one of them struck him a blow on the chest with a staff, which slowed him down, and caused him to fall several times. Despite this handicap he and the other two managed to get to the Castle Wynd, the narrow lane leading down from the Castlehill, and thence along the open expanse of the Grassmarket towards the foot of the Bow. Had Renwick progressed a few yards further he could well have eluded his pursuers in the maze of wynds and closes leading off the Cowgate; but it was not to be. By this time he had lost his hat, which made him more conspicuous; and the pursuit had of course attracted the attention of those in the streets. Just after he had reached the Head of the Cowgate, probably in the area adjoining the Magdalen Chapel, he was waylaid by a passer-by, who held him fast until the officers came up. The other two escaped.[3]

It would have been immediately obvious to Renwick, in the grey dawn of that February morning, that all was over. He had done everything possible to avoid capture; but now that he was in the enemies' hands he submitted unquestioningly to what he saw as the will of God for his future. From that position he was never to deviate.

He was taken first to the headquarters of the Town Guard, where he was held for a time and searched. The search uncovered two small notebooks, one containing the names of contacts and correspondents, some of them identified only by their initials, and the other the heads of the sermons he had preached at the Braid Hills. The first of these was to cause Renwick no little difficulty in his later interrogations; the latter was to form the main basis of his indictment.

The news of his arrest of course caused a sensation, and brought councillors and others to see him. The Captain of the Guard, Peter Graham, amazed at his youthful figure, exclaimed: "What? Is this boy the Renwick that the nation has been so troubled with?"; to which, says Shields, "he answered with smiling in great meekness." Graham, who had a notorious reputation, nevertheless appears to have treated Renwick civilly.[4] Unfortunately, the same could not be said of some others; one of the town bailies baited him with accusations of immorality, a charge Renwick indignantly refuted.

The town authorities could not of course take matters further, since such a notable prisoner was the property of the Privy Council. The Council had already been advised of the news, and a quorum of members was hastily brought together. Graham, after he handed him over, was heard to say ironically: "Now I have given Renwick up to the Presbyterians; let them do with him what they please."

Renwick's first examination, later that same day, was before the Lord Chancellor, the Earl of Perth, and a group of Privy Councillors. Renwick had deliberated on how he should conduct himself before them, and, as he later told friends, was at first tempted to be unaccommodating, and to give evasive answers. But on reflection he had changed this view; and, as Shields records, "he found himself called to be plain and free, and to speak to every man with the same singleness and sincerity that he used to preach; with a desire to do good to the man's soul, be he who he would, that spoke to him". Renwick never had cause to regret that resolution.

The examination that first day was informal, and fairly brief. Perth did however tax him with the all-important question – the one, above all, on which his life depended – whether he had openly preached against the authority of the king, and called him a usurper. Renwick plainly acknowledged that he had. With that, he was remitted to the Tolbooth Prison, and placed in irons, pending further examination. Renwick well knew the methods of the Privy Council against prisoners, and he had a natural horror of torture. On being left alone, for the first time that day, he poured out his heart in prayer, expressing his readiness to lay down his life, pleading for grace to sustain him to the end, and asking particularly that the authorities be restrained from doing anything against him other than to take his life.

Two days later, on Friday 3rd February, Renwick was once more before the Chancellor and Council. The examination this time was more formal, conducted by a duly-constituted committee. In the interval since the last examination the two notebooks found on him had been carefully examined. The committee were particularly anxious to know who the individuals were who were mentioned by their initials in his pocket-book, and they made it clear that they had instructions to torture him if he did not co-operate. Renwick, judging that nothing he could say could place these people at greater risk than they already were, frankly told all the names, though he was careful not to divulge places of residence except in the most general terms. In the face of considerable pressure he also declined to specify the houses he had lodged in over the years, except to say that he had several times stayed at John Lockup's house where he had been found. He was not further pressed by the committee, but the matter caused him some trouble of conscience. He later rebuked himself for having the pocket-book with him in the first place, and in giving an account of the incident to a friend he wrote: "I shall say no more as to this, but only advise persons in my circumstances either not to write such memorandums, or not to keep them upon them, which I did inadvertently and inconsiderately." He was particularly anxious that no harm should come to his contacts as a result of his disclosures, and that he would not be seen to have acted unfaithfully. "Now," he wrote, "if there be anything in this that may be offensive to friends, I seek their forgiveness for it; for if I had apprehended any sin in all this, or that any person would thereby incur injury, I would then, and now also, rather undergo all the threatened torture." This, predictably, did not prevent the usual wild rumours from circulating, and it was soon put about that Renwick had revealed the names of all his resetters and correspondents. The malice of his adversaries was to follow him to the end.

The other notebook found on Renwick had contained the heads of the two sermons he had preached at the Braid Hills. In these, as was his wont at this time, he had spoken of the illegality of the king, as a professed

Roman Catholic, occupying the throne, and of the evil of paying the cess. Additionally, perhaps because of the particular dangers in and around Edinburgh, he had encouraged his hearers to carry arms with them for their own defence. The committee asked him if he continued to maintain these positions. Renwick responded that he did; in particular he could not in conscience own the king as his lawful sovereign, nor did he regard the mere lineal succession as giving a right to govern. The payment of cess was in his view unlawful because it was specifically imposed for maintaining troops to suppress the Gospel, and all who paid it were involved in that guilt. He admitted that he had encouraged his hearers to come armed, in case they met with opposition from the forces, and that it was lawful to carry arms for self-defence. He expanded on his reasons for these positions with a freedom and composure which astonished his hearers.

When he had done, Perth, who was a professed Roman Catholic, asked him of what persuasion he was. Renwick answered that he was a Protestant Presbyterian. How was it then, asked Perth, that he differed so much from other Presbyterians who had accepted the King's toleration and owned his authority, and what did he think of them? Renwick replied that as a Presbyterian he adhered to the old Presbyterian principles, which all were obliged by the Covenants to maintain. These, he went on, had been generally professed by the Church and nation from 1640 to 1660, but some had now apostatised from them for a little liberty, just as, he suggested, the Councillors themselves had done for a little honour.

His words produced a remarkable effect on the committee. Perth told him, to plaudits from the others, that they believed these were the Presbyterian principles, and that all the Presbyterians would own them as well as he, if they had but the courage. Afterwards some of them were heard to say, in a phrase which was to become memorable, that "he was of old Knox's principles"; and that these at one time had been in good currency, but had been made treasonable by the present law.

Renwick had good reason to be satisfied with the outcome of the day. Here, from a most unlikely source, was testimony to the consistency of his position; a testimony, indeed, which went contrary to the received perception of Renwick as a deviant from Presbyterianism and instead placed him in the direct tradition of the Scottish Reformation.

His second examination over, Renwick was returned to prison. For the Council, there was now only one course open. They had heard Renwick confess to actions and principles which the law of the land characterised as treasonable. They could not fail to take action. Conferring after Renwick's examination was over, they agreed to instruct the King's Advocate, Sir John Dalrymple, to pursue a process for high treason against

Renwick before the Court of Justiciary. This involved immediate work on an indictment, or charge sheet; a list of potential jurors for the trial; and a list of witnesses. Dalrymple, who had probably done preliminary work on the indictment already, had all three prepared by the next day, Saturday 4th February.

The indictment against Renwick was in common form, and was reasonably brief. It opened with a recital of Acts of Parliament going back to James VI, asserting the absolute sovereignty of the king, and declaring it treasonable to decline his authority, to rise in arms against him, to put limitations upon the allegiance and obedience of the subjects, or to oppose or divert the lineal succession. Against that background it went on to assert, in the most lurid terms, the crimes of which Renwick was alleged guilty. "Nevertheless, it is of verity that you the said Mr James Renwick, having shaken off all fear of God, respect and regard to his Majesty's authority and laws; and having entered yourself into the society of some rebels of most damnable and pernicious principles and disloyal practices, you took upon you to be a preacher to these traitors, and became so desperate a villain that you did openly and frequently preach in the fields, declaiming against the authority and government of our sovereign lord the king, denying that our most gracious sovereign King James the Seventh is lawful king of this realm, and asserting that he was a usurper; and that it was not lawful to pay cess or taxes to his Majesty; but that it was lawful and the duty of subjects to rise in arms, to make war against his Majesty and those commissionate by him."

The indictment then went on to rehearse the previous action taken against Renwick, including his denunciation as a rebel and the reward for his capture, and proceeded: "Yet you did still continue in your former desperate obstinacy, keeping conventicles in the fields, and requiring your hearers to provide arms, and to come armed to these rendezvouses of rebellion; and particularly upon one or other of the days of September last, you kept a field conventicle near Paisley where there were many persons in arms; and upon one or other of the days of November last, and likewise upon the eighteenth day of January last bypast, you did keep two conventicles at Braids Craigs, within two miles of the capital city of the kingdom, where you not only renewed your former treasonable doctrines and positions but likewise with your hand you wrote down in a book, found upon you when you were taken, the heads of these treasonable sermons, with the dates and places where you had preached the same. And being apprehended within the city of Edinburgh, you did desperately fire upon the officers that came to take you." After reciting Renwick's confessions before the Council the indictment then moved to its conclusion. "Wherefore you the said Mr James Renwick have committed and are guilty of the crimes of high treason above-specified, or one or other of them; and are actor, art and part of the same; which being found by an assize, you ought to be punished with forfeiture of life, lands and goods, to the terror and example of others to commit the like hereafter."

An indictment for high treason was of course a solemn matter, and the serving of it was attended by formalities suited to its gravity. Later that Saturday James Guthrie, the pursuivant or herald of Court, went in procession with his servitor, Patrick Davidson, and a lawyer, Peter Williamson, to the Tolbooth, where with sound of trumpet he formally served on Renwick a copy of the indictment, and summoned him to appear before the Court on the following Wednesday, 8th February. He also left with Renwick a list of 45 jurors' names, from which 15 would later be chosen, and a list of witnesses. Most of the witnesses were members or clerks of the Privy Council who had attended Renwick's interrogations, and who could confirm to the Court the answers he gave. Renwick however would have noted with some dismay that one of the potential witnesses was "James Boyle, prisoner in the Canongate Tolbooth". Boyle it was who had gone to Ireland some months earlier to fulfil the Societies' commission regarding Houston, and had acted on that occasion with much diligence. He had also, it appears, acted as leader of the praise and reader of Scripture at some of Renwick's field-meetings, and so had obviously occupied a trusted position. However, after being arrested the previous autumn he had complied in order to save his life, and had received a remission from the king. Clearly the authorities now hoped that Boyle, who was still held in prison, would prove a valuable witness against Renwick, if further evidence were needed; and they had included him in the list with that in view.[5]

Renwick, throughout his preaching career, had remained mindful of one tender obligation which he owed. It concerned his mother, who in 1676 had been left widowed, with two young daughters to care for. While he remained reticent on the subject, and the facts cannot be known for certain, it would appear that at some point after his return from Holland he arranged for his mother and sisters to be settled in Edinburgh, where they could be protected by loyal friends, and where, on occasion, he could visit them. His mother came to be well known in the circle of sympathisers in Edinburgh, and was seen as a woman of considerable strength of character. It was a quality on which she would need to rely heavily in the days ahead.

The day after Renwick received his indictment, his mother applied to the keepers of the Tolbooth to visit him; and although this was unusual, her request was granted. She was anxious to know how he was. He informed her: "Well; but now since my last examination I can hardly pray." On seeing her surprise he quickly added that indeed he could hardly pray, since he was so much taken up with praising, and with the joy of the Lord. He admitted to regrets that he should be leaving his "poor flock", though this was tempered with relief that he should never again be troubled with a body of sin and death. However, he assured her that if he were ever again to preach in the fields, he would "not vary in the least nor flinch a hair-breath from his testimony" but would see himself obliged to use the same freedom and faithfulness as he had done before. His mother confessed to fears that he might be subjected to the cruelties that others had suffered, and she asked him tearfully: "How shall I look to that head and these hands set up among the rest upon the ports of the city?" He assured her: "You shall not see that; for I have offered my life to the Lord, and have sought that he will bind them up that they may do no more; and I am much persuaded that they shall not be permitted to torture my body, nor touch one hair of my head further." He had, says Shields, an instinctive horror of torture, and had often speculated on how he could endure such things if captured. Yet, Shields goes on, "he obtained persuasion these should not be his trial; and through grace was helped to say that the terror of them was so removed, that he would rather choose to be cast in a caldron of burning oil than do anything that might wrong truth".

Over the next two days a number of other friends were allowed to visit him. The prospect of his death quite overwhelmed them, and some of them ventured to remark on what a grievous loss it would be to the persecuted Church. Renwick however saw it differently. Quoting the sixty-ninth Psalm, he told them that they had more need to bless the Lord that he should now be taken away from the reproaches which had broken his heart. He had become convinced that only his death could conclusively show these reproaches to have been false, something which could not be achieved even if he gained his life without the least compromise of his position.

On Wednesday 8th February, one week after his capture, Renwick appeared before the Justiciary Court. The Lord Justice General, the Earl of Linlithgow, presided, and with him were four other judges – Sir John Lockhart, Sir David Balfour, Sir Roger Hog and Sir Patrick Lyon – who, though not ennobled, bore courtesy titles as Lords of Justiciary.[6] The first business was the formal reading of the indictment. When this had been done, the Justice Clerk asked Renwick if he adhered to what he had said before the Privy Council, and if he acknowledged all the facts of the indictment. He replied: "All, but where it is said, I have shaken off all fear of God; that I deny, for it is because I fear to offend God, and violate his law, that I am here standing ready to be condemned." The Advocate, Sir John Dalrymple, then intimated that in prosecuting the case he would restrict the indictment to the three specific charges of denying the king's authority, declaring the payment of cess unlawful, and encouraging the carrying of arms. Though presented as a restriction, this was by no means a concession; Dalrymple well knew that these were by far the most damaging of the charges, and that it was on these that Renwick had already been examined by the Privy Council. If therefore he could demonstrate to the Court that Renwick had already admitted to these charges, and had not changed his ground on them, he could be certain of securing a judgement against him without the need for calling more witnesses.

At this point the judges had to consider whether the indictment, as restricted by Dalrymple, was relevant to infer treason. This of course left no room for doubt, and the stage was now set for the trial. The first step was the selection of a jury. Of the forty-five who had been summoned, fifteen were to be chosen. In cases of this kind the authorities were known to take a perverse pleasure in putting in the lists the names of known sympathisers to the Presbyterian interest, and this case was no exception. After the fifteen had been sworn, five at a time, Renwick was asked if he had anything to object to any of them. He replied that he did not, but, looking at the jury, solemnly protested that they should include "none who professed Protestant or Presbyterian principles, or adhered to the covenanted work of Reformation". The selected fifteen did in fact include some who were active in the tolerated meetings, and Renwick may have been aware of this. These remained unmoved, but Renwick's words and bearing had a remarkable effect on another juror, William Somerville, chamberlain of Douglas, in Lanarkshire, who does not seem to have been noted for any profession of religion. Somerville, on hearing Renwick, rose and fled from the Court, and, though this cost him a large fine, he later declared that "he trembled to think to take the life of such a pious-like man, though they should take his whole estate".

Renwick was then interrogated by Dalrymple in the presence of the judges and jury. The first question, inevitably, was whether he owned authority, and particularly whether he owned King James VII as his lawful sovereign. Renwick replied that he owned all authority that had its prescriptions and limitations from the Word of God. He could not, however, own "this usurper" as his lawful king, since he was disqualified both by the Word of God and by the ancient laws of the kingdom; these laws plainly debarred any from the Crown unless they swore to defend the Protestant religion, "which", added Renwick, "a man of his profession cannot do". He was pressed strongly on this point by the judges. Could he deny him to be king? Was he not the late king's brother? Had the late king any children lawfully begotten? Was he not declared to be successor by Act of Parliament? Renwick was not intimidated by this spate of questioning. He was certainly king *de facto,* he admitted, but not *de jure.* That he was the late king's brother, he knew nothing to the contrary. What children the late king had, he did not know. "But," he insisted, "from the Word of God, that ought to be the rule of all laws, or from the ancient laws of the kingdom, it cannot be shown that he has or could have any right."

The interrogation then moved on to the payment of the cess or tax. On this Renwick was equally uncompromising. He held the payment of it unlawful, "both in regard it is oppressive to the subjects, for the maintenance of tyranny, and because it is imposed for suppressing the Gospel". He drew a parallel from the incident recorded in Scripture of the three Jews cast into a furnace for not worshipping the king's idol: "Would it have been thought lawful for the Jews, in the days of Nebuchadnezzar, to have brought every one a coal to augment the flame of the furnace?" And by the same analogy, he argued, it could not possibly be lawful for those who were being persecuted for not worshipping the present king's idols to have their oppressions multiplied by the financial contributions of their brethren.

Next, Renwick was asked if he had advised his hearers to come armed to his field-meetings, and to offer resistance if opposed. He freely acknowledged that he had. It would be, he said, "inconsistent with reason and religion both, to do otherwise; yourselves would do it in the like circumstances; I own that I taught them to carry arms to defend themselves, and to resist your unjust violence".

The final question was whether he adhered to what was written in his notebook as a summary of his two sermons at the Braid Hills, and whether he had preached in these terms. Again, he was uncompromising. "If you have added nothing, I will own it, and am ready to seal all the truths contained therein with my blood."

The Clerk now placed before him a summary of his interrogations to sign. It read: "Mr James Renwick being examined in presence of the justices and assizers, and interrogate by his Majesty's Advocate if he owned King James the Seventh who now reigns, to be his lawful king; declares he cannot deny his being *de facto* on the throne, but denies that *de jure* he ought to reign, or that he is lawful sovereign, and that he cannot in conscience obey him as his lawful king; declares he thinks it unlawful for subjects to pay cess to the king; declares he taught to his people that came to his field-meetings that they should come in arms and oppose the king's forces, and fight with them in case they came against them." On being asked to sign this statement Renwick several times refused, as it seemed to him a countenancing of the Court's authority. However, he eventually yielded under protest, saying: "I will subscribe the paper as it is my testimony; but not in obedience to you." When he had signed, Linlithgow added his own signature as authentication by the Court.

The case against Renwick was now more or less complete. However, to strengthen it even further, Dalrymple led evidence from two assistant clerks to the Privy Council, who had been present when Renwick had been examined by the Council's committee. The first, George Rae, confirmed that on that occasion Renwick had uttered "the same treasonable expressions, denying the king's majesty's authority, and others mentioned in his above-written declaration". The second, David Gourlay, gave a similar testimony, referring to the individual points in the statement, and confirming that Renwick had affirmed each of them before the committee. No further witnesses were called.

The jury were then asked to retire. They appointed as their spokesman, or foreman, Ninian Bannatyne, of Kames in the Isle of Bute, a noted Presbyterian and an elder in the church in Rothesay. In a very brief space of time they had returned with their verdict. Bannatyne announced it to the Court: "The whole persons of the inquest having chosen Ninian Bannatyne, of Kames, and he, with the said persons of inquest having considered the libel pursued at the instance of his Majesty's Advocate against Mr James Renwick, with my lord Advocate's restriction of the libel, and the lords of Justiciary their interlocutor thereupon, find by his own judicial declaration and confession, and witnesses adduced, that the said libel as it is restricted by the lord Advocate, sufficiently proven; and that the said Mr James Renwick is guilty of the crimes libelled."

The stage was now set for the final act. The judges agreed the sentence. In accordance with custom the duty of pronouncing it was passed to the "doomster" or "dempster" of Court, John Leslie, who proclaimed: "Forasmuch as it is found by an assize that Mr James Renwick, preacher, is guilty of the treasonable crimes mentioned in the verdict of the assize passed against him, the Lords Justice General and Commissioners of Justiciary therefore decern and adjudge the said Mr James Renwick to be taken upon Friday next, the 10th of February instant, betwixt two and four o'clock in the afternoon, to the Grassmarket of Edinburgh, and there to be hanged on a gibbet till he be dead; and all his lands, heritages, goods and gear whatsoever to be forfeited and escheat to his Majesty's use, which is pronounced for doom." In the silence which followed the sentence, the Lord Justice General asked Renwick if he wished for longer time. Renwick answered: "My lord, it is all one to me; if it be protracted, it is welcome; if it be shortened, it is welcome; my Master's time is best." With that, he was returned once more to prison.

CHAPTER 18

PREPARING FOR GLORY

As his words showed clearly, Renwick was now fully reconciled to his Lord's will. The trial, like his examinations before the Council, had shown that his prayers for upholding grace had been abundantly answered. His self-composure and confidence had astonished his judges. He had earned their respect by remaining true to his principles, even to the extent of declining to give any of them their titles except the Lord Justice General, who was a nobleman by birth. At the same time his pertinacity in a course bound to be fatal was deplored, and there was an increasing desire that he might be brought to some sort of compromise to save his life. Renwick had declined asking for a longer time, but such was the feeling on many sides that the Privy Council, in a most unusual step, took it into their own hands to defer his execution for a week, until the following Friday, 17th February.

There now began a systematic process of trying to wear down Renwick's resistance. Except for his mother and sisters, all friends were forbidden to see him lest they should strengthen his resolve. At the same time, a stream of other visitors descended on him from all quarters, all intent on persuading him to give way. John Paterson, former Bishop of Edinburgh, and now Archbishop of Glasgow, pressed him strongly to petition for a further delay, and was even reported to have tried to petition the Council himself on Renwick's behalf. Renwick however remained unmoved. Paterson tried to remonstrate with him. Did he think that none could be saved but those of his principles? Would he kill himself with his own sword, seeing he could have his life on such easy terms? Renwick still held firm. "Sir," he replied, "I never said nor thought that none could be saved except they were of those principles; but these are truths that I suffer for, which I have not rashly concluded on, but deliberately; and of a long time I have been confirmed that these are sufficient heads to suffer for." The Bishop said he was sorry to see him so tenacious, and that he would so cast away his own life, but nevertheless wished him well. Like others who visited him, he was impressed with Renwick's transparent integrity. He confided to others that "it was a great loss that he was of such principles, for he was a pretty lad".

Another Episcopal visitor, a curate, visited him in his canonical gown, which drew forth Renwick's disapproval. The curate avoided debate, but asked him his view of the Toleration and those who accepted it. Renwick expressed himself against it, but as for those who had accepted it, "he judged them godly men". The curate was impressed that Renwick should speak in such terms of men who were opposite to him; and he too went away with an enhanced opinion of Renwick's character.

Other visitors were not dealt with so mildly. A group of Roman Catholic priests visited him several times. Renwick received them civilly at first, but eventually had to tell them bluntly to be gone, as he would debate no more with such as them. "I told them," he later wrote in a letter to friends, "that I have lived and would die a Presbyterian Protestant, and testified against the idolatrous heresies, superstitions, and errors of their anti-christian way." The priests, on leaving, were heard to describe him as a very obstinate heretic. The keepers of the Tolbooth had heard the exchange, and the report of it began to spread. Before long, a saying had come into popular usage: "Begone, as Renwick said to the priests."

In the meantime, Renwick's detractors among the tolerated Presbyterians had been watching events with increasing dismay. As he himself had said, his death at the hands of the authorities would destroy the credibility of these reproachers; and they well knew it. On hearing news of his temporary reprieve they comforted themselves with the thought that others who had been similarly reprieved at that time had never had the ultimate sentence carried out; and they predicted confidently that he would comply just as James Boyle had done. The attentions of the prelates and priests fuelled this speculation. It was put about that Renwick was secretly in league with them, and so could come to no harm. Prayers for him, or sympathy with his plight, were definitely not encouraged.

The stream of visitors continued. Some officers of the Town Guard, taking advantage of their position, tried to vex him with frivolous questions about his preaching and followers. Renwick tried to satisfy them as best he could, then told them solemnly: "Gentlemen, you do well to know that you must stand before God, and to him give an account of all the deeds done in the body. I will satisfy you no more at the time. Gentlemen, the worst I wish you is that that you knew more of God." A group of tolerated ministers who visited him came away impressed with his composure and calmness, and spoke of him as a "godly youth". Their experience was replicated by others. As Shields records: "It is known that some went in to him full of rage, that returned confounded, and forced to acknowledge that God was with him."

But the most distinguished visitor that Renwick received, no doubt to his considerable surprise, was Sir John Dalrymple, the King's Advocate. It was unusual in the extreme that the Government's chief law officer should personally visit a prisoner lying under sentence of death. Dalrymple had acted as the King's Advocate only since early 1687, and he knew that his tenure was to end within a few weeks when his predecessor, the redoubtable Sir George Mackenzie, would again take up the position. It was clear to Renwick that Dalrymple was troubled in conscience, and at the part he had been obliged to play. He assured Renwick that he was very sorry for his death, and that it should happen in his own short time as Advocate. He strongly urged Renwick to petition for his life, and to recognise the king's authority. Renwick explained to him why in conscience he could not do so. Dalrymple heard him resignedly, then told him, in confidence, that in his view the report of Renwick being a Jesuit had played a great part in his condemnation. He deplored that such a report should have been put about by professed Presbyterians; the result of it had been that the Roman Catholics, whose influence now was so great, could not endure that anyone of his principles should be put about as one of them, and they regarded it as a stain on their religion to let him live. For his own part, Dalrymple told him weakly, he "could not help it".[1]

On Tuesday 14th February, at night, Renwick was suddenly called again before a committee of the Privy Council. This was a most unusual procedure in the case of one already sentenced to death, and seems to have been intended to give the Council some basis for a further reprieve. A strong hint of that was given at the outset, when they reminded him of their unprecedented favour in already giving him a reprieve unsought. They then made clear what they expected of him. He had previously given them some satisfaction as to the names of his contacts; now, they wanted him to satisfy them further on that score. The Chancellor, the Earl of Perth, produced a copy of the *Informatory Vindication,* and asked if he knew it. Renwick admitted he did, and, under further questioning, conceded that he had had a major part in writing it. He was pressed to tell the names of his assistants. This he refused to do, saying merely that they were those whom the Council were persecuting. He was then pressed, under threat of torture, to give information about the Societies and their General Meetings, and to disclose what houses and other places he used to frequent while preaching. Here however he was a match for his questioners. On the previous occasion, the threat of torture had been a very real threat; now, it was an empty one. Renwick well knew, and reminded his interrogators, that to torture a prisoner after sentence of death was against all law; and so he could afford not to be co-operative. He therefore contented himself with saying that on these points he would give no further information than his pocket-book had already given them. The committee, knowing that they could not press him further, returned him again to prison. If the meeting had been called with a view to a further reprieve, that possibility had now disappeared for good.

It had been a difficult, even acrimonious, interview; but after it Renwick was in a contented, even joyful, frame of mind. He was thankful to God that, yet again, he had been enabled to stand firm; and he expressed his sense of honour at being counted worthy to suffer shame for his Master. He thanked the Lord for preserving him while in prison, and for answering his prayer to be preserved from torture. On a friend asking him how he was, he replied, "Very well; and will be better within three days". One of his visitors at this time was Helen Alexander, a gracious woman from Pentland, near Edinburgh, who had often sheltered him in her house, and whom only two months earlier he had united in marriage with her husband, James Currie. "You will get the white robes," she said to him. "And palms in my hands," he replied.[2]

Renwick was now completely and conclusively reconciled to what lay before him. In the words of Shields: "He appeared so ripe and ready for heaven, that he despised life, feared not death, and had nothing in his mind nor mouth but begun praises." He confided to his mother that at the last execution he had attended – that of Robert Gray, a Northumberland man, on 19th May 1682 – he had had a presentiment that the next execution he would be present at would be his own; and so strong had that impression been that he had avoided attending any executions since. He had, he told friends, become convinced that his suffering at this time had been ordained "in the holy and well-ordered providence of God", among other things to confound those who had reproached him, and had characterised his work as self-motivated; and, he added: "I am persuaded that my death will do more good than my life for many years could have done." He was asked what he thought would become of the "suffering remnant" after his death. "It will be well with them," he replied; and quoted the promise in the 94th Psalm, "For the Lord will not cast off his people, neither will he forsake his inheritance."

As the fatal day drew near, the pressure on Renwick intensified. Petitions were written by persons of influence, and sent in to him to subscribe, but he refused every one of them. According to Shields, it was even offered to him that "if he would but let a drop of ink fall upon a bit of paper, it should satisfy" but he would not. On the night of the 16th, Bishop Paterson sent to him to say that if he desired him to do anything for him within his power, he would do it. Renwick sent an answer, thanking him for his courtesy, but said he knew of nothing that he could do, or that he might desire him to do for him.

That same night, Renwick managed to smuggle two letters out of the prison. One was a brief account of his last interrogation before the Council. The other, written somewhat earlier, was a general account of his experience since his arrest, and was in the nature of a last testimony. Renwick had intended that he should leave a more formal testimony to the world; but as he was working on it, it was taken from him by the keepers, and pen, ink and paper denied him. This shorter version, intended apparently for the Societies, had been made possible only by the good offices of friends – possibly his mother and sisters – who, at risk to themselves, had brought writing materials in to him unseen. It was written perforce under some pressure, and bears some marks of hasty composition, but it is nevertheless a moving expression of his feelings as he now calmly awaited death.

His opening words were characteristic, as he affirmed his complete surrender to God's will, and his confidence that the reproaches cast at him so unjustly would be removed by his death. "My dear friends in Christ," he wrote, "it has pleased the Lord to deliver me up into the hands of men; and I think fit to send you this salutation, which I expect will be the last. When I pose my heart upon it, before God, I dare not desire to have escaped this lot; for no less could have been for His glory, and vindication of His cause on my behalf. And as I am free before Him of the profanity, which some, either naughty, wicked, or strangers to me, have reported that I have been sometimes guilty of, so He has kept me, from the womb, free of the ordinary pollutions of children; as these that have been acquainted with me through the tract of my life do know. And now my blood shall either more silence reproachers, or more ripen them for judgement. But I hope it shall make some more sparing to speak of those who shall come after me; and so I am the more willing to pay this cost."

He went on to speak of the wonderful sense he had had of the presence of God with him, quoting particular passages of Scripture which had been his comfort. "Since I came to prison, the Lord has been wonderfully kind; He has made His word to give me light, life, joy, courage and strength; yea, it has dropped with sweet smelling myrrh unto me. O what can I say to the Lord's praise! It was but little that I knew of Him before I came to prison; I have found sensibly much of His divine strength, much of the joy of His Spirit, and much assurance from His word and Spirit concerning my salvation." After referring briefly to the grounds of his condemnation, he added: "I think such a testimony is worth many lives, and I praise the Lord for His enabling me to be plain and positive in all my confessions; for therein I found peace, joy, strength, and boldness. My heart does not smite me for anything in the matters of my God, since I came to prison. And I can further say to His praise, with some consciousness of integrity, that I have walked in His way, and kept His charge, though with much weakness, and many infirmities, whereof you have been witnesses."

He told briefly of his various contendings while in prison, and the pressures put upon him to apply for a further reprieve, and to debate with others about his principles. "I answered," he wrote, "that: my time was in the Lord's hand, and I was in no hesitation or doubt about my principles myself. I would not be so rude as to decline converse with any, so far as it might not be inconvenient for me in my present circumstances, but I would seek it with none."

He came to his personal words of testimony, linking with them an earnest evangelical appeal: "Now, my dear friends in precious Christ, I think I need not tell you that, as I have lived, so I die, in the same persuasion with the true reformed and covenanted Presbyterian Church of Scotland. I adhere to the testimony of the day, as it is held forth in our Informatory Vindication, and in the testimony against the present toleration; and that I own, and seal with my blood, all the precious truths, even the controverted truths, that I have taught. So I would exhort every one of you to make sure your personal reconciliation with God in Christ, for I fear many of you have that yet to do; and when you come where I am, to look pale death in the face, you will not be a little shaken and terrified if you have not laid hold on eternal life. I would exhort you to much diligence in the use of means; to be careful in keeping your Societies; to be frequent and fervent in secret prayer; to read much the written Word of God, and to examine yourselves by it."

The Societies, too, must be constant in their public witness for the persecuted truths of Christ: "Do not weary to maintain, in your places and stations, the present testimony; for when Christ goes forth to defeat antichrist, with that name written on His vesture and on His thigh, King of Kings and Lord of Lords, He will make it glorious in the earth. And if you can but transmit it to posterity, you may count it a great generation work. But beware of the ministers that have accepted this toleration, and all others that bend that way; and follow them not, for the sun has gone down on them. Do not fear that the Lord will cast off Scotland; for He will certainly return, and show Himself glorious in our land. But watch and pray, for He is bringing on a sad overthrowing stroke, which shall make many say that they have easily got through that have got a scaffold for Christ; and do not regard the sufferings of this present world, for they are not worthy to be compared to the glory that shall be revealed."

His concluding words were of thanks to the Lord who had guided him, of farewell to all he held dear on earth, and of welcome to the eternal joys into which he would soon be entering. "I may say, to His praise, that I have found His cross sweet and lovely unto me; for I have had many joyful hours, and not a fearful thought since I came to prison. He has strengthened me to outbrave man and outface death; and I am now longing for the joyful hour of my dissolution; and there is nothing in the world I am sorry to leave but you; but I go unto better company, and so I must take my leave of you all. Farewell beloved sufferers, and followers of the Lamb. Farewell Christian intimates. Farewell Christian and comfortable mother and sisters. Farewell sweet societies. Farewell desirable general meetings. Farewell night wanderings, cold and weariness for Christ. Farewell sweet Bible, and preaching of the Gospel. Farewell sun, moon, and stars, and all sublunary things. Farewell conflicts with a body of death. Welcome scaffold for precious Christ. Welcome heavenly Jerusalem. Welcome innumerable company of angels. Welcome General Assembly and Church of the first-born. Welcome, crown of glory, white robes, and song of Moses and the Lamb. And, above all, welcome, O thou blessed Trinity and One God. O Eternal One, I commit my soul into Thy eternal rest."

CHAPTER 19

THE FINAL TESTIMONY

It was Friday 17th February 1688. In Edinburgh, crowds would soon be assembling in the Grassmarket, where a scaffold had just been erected. The day was sombre and overcast, as if in sympathy with the tragedy about to take place. In the Tolbooth prison, Renwick was early astir, for he had some final business to attend to, and he had little time. He had enjoyed fellowship with his Lord since he came to prison, and he had no fear of death. However, there was one matter which troubled him, and he could not be completely at peace with himself until he had dealt with it. Years before, when he preached his first sermon at Darmead, he had read out a testimony which he had compiled in Holland and which he had intended as a manifesto of his beliefs. That document had contained, among other things, the names of some ministers with whose principles he disagreed, or with whom he was unwilling to have fellowship. Renwick had been sharply criticised for this by some, and he had admitted that to have mentioned these men – some of whom were already dead – had been a misjudgement. But he had seen no reason to retract the document as a whole; indeed he had written more than once to Hamilton of his intention to enlarge it and make it more explicit. However, he had not had opportunity for this; and now there was no more time left. But he could not in conscience leave the matter there; and so, that last morning, he took up his pen and wrote one final letter to Hamilton, bidding him farewell, and leaving his instructions on what he wished done.

The self-possession which characterises this letter, written only some five hours before he faced death, is remarkable: "Right honourable and dear Sir," he wrote, "This being my last day upon earth, I thought it my duty to send you this my last salutation. The Lord has been wonderfully gracious to me since I came to prison; he has assured me of his salvation, helped me to give a testimony for him, and own before his enemies all that I have taught, and strengthened me to resist and repel many temptations and assaults, O praise to his name." He came directly to the matter that weighed upon his spirit: "Now as to my testimony, which I left in your hands when I entered into the work of the ministry, I do still adhere unto the matter of it; but I think the manner of expression is in some things too tart, and it contains sundry men's names, some whereof are now in eternity; also it is not so pertinent to our present affairs, for the state of our controversies is altered; therefore I judge it may be destroyed, for I have testimony sufficient left behind me in my written sermons, and in my letters. But if this trouble you, and if you desire to keep it for yourself, and your own use, you should keep this letter with it, and not publish it further abroad; yet you may make use of any part of the matter of it that may conduce to the clearing of any controversy."

Hamilton had been a man of contention, very different in temperament to Renwick; a man who had been often vilified as a bigot and a fanatic; yet Renwick had found him a true friend.[1] He paid him a moving tribute: "If I had lived, and been qualified for writing a book, and if it had been dedicated to any man, you would have been the man; for I have loved you, and I have peace before God in that, and I bless his name that I have been acquainted with you." He asked to be remembered to friends in Holland, "to whom I would have written, if I had not been kept close in prison, and pen, ink and paper kept from me". He had time to write no more. He ended memorably: "But I must break off. I go to your God and my God. Death to me is as a bed to the weary. Now, be not anxious; the Lord will maintain his cause, and own his people; he will show his glory yet in Scotland. Farewell."

That morning, Renwick had one last visitor. It was the governor of the prison. The governor, who was clearly acting on instructions, asked him that, at his execution, he would forbear to mention the cause of his death, and that he would avoid saying anything that would reflect upon or irritate the authorities. Renwick reacted robustly. He told him: "What God will give me to speak, that I will speak, and nothing else, and nothing less." One final temptation now awaited him. The governor produced a petition, offered it to him, and told him he could yet have his life if he would only sign it. Renwick was not to be moved. He had never read, he said, either in Scripture or history, that martyrs had petitioned for their lives when called to suffer for truth. Certainly they had remonstrated with their persecutors, and warned them of the wickedness of taking their lives; but a petition now would be "a receding from principles of truth, and a declining from a testimony for Christ". The governor, nonplussed, told him that "many martyrs would have thought it a great privilege to have the offers he had". Renwick, seeing the time advancing, declined to be drawn further into debate, but asked the governor if his mother and sisters could be permitted to join him. The governor at first demurred, objecting that Renwick might use the opportunity to smuggle out more papers; but eventually gave his consent. Renwick also received permission to have a friend with him at the scaffold. Alexander Shields, who records this, is reticent as to who this friend was. It could scarcely have been Shields himself, who had a price of one hundred pounds on his head, but it was obviously one in whom both he and Renwick could have the fullest confidence: Renwick for spiritual strengthening and support in his final moments, and Shields for first-hand information for his *Life of Renwick* which, at this stage, he had probably already decided to write.[2]

Shortly after midday Renwick, with his mother and sisters, sat down to a final meal together. In asking a blessing on the food, he said, "O Lord, now thou hast brought me within two hours of eternity, and this is no matter of terror to me, more than if I were to go to lie down in a bed of roses; nay, through grace, to thy praise I may say, I had never the fear of death since I came within this prison; but from the place I was taken in, I could have gone very composedly to the scaffold."

His mother and sisters were later able to recall some of the choice words he spoke as they shared these final moments with him. "O how can I contain the thoughts of this, to be within two hours of the crown of glory! Death is in itself the king of terrors, though not to me now, as sometimes it was, when I was in my hidings; but now, let us rejoice and be glad, for the marriage of the Lamb is come, and his wife hath made herself ready. Would ever I have thought that the fear of suffering and death could be so taken away from me! But what shall I say of it? It is the doing of the Lord, and marvellous in our eyes." He went on: "I have many times counted the cost of following Christ, but never expected it would have been so easy. And now, who knows the honour and happiness of that, He that confesseth me before men, him will I confess before the Father?" He was particularly thankful for the grace which had sustained him at the end: "Now, I am near the end of time; I desire to bless the Lord, it is inexpressibly sweet and satisfying peace to me, that he has kept me from complying in the least with enemies."

His mother, overcome by her grief, was quietly weeping. Renwick loved her dearly, but reminded her of the words of the Lord, that they who loved anything better than Christ, were not worthy of him. "If you love me, rejoice that I am going to my Father, to obtain the enjoyment of what eye hath not seen, ear hath not heard, nor hath it entered into the heart of man to conceive."

His final prayer with them was in large part an outpouring of praise. He gave thanks that he would be above all quarrels, all conflicts with sin and sorrow, that he would never more experience distance from God, and that his blood would cry to the Lord when he was gone. He prayed fervently for the suffering remnant, and that the Lord would raise up witnesses who would transmit the testimony to succeeding generations. He again and again interceded that the Lord would not leave Scotland, expressing confidence that his prayer would be answered, and that the Lord indeed would be gracious to Scotland.

The beating of drums was heard outside. It was for the guards to take him to the scaffold. He was transported with joy, exclaiming: "Yonder the welcome warning to my marriage; the bridegroom is coming, I am ready, I am ready." He took a fond leave of his mother and sisters, begging them not to be discouraged; for, he said, ere all was done, they should see matter of praise in that day's mercy.

In accordance with custom, he was taken first to the town council house, as the town officers would have charge of the execution. His sentence was formally read, and he was told that, if he had anything to say, he should say it there. Renwick answered that all he had to say there was to be found in the prophecy of Jeremiah, chapter 26, verses 14 and 15: "As for me, behold, I am in your hand; do with me as seemeth good and meet unto you. But know ye for certain, that if ye put me to death, ye shall surely bring innocent blood upon yourselves, and upon this city, and upon the inhabitants thereof." He was told that, since he would not be heard at the scaffold for the beating of drums, he should pray now. He declined to do so, and asked whether the drums would be beaten all the time, or only when he said something critical of the authorities. He was told that it would be done all the time, and therefore he should pray now. Renwick still refused, though he seems to have been taken somewhat aback by this response.

The beating of drums to drown out the words of condemned persons was a fairly regular practice at executions. It was not, however, universal; even Donald Cargill had been permitted to speak freely, and was only interrupted by the drums when he was thought to have reflected adversely on the king and government. However, Renwick was not to be daunted. When they urged him to "forbear reflections" he answered, "I will not be limited by you what to speak; I have not premeditated anything, but what the Lord gives me, that I will speak". They asked if he wanted any of the ministers of the city to attend him. Again he declined, and added: "If I would have had any of them for my counsellors or comforters, I should not have been here this day."

Leaving the council house, he was led along the usual route of condemned criminals – through the High Street, and down the steep and winding incline of the Bow, to where the scaffold stood at the eastern end of the Grassmarket. It was shortly after two in the afternoon. An immense multitude – greater than at any other execution – filled the expanse of the Grassmarket and the streets adjoining, and many others watched from windows and other places of vantage. As soon as Renwick stepped on to the scaffold – the raised platform on which stood the apparatus of execution – the drums started to beat incessantly. Some of those guarding Renwick told him it was not worth his while to say anything, since the people could not hear him; but he was not to be intimidated. A curate, standing by the scaffold, called out to him, "Mr Renwick, own our king, and we shall pray for you". Renwick answered, "I will have none of your prayers; I am come here to bear my testimony against you, and all such as you are". The curate insisted: "Own our king and pray for him, whatever you say against us." Renwick dismissed him with the words: "I will discourse no more with you; I am within a little to appear before him who is King of Kings and Lord of Lords, who shall pour shame, contempt and confusion upon all the kings of the earth that have not ruled for him."

Before speaking to the people Renwick engaged in a short act of worship. Even as he was doing so, the beating of the drums continued unabated. He sang part of the 103rd Psalm, in the Scottish metrical version, from the beginning, and read the 19th chapter of the book of Revelation. He then went to prayer, committing his soul to God through the Redeemer, and pleading that the Lord would vindicate his cause in his own time. He confessed that this was the most joyful day that ever he saw in the world, a day that he had much longed for; and blessed God that he had honoured him with the crown of martyrdom, an honour that not even angels could aspire to. He complained of being interrupted in his worship, through the noise around him; but, he added, looking up to the sombre sky above him, "By and by I shall be above these clouds: then I shall enjoy thee and glorify thee without interruption or intermission for ever".

He then turned to speak to the people. It did not matter that few could hear; Renwick knew that there were those around him who would take note of his words, and preserve them for his contemporaries and for posterity. "Spectators," he began, "or if there be any of you auditors, I must tell you I am come here this day to lay down my life for adhering to the truths of

Christ; for which I am neither afraid nor ashamed to suffer; nay, I bless the Lord that ever he counted me worthy, or enabled me to suffer anything for him; and I desire to praise his grace that he has not only kept me free from the gross pollutions of the time, but also from the many ordinary pollutions of children; and for such as I have been stained with, he has washed and cleansed me from them in his own blood. I am this day to lay down my life for these three things. First, for disowning the usurpation and tyranny of James, Duke of York. Second, for preaching that it was unlawful to pay the cess, expressly exacted for the bearing down of the Gospel. Third, for teaching that it was lawful for people to carry arms, for defending themselves in their meetings for the persecuted Gospel ordinances. I think a testimony for these is worth many lives; and if I had ten thousand, I would think it little enough to lay them all down for the same."

He went on: "Dear friends, spectators, if any of you be auditors, I must tell you I die a Presbyterian Protestant; I own the Word of God as the rule of faith and manners, I own the Confession of Faith, Large and Shorter Catechisms, Sum of Saving Knowledge, Directory for Public and Family Worship, Covenants National and Solemn League, Acts of General Assemblies, and all the faithful contendings that have been for the Covenanted Reformation. I leave my testimony approving the preaching in the fields, and the defending the same by arms. I adjoin my testimony to all these truths that have been sealed by bloodshed, either on scaffolds, fields, or seas, for the Cause of Christ. I leave my testimony against Popery, Prelacy, Erastianism, against all profanity, and everything contrary to sound doctrine and the power of godliness; particularly against all usurpations and encroachments made upon Christ's rights, the Prince of the kings of the earth, who alone must bear the glory of ruling his own kingdom, the Church. And in particular against this absolute power, usurped by this usurper, that belongs to no mortal, but is the incommunicable prerogative of Jehovah; and against this toleration, flowing from this absolute power."

He was ordered to have done. He said: "I have near done. You that are the people of God, do not weary to maintain the testimony of the day in your stations and places; and whatever you do, make sure an interest in Christ; for there is a storm coming, that shall try your foundation. And you that are strangers to God, break off your sins by repentance, else I will be a sad witness against you in the Day of the Lord."

He was ordered to stop, and to go up the ladder. He did so, then paused for a moment to pray. "Lord," he said, "I die in the faith that thou wilt not leave Scotland, but that thou wilt make the blood of thy witnesses the seed of thy Church; and return again, and be glorious in our land. And now, Lord, I am ready; the Bride, the Lamb's wife, hath made herself ready."

As the napkin was being tied about his face, he called down to his friend attending him: "Farewell; be diligent in duty, make your peace with God through Christ; there is a great trial coming. As to the remnant I leave, I have committed them to God; tell them from me not to weary, nor be discouraged in maintaining the testimony; let them not quit nor forgo one of these despised truths. Keep your ground, and the Lord will provide you teachers and ministers. And when he comes, he will make these despised truths glorious upon the earth."

The executioner moved to turn him over the ladder. As he did so, Renwick was heard to say, "Lord, into thy hands I commit my spirit; for thou hast redeemed me, Lord God of Truth". And with these words on his lips, he passed into the presence of his Lord.

"Thus died," says Shields, "Mr James Renwick, in the third day over the twenty-sixth year of his age, a young man, and young minister, but a ripe Christian, and renowned martyr of Christ, for whose sake he loved not his life dear unto the death; by whose blood, and the Word of his testimony, he overcame; in such a treasure of patience, meekness, humility, constancy, courage, burning love, and blazing zeal, as did very much confound enemies, convinced neutrals, confirmed halters, comforted friends, and astonished all."

His friends who were present – Helen Alexander among them – were allowed to do their final office for him without hindrance. His body was reverently prepared for burial, very probably in the Magdalen Chapel nearby, and later that afternoon it was interred in the nearby Greyfriars churchyard. In all likelihood, his last resting-place was in the north-east corner of the churchyard, nearest the Grassmarket, where the dust of many other victims of the persecution also rests.

Renwick was to be the last to be publicly put to death for the cause of Christ in Scotland. As several writers have observed, it was as if the persecution of twenty-eight years needed this ultimate sacrifice before it could be finally brought to an end. Within a year, the regime which had so long tyrannised over men's consciences and freedoms had been shattered into fragments.

King James the Seventh, the last representative of that tyranny, was driven from his native land; the apparatus of persecution was dismantled; and with the accession of his Protestant son-in-law as King William III, a new era had begun. Episcopacy was swept aside and the Presbyterian government of the Church restored; the old Presbyterian ministers were restored to their charges; the obnoxious laws of royal and state supremacy were abrogated; and the Westminster Confession of Faith was written into the law of the land.

It was an extreme irony that the mainspring for the Glorious Revolution, as it came to be known, was the conviction by influential leaders in the state that as a professed Roman Catholic, claiming an arbitrary and absolute authority, the king was no longer fit to rule. This was given formal effect in a declaration by the Estates of Scotland – a provisional Parliament – that "King James the Seventh, being a professed Papist, did assume the regal power, and acted as king, without ever taking the oath required by law, and has invaded the fundamental constitution of the kingdom, and altered it from a legal limited monarchy to an arbitrary despotic power, and has exercised the same to the subversion of the Protestant religion, and the violation of the laws and liberties of the kingdom, inverting all the ends of government, whereby he has forfeited the right to the crown, and the throne is become vacant". There could scarcely have been a greater similarity to the position for which Renwick and others had contended, at the cost of their lives. It was an even greater irony that one of the three Commissioners appointed by the Estates to offer the crown to the new king should have been the same Sir John Dalrymple who, only a year earlier, had prosecuted Renwick to the death for asserting that very same position; and that the Earl of Linlithgow, who had presided at his trial, should have signed a letter from the Estates pledging their loyalty to the new king and thanking him for his preservation of the Protestant religion. In a very real sense, Renwick had prepared the way for what, only a year after his death, had become the united will of the leaders of the nation.

In 1690, after the new government had become established, the Scottish Parliament passed an Act rescinding all the fines and forfeitures of the persecution, and restoring the memory of those who had been its victims. Distinguished among the names in the Act is "Mr James Renwick, a Preacher". It was a designation that Renwick himself would have favoured. His place in the public annals of his country was for ever secured. In 1706, a large and dignified memorial was erected in the Greyfriars churchyard to the memory of all the victims of the persecution who suffered death in Edinburgh. As the last of those to suffer, Renwick's name is prominently displayed on the memorial. It is a timeless testimony which for three hundred years has kept his name before each of the passing generations. It is altogether fitting that the city which he knew so well, where he was educated, where he grew up to manhood, and where in the end he laid down his life, should not allow his memory to fade.

CHAPTER 20

Renwick's Place in History

"He was of old Knox's principles." It is doubtful if Renwick would have wished for a better epitaph than these words used of him by members of the Privy Council. They referred of course specifically to his views on the magistracy which he had asserted before them; to the principle of limited monarchy which had been so clearly taught by Knox in his own day. But Renwick would have seen the words as extending much further than that. For him, they would have summed up the essence of the Scottish Reformation. And by the Scottish Reformation he would not have understood merely the work of Knox and his contemporaries, fundamental though that was; he would have understood in particular the period known as the Second Reformation, when Reformation principles had been developed and expanded, and when, by asserting and practising these principles, the Church of Scotland had attained a height and a distinction which made it famed among the Reformed churches of Europe. For Renwick, the Second Reformation had set the standard for the Church of Scotland. Its achievements – the Covenants, the Catechisms, the writings of its great divines – were of permanent relevance. Its Acts of Assemblies, even though reflecting circumstances of their own day, enshrined principles which were normative for the future government of the church. Renwick never saw a need to argue these positions. He took it for granted that anyone claiming to be in the Reformed tradition would accept them as a matter of course. In debating with opponents he freely quoted Rutherford and Durham as unquestioned authorities. It mattered not how men had sought to change the external order of the Church, or to undermine the Reformed position; the achievements of the Second Reformation remained the standard for the Church.

This made it all the more perverse, in Renwick's view, that he and the Societies should be seen as deviants from the mainstream of the Reformed tradition. "As for my principles," he wrote, "I am able to manifest them to have their warrant both from the supreme divine authority in the Word of God in the Scriptures, and the subordinate ecclesiastical authority of our church constitutions. So this is no new way that I am following, but the good old way, wherein I see the footsteps of our Lord, and the print of the feet of our worthy and resolute reformers, and those who in our day have valiantly and faithfully maintained and sealed with their blood the received and sworn principles of our Reformation." And again, not without a touch of irony: "Because some of our worthies in our day have been honoured and helped to hold what our worthy fathers did conquer with their blood, and bind over upon us by holy covenants, and we are endeavouring to do the same, they and we have been reproached as followers of new ways." These reproaches were of course particularly directed against the Societies' actions in disowning the authority of the king and government. Indeed, Renwick was generally known among the people as "the leader of those wild people that disown the king".

Yet for Renwick the issue did not admit of any doubt. For him, as for Cameron and Cargill before him, the insurmountable stumbling-block was that the government of the Church had been made an indissoluble part of the Crown. The Crown had usurped the authority which alone belonged to Christ. To acknowledge the king was to acknowledge him in the totality of his claims, and, as Cargill had shown, those claims were one and indivisible. There was thus no escaping the conclusion that acknowledgement of the royal sovereignty would be treason to Christ. Such an acknowledgement of course would be aggravated by recognising, as king, one who professed a heretical and idolatrous religion; and to that extent Renwick was under even greater compulsion than either Cargill or Cameron had been. It did not matter to Renwick that failure to render that acknowledgement was treason by the law of the land. For him, the issue was clear-cut and admitted of no accommodation or compromise.

It was a view in Reformation times that each national church was called to contend for a particular area of Divine truth. In the Church of Scotland's case, that area was seen to be the upholding of the Crown rights of Christ as king and head over his Church. This – the "distinguishing dignity" of the Church of Scotland, as the *Cloud of Witnesses* has it – was a truth which the Scottish Reformers had vigorously defended, some of them at great personal cost. It was Renwick's lot under Providence to be called to be a spiritual leader to those who were contending for that truth at a time when it was under particular threat. Loyalty to Reformation principles, and to the sacrifices of those who had gone before, demanded that any who professed themselves true members of the Church of Scotland should stand in defence of the Crown rights of Christ. They could not allow them to be usurped by a mere man; still less by one who professed a creed from which the Reformers, a hundred years earlier, had delivered Scotland. But above all, the assertion of Christ's rights was a duty owed to Christ himself. To those who accepted him as Lord, that duty was paramount; and, certainly for Renwick, it was the conclusive argument.

Renwick, in common with the Scottish Reformers, saw the Church of Scotland as a part of the Church of Christ worldwide. He several times referred in his sermons to the plight of persecuted Christians overseas, such as the Huguenots in France and the Waldensians in the North of Italy. Yet he had a keen sense of national identity. He several times declared his conviction that not only Scotland, but Britain and Ireland, had a special part in God's purpose. Preaching on 7th September 1684 he said: "We are a people that is promised to Christ. We are a people that are given of the Father to Christ in a peculiar manner; this land is as it were a promised land to Christ. Psalm 2, verse 8: 'I will give thee the uttermost parts of the earth for thy possession.' This is principally to be understood of these islands, which are in the utmost parts of the world. It is also clear from Isaiah 49, v1, 'Listen, O isles, unto me; and hearken, ye people, from far', and v6, 'that thou mayest be my salvation unto the end of the earth'. Likewise Isaiah 42, v 4, 'He shall not fail nor be discouraged, till he have set judgement in the earth, and the isles shall wait for his law'. Britain and Ireland shall wait for his law. Likewise Psalm 65, v. 5, 'Thou art the confidence of all the ends of the earth, and of them that are afar off upon the sea'. All these hold out, in a very peculiar manner, that these lands are promised to Christ, and that we are a people promised to him; and so think not that Christ will quit with what is given him; think not he will let the bands of his charter be intrenched upon. Let us rejoice that ever there was a line in the Old or New Testament pointing at Britain and Ireland's case; we are a promised people, and our land a promised land; and therefore we may expect that the Lord will come to it again. Though it be a day of great trouble, we shall be delivered out of it."

But of course Scotland was the Lord's in a very particular manner. It was a covenanted nation. There had been a solemn national dedication of the land to him. "As our land is a promised land, so it is a dedicated land. All of us are dedicated to him." This brought with it special privileges, but also special responsibilities. If these responsibilities were set aside, the land was exposed to God's judgement. Renwick frequently quoted the verse in the Book of Amos: "You only have I known of all the families of the earth; therefore I will punish you for all your iniquities." Renwick had no hesitation in asserting that the persecution was a judgement on the land and the church for its breach of covenant. Yet in judgement God would remember mercy. The very fact that God had accepted sacrifices, in terms of the martyrs and their testimonies, was an evidence that he had not forgotten the land. His purpose was not to destroy, but to cleanse and purify. "Why," Renwick asked, "will he heat the furnace so hot, but that he may bring forth a piece of pure metal? And why will he throw down the fabric of this Church to the ground, but that the rubbish thereof may be taken away, and the superstructure thereof made more glorious?" Renwick not infrequently used the image of a sieve, sifting out the chaff and letting the wheat remain. The persecution would reveal men in their true character. It would serve God's purpose of cleansing a church for himself. Only when that purpose was accomplished would the persecution end. Then, the enemies themselves would be ripe for judgement, and God would be glorified both in that judgement and in the deliverance of his people.

Renwick had a keen sense of history. He had a conviction that the experiences through which he was passing were not merely of concern to himself and his contemporaries but to future generations of the Church. It was important that posterity should know how the people of God in Scotland had conducted themselves at a time of extreme persecution, and how they had been enabled, by grace, to overcome. He was therefore particularly concerned that a testimony should be left to future generations. Even in his last letter to Robert Hamilton, written on the very day of his death, he expressed satisfaction that he should be leaving behind him a testimony in the form of his written sermons and letters. He wanted his own experience to be not merely a matter of historical record, but a help to the Church down the years in whatever tribulations it might be called to face.

Renwick had a strong belief in God's overruling Providence. Nothing happened by accident. Even the apparently haphazard events of life had a meaning and purpose. A frustrated travelling arrangement, or a meeting prevented by unforeseen circumstances, gave cause for pondering, as he used to put it, over the "language" of such dispensations. For Renwick, they were part of the ongoing plan of God for his life. He was often able, after the event, to detect a meaning and purpose hidden at the time. His enforced diversion to Ireland on his return to Scotland from Holland was occasioned so that he could encourage the Lord's people there and gain experience for his future ministry. After being at first mystified by the delay in the date of his execution he some days later wrote to friends: "I see what has been the language of my reprieve; it has been that I might be further tempted and tried, and I praise the Lord he has assisted me to give further proof of steadfastness."

As a field-preacher Renwick followed closely in the steps of those who had gone before him. He spoke almost reverentially of Cargill and Cameron. Cameron he greatly admired for his fearless testimony, and Cargill was clearly his model as a preacher. But of course Renwick had his own distinctive temperament. If he lacked the diffidence of Cargill, he lacked also the assertiveness of Cameron. In his dealings both with opponents and friends he studied moderation. Much as he was reproached, he at no time responded in kind. "It is my study," he wrote to one correspondent, "not to be bitter against the bitterness of others, not to be reviled into a reviler, nor scoffed into a scoffer, so as to return the same to them as they are to me, neither to throw back my brother's fire-balls into his own face." He judged it no compromise to be accommodating to opponents, or to give them a hearing if they sought one. He was willing to listen, and to respond to reasoned argument. But he did not believe in seeking out argument for its own sake, or submitting his principles to be tested by others. This was not arrogance, but the result of a deeply-held conviction. Scripture was the supreme rule of faith and life. Where Renwick was satisfied in conscience that he had Scripture on his side, he was not to be moved.

This did not mean that Renwick did not develop some of his views as he came to greater maturity and understanding. In his early days as a preacher, James Russel and his faction had charged him with inconstancy. Patrick Grant, in one of his many pamphlets, was later to allege that Renwick had originally believed in the assumption of magistracy – a view reflected, indeed, in the Lanark Declaration – and that the *Informatory Vindication* represented a retreat by him from that position. Whatever the merits of this may be, it is clear that on some points Renwick did moderate his views with the passage of time. The general tone of the Vindication is certainly milder than that of Renwick's original testimony, which owed much to the influence of Robert Hamilton. In the area of ministerial fellowship this is perhaps particularly evident. But on the main points of principle Renwick never did and never would compromise his position, whatever the pressures upon him might be. Even his enemies were to testify to this. The Viscount of Tarbat, a member of the Privy Council, was reported to have said that "he was one of the stiffest maintainers of his principles that ever came before us; others we used always to cause at one time or other to waver, but him we could never move; where we left him there we found him; we could never make him yield or vary in the least".

The traditional view of Renwick – or, perhaps more accurately, the one fostered by 19th century writers – is of a seraphic, heavenly-minded young man, with perhaps little concern or interest in the things of the world. The reality was somewhat different. Heavenly-minded he certainly was; but he was also closely attuned to human relationships and the ordinary affairs of life. He was a shrewd judge of men, and did not hesitate to voice his opinions frankly. Thomas Lining was "the most hopeful lad, by appearance, that we have"; and Alexander Shields was "of a right stamp". On the other hand James Russel was "a costly James Russel to the poor Church of Scotland". He could be robust when the occasion demanded, as with Russel and others whom he felt had compromised the cause. While he did not enjoy controversy, he at times found it a stimulant to greater zeal. "I think," he wrote to Hamilton after a particularly heated confrontation, "they are very pusillanimous, who do not find such hot bickerings a mean to ding a spirit into them." In all his work, even of the most routine kind, he laboured conscientiously. He was expert in administration, and, in his time as clerk, he attended to all the business of the Societies with scrupulous care. His letters were carefully crafted, and clearly and distinctly written. His sermons were well organised, and followed a closely logical order of thought. At no time did he allow his spiritual concerns to be an excuse for careless or unmethodical work.

Was Renwick unduly idealistic in looking for a return to the "godly commonwealth" of the Second Reformation era? He would of course have denied this, and have pointed to the evidence of God's signal blessing which in those days had rested on land and people. However, that is not necessarily to say that he would have insisted that in every respect the church emerging from the persecution should follow the pattern of the Church of the 1640s. He was ready, in his last letter to Hamilton, to acknowledge that, even since the start of his ministry, "the state of our controversies is altered".

An associated question is whether Renwick would have joined the national Church at the Revolution. Opinions on this have varied, and it is not particularly fruitful to speculate. Certainly, he would have been exercised by the fact that the Revolution Settlement did not explicitly recognise the Covenants, nor many of the achievements of the Second Reformation period; and it left in place many ministers who had conformed to prelacy. On the other hand, Renwick did prize very highly the unity of the Church of Christ; and, like Alexander Shields, Thomas Lining and William Boyd, he may have thought it right not to stand aloof from a constituted church based on the principles of the first Reformers. Lining, for whom Renwick had a high regard, was firmly of the view that Renwick would have come in to the Revolution Church, and in proof of this he cites the repeated indications in the *Informatory Vindication* that the grounds of withdrawal stated there were related only to the then disrupted state of the Church and not to the Church as properly constituted. On the other hand, it must not be forgotten that Renwick was closely attached to Robert Hamilton, who stood out firmly against the Revolution Settlement because of its "uncovenanted" character. There would clearly have been strong pressures on Renwick in either direction. It was an issue however on which in God's providence he was spared from making a judgement.

It was Renwick's lot in Providence to appear on the stage of history at a critical time for both Church and State in Scotland. The persecution of the Church had of course continued over many years, and the advent of a Roman Catholic king in 1685, just over a year into Renwick's ministry, gave it a new and potentially even more terrible dimension. The unparalleled horrors of that year appeared to vindicate that foreboding. Yet Renwick habitually reminded his audiences that the darkest hour of the night is the one before the dawn. The heightened tyranny carried with it the seeds of its own destruction. The king's increasingly authoritarian rule, and his determination to surmount all constitutional barriers to favour his co-religionists, started to generate unease among those in the State who hitherto had seemed indifferent to the tyranny which had engulfed the Church.

The first indications of that unease were evident in 1686 when the Parliament refused to bow to the King's demands to relax the laws against Roman Catholics. Although opposition remained muted, an undercurrent of suspicion and questioning now existed in influential quarters in the State; and as the king's authoritarianism increased, and the threat to constitutional safeguards became more marked, so that undercurrent grew stronger.[1] But it needed an impetus to bring it to the surface; and Renwick's public death was to provide that impetus. Renwick had of course addressed the issue again and again in his preaching, but his death brought it before a far larger constituency than ever his preaching could have done. He had himself predicted that his death would do more good than a life extended over many years; and, at the end, he appears to have come to see it as a necessary sacrifice. It gave an unquestionable credibility to his testimony; but, more than that, it brought starkly before the nation the constitutional disaster to which it was heading. To that extent it played an indubitable part in releasing the forces which, only a few months later, had swept the king from the throne and set both Church and nation on a new course for the future.

James Renwick lived his whole life under the persecution which for twenty-eight years ravaged the Church of Scotland. Yet he passionately believed that the day of deliverance would come; that God would yet return, and show himself glorious. He himself did not live to see that deliverance. But when it did come, those few months after his death, his stand for the liberties of church and nation was seen to be fully vindicated. In his lifetime it was his lot to suffer hardship, persecution and reproach. But he was given the grace to endure, and in the long annals of the Scottish Church there are few names more honoured than his. His life was brief, but he has left an enduring memorial.

——— • ———

• A TRIBUTE BY A HEARER •

By James Nisbet

This eloquent and moving tribute to Renwick, written in 1725, appears in James Nisbet's memoirs of the persecution, published in 1827 under the title Private Life of the Persecuted. *Nisbet was a devoted hearer of Renwick and has also left impressions of his field-preaching, as recorded above.*

"HE was born 1662, Febr 15, of parents both eminently godly; his mother's name was Elizabeth Corson, with whom I was well acquaint. He was the only man that ever I knew that had an untainted integrity; he was a lively and faithful minister of Christ, a worthy Christian, so as none who was entirely acquaint with him could say otherwise but that he was a beloved Jedidiah of the Lord. I never knew a man more richly endowed with grace and suitable qualifications; I never knew a man more equal in his temper, more equal in his spiritual frame, and more equal in walk and conversation. Many times when I have been thinking of the great Mr John Knox, Mr John Welsh, Mr John Davidson, Mr Samuel Rutherford and others of our worthy Reformers, I have thought that the great Mr James Renwick was as true and genuine a son and successor to these great men as any that ever the Lord raised up in this land to contend for truth and preach the Gospel to lost sinners. He seemed to come upsides with them in point of principle, in point of practice, and in point of zeal for the glory of God, in giving testimony for truth and against sin and defection; so that although he was the Joseph that was sorely shot at and grieved, yet he was the Caleb that followed the Lord fully.

"When I consider him as a man, none more comely in features, none more prudent, none more brave and heroic in spirit, none more humane and condescending to those of the weaker capacity; he was every way so rational that there was ground to think the powers of his reason were as much strengthened and sanctified as any mere man that ever I heard of. When I consider him as a Christian, none more meek, and yet none more prudently bold against those that were bold to sin, and yet none more prudently condescending to those that were weak; none more frequent and fervent in religious duties, to wit, prayer, converse, meditation, self-examination, preaching, prefacing, lecturing, baptising and catechising, in teaching and instructing, accompanied with a sweet charming eloquence in holding forth Christ as the only remedy for lost sinners. None more sound in the orthodox principles, none more free and sharp in reproving of sin and vice, none more faithfully zealous in contending for Christ's crowned rights and royal incommunicable prerogatives, so that he would not part with hair or hoof, and yet none more condescending, as far as Scripture limits would allow; none more hated of man, and yet none more strengthened and upheld by the everlasting arms of the great Jehovah, and none more steadfast to the death, wherefore he might justly be called Antipas, Christ's faithful martyr.

"And as I lived then to know him, and all these things of him to be so of a truth, so by the good hand of God I yet have, seven and thirty years after him, to testify that no man upon just grounds had anything to lay to his charge, when all the critical and straitening circumstances of that suffering period are well considered, save that he was liable to natural and sinful infirmities as all men are while they live, and yet he was as little guilty this way as any I ever knew or read of. He was the liveliest and engagingest preacher to close with Christ of any that ever I heard; his converse was pious, prudent, and freest of heat and of affectation of any I ever knew, and, be in heat or out of humour who would, in debate or reasoning, yet they were never seen to move in him, although he did not let anything pass without a full, clear and convincing answer, so that it carried alongst with it a full evidence of the truth of what he asserted. And for steadfastness in the way of the Lord few came his length; he examined the truth and counted the cost, and sealed it with his blood.

"Of all the men that ever I knew I would be in the least danger in committing a hyperbole when speaking to his commendation; and yet I speak not this to praise man, but for the glory and honour of God, who makes men to differ so much one from another, and in some periods of the Church more than others. O this doth wonderfully speak forth the infinite wisdom and immensefulness of Christ, the glorious king and rightful head of his Church, that he being the head of all Divine influences can and doth communicate to and lodge in man, a clay vessel, such graces, gifts and qualifications whereby they are throughly furnished for what work he has a mind to call them to and cut out for them, and then seal it with their blood, which is a great honour, that few obtain. Now O my soul, bless the Lord that ever I heard this great man preach the unsearchable riches of Christ to poor lost sinners, of whom I am the chief, and the more I descend by self-examination to feel the sinful workings of my heart and nature, the more cause I see to cry out, O wretched man that I am, who shall deliver me from the body of this death? But thanks be to God through Jesus Christ our Lord, who shall change this vile body that it may be fashioned like unto his glorious body, according to the working of his mighty power, whereby he is able to subdue all things to himself. And to this one God, Father, Son and Holy Spirit, be endless praise and Hallelujahs for evermore. Amen."

APPENDIX 1

RENWICK AS A PREACHER

As with other of the field-preachers, many of Renwick's sermons were taken down in manuscript by hearers. A few individual sermons were published shortly after his death, but it was sixty years before a collected edition was produced. In 1748 William Wilson, schoolmaster at Douglas, in Lanarkshire, published the first volume of *A Choice Collection of Very Valuable Prefaces, Lectures and Sermons, preached upon the Mountains and Muirs of Scotland, in the hottest time of the late Persecution, by that faithful Minister and Martyr of Jesus Christ, the Reverend Mr James Renwick*. A second volume followed in 1751, the two comprising 32 Prefaces, 9 Lectures and 44 Sermons in all. The collection was re-published as a single volume in 1776 (twice), again in 1777, and yet again in 1804. The single-volume editions all contained Renwick's 1683 Testimony at Darmead.

John Howie of Lochgoin published his *Collection of Lectures and Sermons* of the field-preachers in 1779, and another short collection as an appendix to *Faithful Contendings Displayed* in 1780. Since Renwick's sermons had been so recently and frequently published, he did not include sermons by Renwick in either collection. This had the unfortunate result that when Howie's 1779 volume was republished in 1880, under the title *Sermons in Time of Persecution in Scotland* – a volume recently reprinted – no sermons by Renwick were included. The modern reader thus has to depend on an edition 200 years old, or more, to gain access to Renwick's sermons.

The structure of Renwick's preaching followed closely the conventions of the time. A day's preaching would normally consist of a Preface, Lecture and Sermon in the forenoon, and a further sermon in the afternoon. The Preface was intended as an opening exhortation to the audience, to capture their attention, and was frequently blunt and challenging. The Lecture was basically an exposition of an extended passage of Scripture, drawing appropriate lessons for the times. Not infrequently, the text for the forenoon and afternoon sermons would be the same. Renwick generally made it his aim to direct his forenoon sermon to unbelievers, and the afternoon sermon to professing Christians. When he preached at night, as he frequently did, it is likely that these aims were combined in a single sermon, with the Preface and Lecture preceding. The records suggest that a forenoon or night-time's preaching would normally occupy around three hours. There was also, of course, prayer and praise. The praise, led by a precentor, was taken from the Scottish metrical psalms of 1650, which was the only version sanctioned by the General Assembly. In accordance with custom, the precentor sometimes led in praise before the preacher's arrival, or read selected passages from Scripture.

The structure of Renwick's sermons also followed a standard form. Known commonly as the "plain style", this consisted of an introduction explaining the text, followed by a series of "doctrines" or "observations", and finally a series of "uses" in which practical application was made of the doctrines. These uses could range widely, applying to the hearers' personal and spiritual lives or to their public witness.

Renwick, like all the field-preachers, had a very keen sense of his calling as a minister of the Gospel. He saw himself as a sent messenger, an instrument in God's hand, as one speaking to the people with God's authority, whether they would hear or whether they would forbear. He was what was later to become known as a "searching" preacher. He brought uncompromisingly before his hearers the realities of life and death, of heaven and hell. He spent much time identifying the "marks" of the true Christian, and warning against false pretensions. The times in which he preached gave of course a particular poignancy to these issues. The things of eternity seemed very near. At a time when great sacrifices were demanded, Renwick was conscious that some could be tempted to depend on their own works rather than on the finished work of Christ. He wanted them to be aware of their danger, and he did not spare his words of warning to them. He was of course careful to mingle these warnings with words of warm Gospel invitation. Indeed, it is not easy among the recorded sermons of the time to find words which commend the excellence of Christ in such compelling terms as does Renwick in his published sermons. His first sermons at Darmead set the tone for this, and it was a theme which was never far from his lips throughout his life.

What fascinated many about Renwick's preaching, and drew them to him, was the maturity of spiritual judgement he possessed, and his ability to assess the spiritual condition of his hearers. To a remarkable extent for his years, he displayed a depth of knowledge of the human heart. Even his inaugural sermons at Darmead, preached at the age of twenty-one, were suggestive of a lifetime of Christian experience. It was as if in Renwick's case that experience had been compressed into a small compass so that he would be specially fitted, within the time granted him, to be a spiritual guide to those subjected to extreme trial. In Renwick they were to find one who could not only sympathise with their condition, but who could bring to them in a very special way the spiritual counsel and comfort they needed.

Renwick himself was always conscious of the unique mission on which he had been sent. His hearers, certainly those who continued faithful, could not count on another day's freedom to hear the Gospel. They did not know when they would be called upon to face arrest, imprisonment, or even death. Renwick well knew the pressures they faced and the challenges to their faith. They were ordinary, fallible people with very human failings. They could not but be affected by the circumstances in which they were forced to live. They were concerned about their families, their property, and their livelihood. During the worst period of the persecution, in 1684 and 1685, the situation for many became so desperate that their faith began to falter. It seemed that evil was triumphant; that the cause of God in Scotland was lost; and that everything in Providence was set against it. A sense of hopelessness, and even more dangerously, of cynicism, began to set in. Renwick referred to this in one of his sermons: "They say, judgement has left the earth, and the Lord is testifying that he delights in wickedness, when they see them that tempt God even delivered, and the workers of wickedness exalted. The affliction that has befallen the church in our day has made many say this, that they think wickedness will never come down; and we must cast in our lot, and take part with the rest."

It was against this terrible background that Renwick was called upon to strengthen the faith of those who were well-nigh despair. For himself, he never wavered; and his unflinching steadfastness was a beacon of hope to those who were sorely tested. In the same sermon he told his hearers: "He brings his people low, that he may get them taught to fix their eyes alone on him for help. Be their case ever so low, there is enough in him for their recovery. You that are the people of God, despond not at your low condition; the lower your case is, he shall get the more glory in delivering you. Rejoice in your low case, because it makes for the manifestation of

God's attributes. Rejoice, because God shall be exalted in your delivery; for the lower you are brought, the more glory shall redound to him when you shall be redeemed out of all your troubles."

As a rule, particularly in the earlier part of his ministry, Renwick did not enter much into matters of public controversy in his sermons. These were normally left to the special "fast days" which were arranged from time to time, where numerous "causes of fasting and humiliation" were confessed before God. Latterly, however, he tended to refer more to these issues, no doubt because he saw the need for the people to be warned urgently against the dangers of them. He specifically counselled his hearers not to associate themselves with Argyle, and in his final few months he regularly issued warnings against the evils of the Toleration. These were always however set in the context of spiritual lessons, and particularly of the need for steadfastness in the face of temptation.

The following sermon on Isaiah 3:10 comes from around the mid-point of Renwick's ministry, and gives a typical example of his preaching. It is taken from the published collection.

> *"Say ye to the righteous, that it shall be well with him"* – Isaiah 3:10.
>
> There are several questions of great weight, which we should be oft asking, that are of soul-concernment: as that, "What shall I do to be saved?". Do you know what this is, to be put to much exercise, and great diligence about your soul's case? This flows not from passing and transient thoughts of Christ, but from a heart-work, and a humble work. Oh think, "What shall I do to be saved?". It is sadly to be feared, that there are some folk that never ask the question at their own hearts, "What shall I do to be saved?". And there are some, when they set about this work, in some case, they do make themselves, by their overly seeking, to be still under a secure silent condition; and, if they go to seek the charter of their soul's assurance, they satisfy themselves very easily, and they are content to have it written in such small letters that they can hardly win [attain] to discern or read them; but Christians should seek to have the evidences of their assurance drawn and engraven in great and grave letters, seeing this is the only thing needful that we are called to make sure in time.
>
> A second question that we should be setting about, and studying to know, and that is, "How to know God, and to have the soul brought under high contemplations of him?". The beauty of him should make us love and admire him, and praise him. This will be the motto that

the believer will be forced to put upon him, "He is matchless, and every way transcendently glorious". Look how he is brought in by the Spirit, Isaiah 9.6, "Wonderful, Counsellor, the mighty God, the everlasting Father, the Prince of Peace". And look how he is brought in by John, Revelation 19.16, "King of Kings, and Lord of Lords". So that his properties and styles cannot be set out by the believer; and therefore, with the spouse, they must declare him matchless, and "altogether lovely".

And there is a third question, that you should be oft asking at your own hearts, and it is this, "What shall I render unto the Lord for all his benefits to me?". Are you so senseless, that you know not that you have your being of him? Are you not made to wonder at the condescension of our Lord, in all the steps of his goodness? A soul, when right with God, will read mercies out of the greatest of judgements. Jacob was made to say, "I am not worthy of the least of all thy mercies". And I will tell you, a quarrelling disposition with God is far from a gracious disposition.

And a fourth question that you should be often asking, and it is your duty to be seeking much of the Lord's mind in it, and it is this, "Watchman, watchman, what of the night?". The answer is, "The morning cometh, and also the night". We are in the night with it this day; but there is a darker night coming, when the Lord shall draw forth his bright sword: it is furbished that it may glitter, and it shall be put in the hand of the slayer, when he shall pass through the breadth and length of the land, and destroy and lay waste the sinners of his people; that will be a dark night. But, believe this, the church will have glorious days when the Lord comes back to his church in the latter days, to restore the solemn feasts; when every one shall dwell safely under his own vine, and Israel shall no more dwell in tents. Oh if this were believed, a sight of these days by faith would create more courage in his people's hearts resolutely to face the storm. Considering what he will bring with him of the power of the Gospel, this will make all the swellings of Jordan to appear but little, although it should overflow all its banks. However in this portion of Scripture, the Lord hath certified and asserted, that come what will, it shall be well with the righteous.

Now, from the words read, I would draw these two observations.

1. The first observation is this, That it is a minister's duty to divide the Lord's Word aright. Here you see Isaiah gets his commission from

the Lord, to tell the righteous for their encouragement, that it shall be well with them. And likewise to tell the wicked, that woe and wrath was abiding them, and that it should be ill with them. This was Paul's charge to Timothy, that he should study to divide the Lord's Word rightly, 2 Tim. 2.15. For the clearing of the meaning of this, it is to apply promises to whom promises belong, and threatenings to whom threatenings are due. Ministers should excuse or palliate sin in no person, of whatsoever degree, as you may see frequently in Scripture from the Lord's commission to his servants, that they be faithful stewards in his house, in dividing his Word faithfully. In effect, I shall say this word from it, the failing that has been in this time in not dividing the Lord's Word faithfully has made his church a broken and divided church, which if the Word had been faithfully divided and seasonably applied, our rents and divisions, and subdivisions., had not been such as they are this day. But there have been some that came and pretended to carry the Lord's message that have spoken and proclaimed peace to them that capitulate with the Lord's open and avowed enemies; and strengthened their hands, by their fainting to bear the Lord's banner, and taking the lee-side of the brae, and so the fall of many has been occasioned thereby. Oh, what shall these be likened unto, that should have been builders with others in the house of God? There is nothing that they can resemble more, than a company of builders at a house, where there are some building, and some casting down. And so the ministers of Scotland are such; there was one party building, and another party casting down; and so, when these that were building saw that the rest cast down what they builded, they began to cast as fast down as the rest, and so the building is come to a ruinous heap. Or they may be compared to men rowing in a boat, and the wind becomes contrary, and the storm rises; and ere they weary themselves to get the boat brought to harbour, they would rather quit their work and let the boat perish. And so this day you are scattered without shepherds to feed the flock; and what the Lord said to Hosea may be applied to and said of the men of these practices, Hosea 4.6, "My people are destroyed for lack of knowledge". And this is not our observation only, but their own, that when they that should feed Christ's flock deny to do it, they thereby provoke the Lord to deny their children of spiritual food. We see something of this already.

2. The second observation is this, that in this commission that Isaiah gets, to say to the righteous, "that it shall be well with him", we see

that when the Lord threatens sinners with most judgements, he does not forget to comfort his own people. This prophet, from the beginning of this chapter, shows that he will take away the prophet, and the captain, and the eloquent orator; and then, in a word, that he will bring a general judgement upon all, so that none shall escape. Yet he forgets not a promise of comfort to his own; "Say ye to the righteous, that it shall be well with him". Oh if we could stand still and admire the condescendency of God, that he will not bring a stroke upon the wicked till he warn his people of it; you will see a proof of this in the ninth of Ezekiel, for then, when he had determined that he would bring a general stroke upon the city, he gave a charge, that there should be nothing done until all the mourners were marked. And not only so, but when the sentence was put in execution, he gave a charge to the men with the slaughtering weapons, that they should not touch or come near any that had the mark. Oh how wonderful is his condescendency and kindness! He is sometimes so kind to, and familiar with his people, that he will give them a sight of their captivity, with the sight of a promise in the bosom of it, for their outgate [deliverance]. He dealt thus with his disciples, when he foretold them of his going away; "For," says he, "I will see you again, and your hearts shall rejoice." For he knew that the news of his departure was sad and heavy to them, and therefore he promised that he would come again and pay them a visit. Whence we see that the Lord allows comfort to his own people in the saddest of times; and he will have them comforted, and he will have it told them. This is clear from Isaiah 40.1-2, "Comfort ye, comfort ye, my people, saith your God; speak ye comfortably to Jerusalem, and cry unto her, that her warfare is accomplished, that her iniquity is pardoned". And he forewarns the wicked of what shall befall them also.

3. The third observation that I would notice is this, that the righteous man is the only happy man, because that he has the promise of life eternal; and not only so, but he has the promise of all that the Lord sees needful for him in this present life. Who is the man that will get all the promises made out to him? Only the righteous man; they shall be brought to sit on thrones, and to walk in white; they shall be kings and priests to God and to the Lamb. This is only given to the righteous person; all the promises in this life, and the life to come, the righteous may claim them as their own, Psalm 84.11: "No good thing will he withhold from them that walk uprightly."

But perhaps you will say, How can this consist with the case of his people? For we see that the Lord is giving us ground to take up that complaint, "that the wicked are spreading themselves like a green bay-tree", and have all that their hearts can wish, when his people are reduced to great straits. But though this be true, yet it consists very well with the promises; for if the Lord saw not this good for his people, that they be emptied from vessel to vessel, for their being made meet for heaven, he had never reduced them to such straits; but he is wise who has said, Romans 8.28, "And we know that all things work together for good to them that love God". He can give them the hundred-fold in the hardest of their conditions. Dare you not say, you who have peace with him in your own consciences, that you have found this to be true, that you have found the feast of fat things, of wines well refined upon the lees, in your hardest lot, when all other things have been but as trifles to you?

But perhaps you will say, How does it consist with the promises, when his people are dragged to prisons and to scaffolds every day, and are made to undergo the hardest and sharpest of sufferings? Yet though all this be true, it stands very well with his promises; for is he not their light and their life, and has not his strength been forthcoming to them? Whereas he has said, "When they go through the rivers they shall not overflow them, and when they walk through the fire they shall not be burnt". Has he not made out this promise to many a poor thing that, no doubt, has said, "Their lines are fallen to them in pleasant places"? We doubt not but his presence has been so manifested to his people that even enemies themselves have wished that their latter end might be like theirs, although, like Balaam, they will not live their life. And so the Lord causes the prophet to proclaim this, "Say to the righteous, it shall be well with him".

But for the better understanding of these words –
I. I shall show you who is the righteous man. And then,
II. I shall give you some evidences for clearing of this.
But I shall be very brief.

I. As to the first, Who is the righteous man? And how shall I know whether this promise belongs to me or not? I answer, the righteous man is he that has fled to Christ for righteousness; that is, the man that has apprehended Christ for his righteousness. Observe it, till you be in union with Christ, there is not a promise in all the Bible for you; for there is none that can open this book, that is fast sealed, but only Christ; and can let out of his promises to his people. It is said, Revelation 5.4, that John wept because no man was found worthy to open and to read the book, until Christ, the Lion of the tribe of Judah, prevailed to open the book and to loose the seven seals thereof. So then, believe it, that the book is sealed till once you be in union with Christ; and then, when Christ is yours, all is yours, and you are righteous; for it is these who have fled to him, and have union with him, that are the only righteous. Oh labour to make this sure, that you are united unto Christ by faith, and married to him by covenant. Remember that till then, you can perform no duty acceptable to God; and there are four sorts of folk that I would propose this unto, to try themselves by. And,

1. The first sort are those that are not sensible of their own condition; that know not what it is to be convinced of sin, and of their soul's destruction for sin, and that see not the sword of justice drawn above their heads, for a broken law, until Christ came and interposed in their room. And so consider, you that are in that case, that never knew what it was to dwell half an hour under despairing thoughts about your souls, you have never known what it is to come to Christ, as seeing yourselves under the curse of the law. I say, whatever you may imagine in a gospel way, that you may look at in order to your in-bringing to himself; yet this is sure, that you must make use of as much of the law-work as shall discover to you what you are by nature.

2. The second sort are you who rest on purposes and resolutions to grow better, but never bring your purposes the length of practices. Remember this, that Balaam had good purposes and intentions, who prayed to the Lord that he might die the death of the righteous, and that his latter end might be like theirs. Remember also what strong resolutions and purposes Peter had; when Christ was foretelling that they would all leave him, he cried out that although all should deny him, yet he would not do it; yet, you know, Peter was the first that fell foully. Therefore I would say that resolutions rested on, and purposes and intentions to grow better, when they are not brought the length of practices, speak out this, that they are none of the righteous that the Lord is here comforting against trials and straits.

3. The third sort that I would name are these that are resting on duties without Christ. There is not a promise in all the Scriptures to

such. Oh, say some, What need I fear, or be at such pains, for if I neglect not reading and praying, and opportunities of that kind, what will ail me? But remember this, that there are many such hypocrites that are among the damned in hell, that have been very forward in external duties. You know what the Pharisee said, when he went up to the temple to pray, and began to commend himself to God, by the good deeds he had done, thanking him that he was not like others, or like the publican. You see also what Paul says of himself, when out of Christ, that he was a very trim legal man; and yet you see, for as good a conceit as Paul had of himself, and of his zeal that made him persecute the church, yet he tells in another place, when once he saw the law-work, and had the right conviction of sin, then he calls himself the chief of sinners.

4. The fourth sort are these who crucify convictions, and rely on created graces. They ever think it is well, because they had a calling of this sort; therefore they cross their convictions, and fight against their consciences to get them quieted. But remember this, that every challenge is not saving; you may come through many challenges, and may get the conscience quieted and calmed, and yet not be a saving work of grace. Many have had many challenges, flowing from the common operation of the Spirit; as Judas, who had challenges enough for betraying innocent blood, yet no work of saving grace. It is true that his challenges were such that he could not get his conscience calmed again; but however I will say this, unless your convictions produce a real hatred of sin, and a loathing of yourselves, and a fleeing into Christ, they are not saving convictions. It is true, Christ is the end of the law to them that believe; convictions may be made use of by the Lord in a sovereign way, as he pleases; but they in themselves wanting [lacking] this character and mark, a hatred at sin, and a real desire to get God's wrath pacified, through the merits of Christ, it is naught. Now, this is the language of faith, yet it has another language, "O Israel, thou hast destroyed thyself; but in me is thy help". Moses himself was not sufficient to carry forth the children of Israel out of Egypt through the wilderness, but Christ behoved to be employed, as the spiritual rock they drank of, to keep them from fainting. So there must be a constant travelling of the soul betwixt Moses and Christ. It is the greatest subtlety and wiliness of Satan that causes men to rely upon convictions; for, believe it, that it cannot be the evidence or ground of true saving grace. It is always the unchangeable love of God in

Christ that is to be depended upon, for what is all created grace, but like the trusting in the arm of flesh? But remember this, while out of Christ, no promises made to the righteous will serve your turn. "But say to the righteous, it shall be well with him."

But who are the righteous? Only such are they, as have communion with God. And here you may know your union with him by the communion that you have with him; and if it were asked at you, what is it that your hearts are going out after through the day? And what is it that you have most communion with? We fear, if conscientiously answered, that it is with Belial, and the works of darkness; he that gives way to the world, and to his lusts and idols, and is keeping fellowship with them, and is not crying out with Ephraim, "What have I to do any more with idols?" is none of the righteous. But there are some that think that they can have God and idols both; they will give one part of their hearts to him, and another to the world, and their idols in it; but he has told us, that there is no concord betwixt Christ and Belial.

II. But to make it more clear, consider these evidences: for as these that are settling upon their lees, and pursuing the world, are far from having union with Christ, so these are the evidences of such as have union with him.

1. The man or the woman that has union with Christ, they have a real antipathy at every sin, because the fear of God remains in their heart; it is not hatred at some sins that are averse to their nature, but hatred at all sins, especially that sin that their nature is most inclined unto. It was David's endeavour to keep himself from his own iniquity, Psalm 18.23.

2. They that have union with Christ, they know by experience that faith is the instrumental cause of that union, because it is only by faith in Jesus Christ that the believer is helped to this; but you that know not how you won by faith have reason to question that your faith is not sound. Therefore, there is no union with Christ without faith; you will readily say that you believe, and that you have faith; but how came you by it? You cannot tell; but I tell you, that faith that you brought to the world with you, shall not carry you far. But the man that has union with Christ, he can tell of the difficulty of believing, and how hard a work he had ere he won at his faith. Christianity is a mystery, indeed, to the Christian to win at; but to such only this is that which strengthens their faith, that Christ is the

author and finisher thereof. Therefore I would say this from it, that you that know not the difficulty of believing, you know not what it is to believe.

3. Those that have union with Christ, this is an evidence of it, that he only is precious to them; according to that word, 1 Peter 2.7, "Unto you therefore that believe he is precious". They that believe, they have a high designation to give him; and their estimation of him is above all things. So you that find your hearts much after other things, and are ready to forget him, he has never been seen to be precious to you. You have never won to know, what it was to dwell under the refreshing thoughts of him and his love; and to come with him from Lebanon. And if an absent Christ be thus lovely, what must his presence be? Indeed when he is present, a soul will not win to get all his properties commended but this, that he is altogether lovely. And you that know not what it is to have his loveliness engraven upon your hearts, know not what it is to believe in him, and to have union with him; but to them that believe he is precious.

4. They that have union with Christ, they are longing for communion with him, and without interruption. "The Spirit and the bride say, Come," and the loving soul that has union with him, says, "Even so, come quickly." It was thus with Paul, "Who shall deliver me from the body of death?". This put him to a strait, desiring to be dissolved, that he might win to enjoy communion with him without any interruption. Have you not been at this, to have a thirsting and longing to be freed from a present life, that you might win to enjoy him? Oh happy soul that from a real ground can say this, that this is the thing that would make him content to be absent from the body, that he might be present with the Lord.

But I shall name this as the last and sum of all in it; that these who are united to Christ, they have faith, and it is such a faith as purifies the heart; there is nothing but Christ that lives and reigns in the soul; they are helped to trample upon principalities and powers, the world and their lusts, and Christ is become the only desire of their soul. But you that say you have union with him, and yet keep and entertain your idols in your bosom, I would ask this, where is your holiness? For faith employs him, not only for justification, but for sanctification and cleansing also.

Now I shall speak a word to two sorts of people.

You that can lay hold on these marks and evidences, do not doubt him, although, as to human appearances, he should seem to cross his promises; for he that has begun a good work of grace in the soul shall carry it on, for his work is perfect. Therefore spend more time in blessing and praising him, and in believing on him; for the enemies, in the midst of all their profanity, cannot have the satisfaction that you may have. He is inviting you to come and take your fill of love; is he not crying, "Behold me, behold me"? and holding out his arms, and bidding all come; and every one that will let him come, and he is begging upon his knees, as it were, that you would come unto him, and partake of his rich salvation.

But possibly some will say, I am a poor sinner, will he accept of me, that is so vile and polluted? I answer to this, I will tell thee in his name, that it is such he is seeking; and although thou be black like the tents of Kedar, yet thou shalt be made comely like the curtains of Solomon. It is not the penitent only, but the impenitent that he invites to come; the greater thy sin be, the greater necessity thou hast of him. And I promise you, in his name, that you shall not be the unwelcomer to him that your sin is so great; for we never hear that Christ upbraided any heinous sinners for coming to him. But, on the contrary, his serious entreaties are used, and he hereby regrets that sinners will not come to him that they might have life. This made him weep over Jerusalem and say, "How often would I have gathered you, as a hen gathereth her chickens, and ye would not", therefore let not this be your excuse; let not the greatness of your sins hold you away; for although you had all the sins that all within this place are guilty of, yet I, in his name, promise you, you shall be welcome to him, and that this shall not keep you away. Come, and regret your case to him, for it is only he that can help you out of that condition. Seek a heart to repent, and grace to believe in his name, that he that is God, that justifies the ungodly, may justify you.

Now there are two or three words of use, and I shall only name them.

Use 1 is of reproof to them that are at no pains to get it known that they are righteous, and have an interest in the promises. What a poor portion have they, that will not be at pains to come to him; you have not a right to this promise, that it shall be well with you, but the wrath of God shall seize upon you, and you shall be joined to the company of devils and damned spirits to all eternity. Therefore take this exhortation, and let not him be provoked to say of you, "Bring these murderers, and slay them before me, that would not that I should reign over them". Lay to heart and consider what you will say, when that sentence shall be pronounced against you, "Depart from me, ye cursed". Remember that you are now invited to come and close the bargain with him; and if you refuse, there is not a promise in all the Bible for you; no, not from the first of Genesis to the last of the Revelation, that shall be for your comfort. But I, in his name, do denounce eternal wrath against you; and what will you answer? Will you send the answer of Pharaoh, which he gave to Moses, "Who is the Lord that I should obey him?". Well, if this be your resolution, gird up your loins, and make yourselves strong, and put on your harness, for you shall not boast when you put it off again; you shall not boast of your victory; remember that you have an angry God for your party.

Use 2 is of reproof also, to a generation that seek their well-being only in the world; and that are settling themselves upon their lees, and they will keep the big world in their arms till the fire of hell be kindled in their bosom. Oh remember what a poor portion you have, who have chosen the world for your portion. You that would do anything that you may get the world bruiked [enjoyed], that agree and capitulate with enemies, and do thereby deny all duty that ever you have done; remember, it is the shortest cut to die well, to live well.

Use 3 is a word of consolation to his own faithful ones; that, however it fare with the world, it shall fare well with them. Oh man, art thou a believer? What is thy case? Thou hast many rich promises to apply to thyself; and although thy life may be attended with crosses, yet thou hast the promise of his presence, and of all the strength that is in Christ to be forthcoming for thee, and for thy throughbearing; and the end shall be well, for the latter end of the righteous is peace, however matters go with the world. And even as to time, it shall go well with him; he shall have his hundred fold in this life, and the Lord's presence shall not be wanting, sometimes less and sometimes more, according as he sees it needful for him. And if it were no more than the crumbs that fall from the children's table, it is enough to make thy heart cheerful. His company and presence make the hardest of lots a paradise. The Psalmist said he would not fear, though mountains were cast into the depths of the sea. However his enemies may think light of this, to hang a flag of defiance against him, and think little of his love that his people partake of; yet he is a friend that loves at all times, and he is such a friend that he will stick closer than a brother. He is not like many temporal friends, that although they have willingness to help, yet they want ability; but he is both able and willing. What is it that you want, but it is to be found in him? Then will you effect the cause, and endeavour to be in the case of his people, and you shall be counted righteous in his sight; and never rest till you know that their case is your case, and that you have a right to him. He gave the prophet a charge to proclaim this in the ears of the people, before he brought on desolation and wrath upon the wicked: Go to the righteous, and say to them that it shall be well with them. And now to him that is able to perform this promise, and all others, do we desire to give praise. Amen.

APPENDIX 2

RENWICK AS A CORRESPONDENT

RENWICK was a prolific letter-writer, though obviously only a fraction of his letters have survived. Four of these were appended to Shields' *Life of Renwick* as published by John McMain in 1724. Forty years later, sixty-one letters of his were included by John McMillan of Pentland in his *Collection of Letters* (1764). These were republished by Dr Thomas Houston of Belfast in 1865. The best edition is that of W H Carslaw (*The Life and Letters of James Renwick,* 1893). In his introduction, Carslaw tells of his original intention to publish only selections from the surviving letters; reluctantly however he had agreed to the solicitations of friends to publish all of them unabridged. Posterity has reason to be grateful that Carslaw accepted his friends' advice.

The letters, particularly those to Robert Hamilton, are a very useful source of information on Renwick's life as seen from his own perspective, and as his joys and sorrows unfolded. Many are devotional, either in whole or in part, and were intended to bring spiritual comfort to those who had need of it, or to share his own spiritual experience. It appears from the last letter he wrote that he intended his letters, or at least some of them, for publication, as he regarded them as part of his testimony to the world.

Numerous extracts from his letters have been given above; some others follow.

• EXTRACTS •

IN all cases, let us have our recourse to the Rock that is higher than we, where we shall find comfort for our perplexed hearts; and let us lay our all under the feet of all men, but quit a hoof of God's matters to no man. Let us be lions in God's cause, and lambs in our own.

To Robert Hamilton, February 6th 1683

OH that the Lord would order all things aright for the enlargement of his kingdom. O precious kingdom! And O noble way that he is taking this day to enlarge it, by stretching out the borders thereof with blood! His house is a costly house, and it is well worth costly cementing.

To Robert Hamilton, June 16th 1683

IN fire or water I dare not say he has left or forsaken me; and though perils by sea, and perils by land, and the snares of enemies to the cause and cross of Christ, have been many, yet he has wonderfully brought me hitherto through the same, and frustrated the expectations of the wicked; and not only has been at great cost and pains to lay obligations on me to be for him, but also has taken many ways to train me up for the work that he has laid upon me, in the circumstances of the times wherein my lot is fallen.

To the two ladies van Heermaen in Holland, 1683

As Christ is lovely to his own, so his cause is precious. It is his declarative glory. It is that whereby he makes his name known. How honourable it is to be an owner of the same! What badges of honour are reproaches and revilings upon that account! As love unto him makes his cause precious, so, where that is, nothing will be thought too costly to bestow upon the cause's account. Seeing his glory is concerned in it, it is our honour to be concerned with it. The cause is the Lord's. He shall prevail. He will overturn thrones and kingdoms, and get himself a name.

To the society of Strangers at Leeuwarden in Friesland, July 2nd 1684

HIS people's delivery shall be so glorious that it shall abundantly make up for all the cost, wrestling and suffering that they can be at; and though many of them with their bodily eyes may never see it, and though some of those that, in their places and stations, are employed about the building, may never see the cope-stone put thereupon, yet what's the matter? They are about their duty, and their delivery shall be more complete and glorious. While the Lord has anything to do with me, I shall continue, and I desire to continue no longer; and, through his grace, this is all my desire, to spend and be spent for him in his work, until my course be ended. And for seeing better days with my bodily eyes (though I am persuaded they are near at hand) I am not in the least anxious, neither was that desire either soon or late my exercise.

To Robert Hamilton, July 9th 1684

THE incomparableness of time's trials and sufferings with the loveliness of Christ, and the glory that shall be revealed thereafter, makes me sometimes that I see neither trouble nor danger, mine eyes being shut thereat, and carried to behold a small glimpse of that which is beyond tribulation's reach. Oh what a life will it be, when we shall neither sin nor sorrow, when we shall lay down our arms, and take up the palm of victory and triumph in our hands, and follow the Lamb with songs of praise in our mouths! Everlasting love and joy will be all the work that is there.

To Robert Hamilton, July 9th 1684

I HAVE heard it of prisoners, that God made himself much more known to them in bonds, than ever he did when they were at liberty; and I hope that it is so with not a few of you. O the wisdom of God who can make enemies instruments of so much good to his people! In the supposed enjoyment of all created things there are still wants, but in the enjoyment of him there is nothing wanting; more than a soul can desire, and than all created capacities are able to comprehend, is to be found in him, for he is all in all. He is that treasure of which enemies cannot rob you, though they be permitted to come and bereave you of life, and all created comforts. He will be with you in prison, in torture, in bonds, in banishment, and in death. Is not his presence enough? All your trials shall work together for your good, as he has said. Therefore rejoice, not only in them, but because of them; and, in all your seekings, seek to have his image more and more renewed in you. O employ the power and efficacy of his grace for carrying on in you a progress in holiness, for, the more of this you attain to, the more of his special manifestations you shall enjoy.

To the prisoners in the Tolbooths of Edinburgh, Glasgow and elsewhere in Scotland, March 1685

IF I could commend anything besides Christ, it would be the cross of Christ. Those things which make carnal onlookers think my condition hard and miserable, make me think it sweet and pleasant. I have found hazards, reproaches, contempt, weariness, cold, night-wanderings, stormy tempests, and deserts so desirable, that it is a greater difficulty to me not to be ambitious of these things than to submit unto them. O rejoice in the cross, for it is all paved with love. The fewer that will bear it, it is your greater honour to be friends to it. Follow Christ with the cross upon your backs, and set none else before you as your leader, for man is a poor fallible changeable creature. Let it be your care not to fall upon the stumbling-blocks cast in your way. Though you have your own share of the revilings of this time, yet be not reproached with reproachers; though the sourness of others grieve you, yet let it not infect you. Let zeal be accompanied with meekness, that you may be free from passion and prejudice; and let meekness be backed with zeal, that you may be free of lukewarmness and indifference. Let meekness be extended toward all persons, and zeal against all sins.

To the Society of Strangers at Leeuwarden in Friesland, February 18th 1686

OUR natures would have the way so squared that we might travel without a rub, but it lies through many an encounter. We would have it through a valley of roses, but it lies through a valley of tears. We would have it so as to be travelled sleeping, but it must be travelled waking, and watching, and fighting. We would have it to be travelled laughing, but it must be travelled with weeping. A sight of the recompense of the reward makes bold and resolute to pass through every opposition. If they were possible, ten thousand deaths, ten thousand hells would seem nothing to a soul, who gets a sight of Christ at the other side of all these.

To the two ladies van Heermaen in Holland, May 8th 1686

MANY a time I think, they can have no pleasant life who have not the Christian's life. Whatever the world think, yet the believer gets that in time, which may sufficiently engage him to go through, if it were possible, a thousand deaths in obedience to the Lord. Oh then! Since the imperfect and inconstant enjoyment of Christ is such a thing, what must the full and eternal enjoyment of him be!

To the lady E.B, in Holland, May 13th 1686

I AM persuaded that the wrong way of bearing and handling the ark will keep it longer in the wilderness, but will never carry it through Jordan and settle it in the land of Canaan. For mine own part, I see it so difficult a thing to move one step rightly forward with it, that I am in a continual fear anent what I do. I wish I were more in the exercise of that fear, for it would put me to look more unto the Lord, whom I desire and aim to set before mine eyes at all times. Oh to be framed for the work of the day, for there is none fit for it but such as have honest hearts, ingenuous spirits, and the faces of lions.

To Robert Hamilton, January 10th 1687

COUNT the cost of religion. God is a liberal dealer. Who is in heaven like unto him? And who in earth is to be desired like him? Lay down to him your names, your enjoyments, your lives and your all at his feet, for he is only worthy to have the disposal of them. The sufferings of this present time are not worthy to be compared with the glory that shall be revealed in us. Think not much to quit the vain and carnal delights of the world; they cannot satisfy your senses, and much less your souls. The earth is round, and the heart of man three-cornered; therefore, this cannot be filled with that. Though you could find content in them, yet how vain were it, because inconstant! And how unsolid, because uncertain!

To the two ladies van Heermaen in Holland, August 13th 1687

YOU are now to be banished out of your native land; but your enemies could not have appointed that for you, unless the Lord had from all eternity ordained it. His infinite love and wisdom have consulted and measured out your lot; and as this should make you despise the instruments of your afflictions, so it may help you to stoop, and cheerfully submit unto the providence of God, who "is of one mind, and who can turn him?" Considering the preciousness of the cause for which you are persecuted, you may rejoice that you are counted worthy to suffer such things. It is no less than the

Gospel of Christ, and his great prerogatives, as he is King of his own Church, which he has purchased with his own blood, and as he is supreme governor and sovereign of the whole world. Oh is this not a precious cause? Are not these great heads of suffering? If every one of you had a thousand worlds of enjoyments, and a thousand lives, they would be all too little to signify your love to Christ, and your respect to so honourable a cause.

To prisoners under sentence of banishment, 1687

APPENDIX 3

RENWICK AND THE UNITED SOCIETIES

RENWICK was involved with the United Societies from their inception in 1681 and continued to take an active part in them throughout his life. His initial involvement was as Clerk to the General Meeting, in which capacity he acted until his departure for Holland at the end of 1682. The records of the Societies, published by John Howie in 1780 under the title *Faithful Contendings Displayed,* contain no reference to Renwick's appointment as Clerk, but in his interrogations in Edinburgh Alexander Gordon of Earlston twice referred to him as such (*A True Account and Declaration of the Horrid Conspiracy against the Late King, 1685,* Appendix, pp. 101-2) and Earlston's commission was signed by Renwick as "Clericus Conventionis" on 10th April 1682 (ibid., p. 92). Michael Shields, a brother of Alexander, succeeded Renwick as Clerk, though in Shields' absence in Holland in 1687 Renwick again acted in this capacity for a time.

After his ordination Renwick had a rather special position among the Societies as their only minister. He did not however use this to exercise any official authority, and although he regularly attended the General Meetings he did so in the capacity of an adviser or assessor rather than a full member. In denying a charge by John Flint that Renwick "did sit in our meetings" the Societies maintained that "he never sat as a member in any of these meetings, but only gave his advice in matters as a minister of the Gospel". At the same time, it is clear that his influence at the General Meetings could be considerable. After the Carrick men met the Societies in January 1686 they reported: "All questions were first formed by him, then the Clerk was appointed to ask everyone his judgement anent them: yea further, he did not only form, but likewise he asked our particular judgement himself."

It is clear too that in the wider work and witness of the Societies Renwick played a leading role. He was of course mainly responsible for the Societies' two publications, the *Informatory Vindication* and the *Testimony against the Toleration,* and for at least two of their declarations. He was also deeply involved in the interaction between the General Meeting and the local societies throughout the country. He refers several times in his correspondence to "examining" local societies, and it would appear that his preaching tours were often combined with a programme of local visitations. This no doubt reinforced the popular perception of him as the "leader" of the Societies, whatever may have been his formal status.

At the Revolution the Societies had three ordained ministers – Alexander Shields, Thomas Lining and William Boyd. All three entered the national Church in 1690, but some of their hearers – largely at the instigation of Robert Hamilton, now back in Scotland – continued the Societies in their separate position. They remained pastorless until they were joined in 1706 by the Rev John McMillan of Balmaghie, who had earlier been deposed by the General Assembly. In 1723, when they were also joined by the Rev Thomas Nairn of Kirkcaldy, they formed themselves into a "Reformed Presbytery" which later became the Reformed Presbyterian Church of Scotland. That denomination grew significantly over the years, but in 1876 the majority united with the Free Church of Scotland. A small minority continues to the present.

Renwick was always jealous for the integrity and purity of the Societies, and he was anxious that no stain or scandal should mar their witness. This called for extreme care in admitting new members. It appears that local societies for a time operated their own rules for admission, but Renwick was concerned that they should all work to a standard pattern and he prepared a model set of rules (below) which he intended to be of uniform application. This appears to be the set referred to in J King Hewison's *The Covenanters* (1908 ed., Vol. II, pp. 558-9). It is not clear how widely these rules were adopted, but they are at least of interest in showing the high standards Renwick expected from those who aspired to membership. The rules are accompanied by fifteen standard articles for the Societies, to which all members were required to assent, and which they were to promise "religiously to practise and observe".

APPENDIX 3 – RENWICK AND THE UNITED SOCIETIES

• RULES FOR ADMISSION •

First, that every person desiring to be admitted be required to give the grounds, causes and motives that induced him or her to join in your fellowship.

2nd, that he be required to declare what moved him to separate from these with whom he formerly consorted.

3rd, if he be a stranger, that a testificate be required of him from the Society to whom he did formerly belong or at least due inquiry made and satisfaction be gotten of the soundness of his principles and uprightness of his conversation, that no person who maintains errors in their judgement or is chargeable with any scandals in their practice be admitted.

4th, that he be required to declare his judgement concerning the Covenants and the late work of Reformation.

5th, that he be required to declare his judgement concerning the prophetical, priestly and kingly offices of Christ.

6th, that he be required to give his judgement concerning church government.

7th, that he be required to give his judgement concerning prelacy and hearing the curates.

8th, that he be required to give his judgement concerning Erastianism and joining with the indulged.

9th, that he be required to declare his judgement concerning the practice of those ministers who did in this juncture of Providence lay aside the public exercise of their ministry and blamed the zeal of their brethren who continued faithful.

10th, that he be required to give his judgement concerning the late and present wrestlings and endeavours, testifyings, declarations and sufferings of the late martyrs and the present sufferers in Scotland.

11th, that he be required to give his judgement concerning the carriage of these who complied with the enemy and granted sinful bonds or made unwarrantable compositions with them, declining the testimonies of Christ and suffering for him contrary to the laudable practice of the godly.

12th, that he be required to bind himself to secrecy to divulge nothing of the matters reasoned or concluded in the Society but in so far as the Society doth allow to be done with general consent, or whatever other proper questions be thought fit to interrogate, and if satisfaction be given in all these then may be presented unto him the articles of the Society and he be required to assent thereunto and engage religiously to practise and observe the same.

• ARTICLES OF THE SOCIETY •

1. We all and every one of us taking into our serious consideration the Lord's late manifestation of his wonderful loving-kindness, tender mercy and great love to these lands, together with the great ingratitude, the sinful and shameful defections, the present obstinacy and impenitency of this generation, the lukewarmness, neutrality and sinful compliance of temporising professors, the many spiritual and temporal judgements and plagues that have already overtaken us together with the dreadful plagues and woes and fearful judgements that are now hanging above our heads and threatened to be poured out in a signal manner to our astonishment, ruin and destruction, the overspreading and increase of Popery, superstition, error and heresies, with the present tyranny and oppression exercised over the estates, persons and consciences of the Lord's people, together with the present darkness, ignorance and atheism, with the abounding of iniquity, profanity and wickedness that doth now overflow these, as also the unfaithfulness of professors and their unmindfulness of the Lord's former kindness and the solemn and sacred vows and covenants which they are under to God and to their brethren, together with the present decay of godliness, piety and zeal, and barrenness in religion, we do judge it our duty to search and try our ways and turn again to the Lord, Lament. 3:30, not to forget the assembling of ourselves together as the manner of some is, but according to the example of the godly in former ages, Mal. 3:16, and the practices of the faithful in this present age, to contract ourselves into societies, join and assemble ourselves together for following duty of prayer and other duties incumbent for us to follow in our station according to the vows and ties of God upon us, purposing the mutual encouragement, edification and strengthening of one another, that in following our duties we may endeavour in some measure the fitting of ourselves

for the threatened and approaching storm that seems not to be far off, or whatever the Lord in his wisdom sees fit for us to tryst us with; so we resolve to declare and set down our present purpose and method that we resolve to follow contained in the following articles agreed upon and assented to by the members of our Society. We resolve and declare therefore that the principal and chief end that we have before our eyes and purposes through the Lord's assistance sincerely, really and constantly to pursue it allenarly [entirely], only and alone the glory of God, the exercising of our duties according to his command, our own increase in knowledge and growth in grace, with the mutual good, spiritual profit and advantage of one another's souls, and that we being conscious to ourselves of our own weakness and infirmity are not nor do not undertake the performance of the meanest of our duties in our own strength nor by our own wisdom, but as we desire to be denied to ourselves, and we desire to betake ourselves to God and to seek unto him, relying on him alone for support, supply and furniture of grace and strength to fit and frame us for the right acting and exercising of every part of commanded duties, and also to apply ourselves frequently to him in the name of Jesus Christ, both secretly and publicly by fervent prayer and supplication, for his assistance and for whatever else he sees needful for us in our several circumstances.

2. We resolve and declare that we purpose to make the sacred Scriptures of the Old and New Testaments the only rule of our life, religion and conversation, and to disown and disclaim all doctrines, motives, principles and practices which are contrary thereunto, and to endeavour the performance of the obligations and duties sworn to in our sacred Covenants with God and with one another in our several stations, adhering to the Confession of Faith, Catechisms Larger and Shorter, and as we look upon it to be a great mercy and obliging encouragement that we are commanded in the wise providence of God with the example of so faithful a cloud of witnesses who have overcome by the blood of the Lamb and the word of their testimony and are now made more than conquerors, especially the example of these worthy martyrs who lately suffered in Scotland whom the Lord called forth in this juncture to testify unto, contend and suffer for his truth and cause, they remaining faithful in these sacred covenants, whose wrestlings, faithful testifyings and declarations public and private we fully assent unto

and approve of; we mean these that we have seen and are come to our hands, so are we resolved in his strength to go on and not to disown, desert nor decline his cause nor the duties contained in these Covenants, nor desert any of the truths though we should be exposed to these or the like sufferings.

3. As we judge and declare it our duty to entertain a high estimation of the Lord's public ordinance and to respect the enjoyment of these benefits when rightly dispensed by his faithful ambassadors called and sent of him and exercising their ministry according to his own institution to be great mercies and singular privileges, so we purpose and resolve to attend his public worship, the true preaching of his word and right administration of his sacraments when and wheresoever we can have the occasion thereof by the administration of lawful, honest and faithful ministers all functioning in his name and by his authority according to his rule, so also we resolve and declare that we will not own, hear nor countenance any though pretending themselves to be ministers of the Gospel who want a lawful call thereunto and continue not faithful in the exercise of their ministerial function, but prove forgetful of the sacred solemn Covenants and disloyal to Christ, who decline the duties, practices and conversation of Gospel ministers, and who comply with, continue in, plead for or vindicate these sinful practices and detestable courses of these ministers, Revel. 18:4, 2 Thess. 3:6 and 14, 2 Cor. 6:16, Isa. 52:11.

4. Because the backsliding compliers and temporisers with the defections and evils of this time do not only vindicate and defend their defections and scandalous practices, covering their defections, backslidings and guilt with the bright-coloured cloak of wisdom and prudency, but also are ready to cry out against the zeal, conscientious endeavours and tenderness of the faithful witnesses and sufferers, blaming and censuring and accusing them, their godly practices and endeavours, for imprudency, blind zeal and want of wisdom, we judge it our duty, we find two kinds of wisdom mentioned in the Scriptures, to declare what sort of wisdom we ought to beware of and to decline and what not to decline; such we judge to be that wisdom mentioned in the following Scriptures, Isa. 5:21, Isa. 47:10, Jer. 4:22, 1 Cor. 1:19, 20, 21 and 3:19, 20. So these doctrines and practices that lead people from God, his truth and way unto a worldly sanctuary for present conveniency though

adorned with the name of wisdom; and these doctrines and practices that teach obedience to God and the observation of his statutes, this is the wisdom we prefer and own according to Deut. 4:5, 6, Job 28:28, Prov. 4:7 and 18:7, not regarding the wisdom of this world, although the children of this world be said to be wiser in their generation than the children of light.

5. Because that through the abounding of iniquity and deluge of defection many have defiled themselves with these sinful courses, snares and abominable practices of these times, therefore we judge it our duty and resolve that no persons of erroneous principles who are followers of error and defection of these times nor no person of a scandalous conversation shall be owned by us nor admitted to our Society, nor any stranger, though under the names of a professor and sufferer, without a tesificate from some of the godly, or satisfaction given to the Society of the soundness of his principles, the purity and uprightness of his walk and conversation, therefore we judge it convenient that no member of our Society bring in any stranger into the Society or fellowship of his brethren unless first the Society be informed of him and some of our number directed unto him by them to take a trial of his principles, judgement and conversation, report made and the Society concur therewith and approve of his admission.

6. As we judge it our duty to take a special inspection of those that we admit to our fellowships, likewise we judge it expedient to reject all and every one who suffers themselves to be seduced to any sinful course or infected with error or shall be convicted of any public scandal; yet not so as to give up and altogether to disown them, but by wholesome exhortation to endeavour their regaining, and if they amend their ways, confess and acknowledge their offence, reform their abuses, giving true evidence of their repentance, we judge it our duty to receive them again and entertain them as brethren, Matt. 18, 21 and 22.

7. Since it has been and yet is the constant practice of Satan to sow tares among the wheat, to raise animosities and discord among the godly and by divisions to endeavour to break the peace and the harmony of the Lord's people and to frustrate their godly purposes and ends of the Gospel, we judge it for our duty in special manner to watch against all such motions and to resist all such attempts and

to the outmost of our power to endeavour to keep the unity of the spirit in the bond of peace, and not to entertain evil in our hearts nor take up a groundless prejudice against one another, neither falsely to accuse nor rashly to give ear to uncertain reports and misrepresentations of any of our number till trial be made in a Gospel manner both secretly, privately and publicly, Matt. 18:15, 16, 17 and that we resolve to endeavour by all means possible to live in peace, love and harmony together, bearing with one another's weakness, in love obscuring of one another's infirmity, exhorting and reproving one another's failings in the spirit of meekness and love, Heb. 13:1, Gal. 6:1 and 2.

8. We considering our great weakness and many infirmities, the corruption of our nature and the wickedness of our hearts that are ready to backslide and offend if grace prevent it not, and therefore as we judge it our duty always to watch and be upon a constant guard as suspecting ourselves, so we judge it our duty not to connive at the offensive escapes, the sinful and scandalous practices of any of our brethren or in silence to pass by the reprehensible offences that any of us may perceive in one another, but timeously for the preventing and removing of the guilt of our offending brethren to admonish, exhort and reprove same, striving for their good and gaining in the spirit of meekness and love, Leviticus 19:17.

9. We considering that the principal grounds whereupon we can expect the Lord's blessing upon us and his countenancing of our endeavours and fellowship, unity or the founding of our faith upon the true principles of truth, our careful closing with the way of redemption through Jesus Christ, our due honouring him in all his three offices as king, priest and prophet, our ready yielding all obedience and subjection due to him as our saviour, teacher and lawgiver, our keeping close by his rule in all our walk and performance, and as we ought to the outmost of our power in his strength to endeavour the same, so do we resolve and in order thereunto we do give up ourselves unto him to be ruled, judged and governed by his Spirit according to his Word, resolving carefully to endeavour the right reformation of our judgements in all matters of faith and duty, diligently to give up ourselves to the study and practice of virtue and holiness in all our walkings, performances and actings toward God and man, that as the enemies may have no just quarrel against us nor time-serving professors any occasion to

calumniate, mock and reproach, even so likeways that others of the faithful through their beholding of our godly conversation may be induced and encouraged to join with us or to enter into the like fellowships, that the Lord may be praised, his truth and ways highly honoured and greatly loved, and enemies, mockers and hypocrites ashamed, confounded and rendered the more contemptible.

10. Since this is now a suffering time and like to continue so, as we judge it our duty so do we resolve to entertain a fellow-feeling and Christian sympathy with our brethren in affliction, pouring out our spirits in groans and prayers on their behalf and in the behalf of desolate Zion, so also do we declare and resolve that if in the providence of God any of the members of our fellowship shall be called to suffering and imprisonment, that we shall not only endeavour their comfort and encouragement by our prayers but also all and every one of us according to our several abilities shall cheerfully contribute part of our substance to their maintenance and encouragement for supplying their wants during the time of their imprisonment and suffering, that so the way of the Lord be not evil spoken through our neglect.

11. We considering that some things may fall in among us and reasonings that may prove too difficult and hard for us satisfactorily to resolve, we judge it fit therefore and resolve for preventing schism that such matters be laid aside for a time until occasion be had that the same may be communicated to our godly brethren in their Societies, and their judgement reported therein, and for this end we judge it convenient and resolve that some probable course be laid down for corresponding with our Societies both for resolving of such matters and for entertaining a good understanding amongst the godly.

12. We likewise judge it convenient and resolve that means be used for engaging others to join with us in fellowship, and they must be only such whose holiness and sound principles and tenderness do invite us to admit them thereunto.

13. We resolve and declare that none of us shall reveal or divulge any matters that are reasoned or concluded in the Society but in so far as is allowed by the common consent of the Society, and that offenders herein be publicly and sharply rebuked.

14. We judge it convenient and resolve that always before the dismissing of our Societies that time and place be concluded and resolved upon when and where to meet next, that every person may know where and when to attend.

15. We judge it convenient that inquiry be made of absents and that such as withdraw without lawful excuse, and reasons may be looked upon; after the continuing of the admonitions they are to be counted as deserters of the fellowship and not to be readmitted till satisfaction be given to the Society for their offence.

SELECT BIBLIOGRAPHY

An Informatory Vindication of a Poor, Wasted, Misrepresented Remnant, 1687; republished with additional material 1707, 1744 and 1791.

Carslaw, W H: *The Life and Letters of James Renwick*, 1893.

Carslaw, W H: *Life and Times of James Renwick*, 1900.

Corrie, John: *Glencairn; The Annals of an Inland Parish*, 1910.

Houston, Thomas: *The Letters of the Rev James Renwick*, 1865.

Macmillan, John: *A Collection of Letters*, 1764.

Shields, Alexander: *The Life and Death of that Eminently Pious, Free and Faithful Minister and Martyr of Jesus Christ, Mr James Renwick*, 1724; republished 1806, and in *Bibliographia Presbyteriana*, 1827.

[Sime, William]: *The Life of James Renwick*, 1833.

Simpson, Robert: *Life of the Rev James Renwick*, 1843.

The Testimony of some Persecuted Presbyterian Ministers of the Gospel unto the Covenanted Reformation of the Church of Scotland, 1688; republished 1723.

Watson, Jean L: *Life and Times of Rev A Peden and James Renwick*, [1881].

Wilson, William, ed: *A Choice Collection of Very Valuable Prefaces, Lectures and Sermons preached upon the Mountains and Muirs of Scotland in the Hottest Time of the Late Persecution, by that faithful Minister and Martyr of Jesus Christ, the Reverend Mr James Renwick,* 1748 (Vol. 1), 1751 (Vol. 2); republished as single volume 1776 (twice), 1777 and 1804.

Notes

Chapter 1 – Birth and Background

1. Rev James Baillie (a former minister of the parish) in *The Third Statistical Account of Scotland, County of Dumfries,* 1962, p. 211.

2. Like many rural parishes, Glencairn at the time of Renwick's birth was a more populous place than it is today. While no figures exist pre-1700 the parish had in 1755 a population of almost 2,000, of which Moniaive probably accounted for about half. By the end of the 19th century the population of the village had fallen to 650. In more modern times a local historian has noted that it is now "little more than 460 and mostly comprised of incomers. I can only account for between twenty and thirty true natives." (J Black, *Why Forget? Moniaive in Bygone Days,* 1992, p. 1).

3. The name is found in a bewildering variety of forms. In contemporary usage it was written Renwick, Renvick, or Rennick; otherwise Rainie, Rainy, or Reny. Even these do not exhaust the variations. The latter varieties suggest a phonetic usage which may have been the norm among the people.

4. Quoted in *Richard Cameron* by Sir John Herkless.

5. Quoted in *The Preachers of Scotland: From the Sixth to the Nineteenth Century* by William G. Blaikie.

Chapter 2 – Preparation for Service

1. *Register of the Privy Council of Scotland,* 10th December 1616 (Vol. X, pp. 671-2).

2. *Fasti Ecclesiae Scoticanae,* Vol. 2, p. 315.

3. The university year began in October, though matriculation did not usually take place until the following spring. Renwick's name does not appear in the register of Pillans' first-year class, which was matriculated in March 1678. However, the date of his graduation (1681) clearly points to a 1677 start. Like the *Graduation Register* (see below) the *Matriculation*

Register is not an infallible guide. There is no record of Renwick's having joined the class at an intermediate stage.

4. James Pillans, a native of Edinburgh, was appointed regent of humanity on 8th November 1644 and was promoted to regent of philosophy on 29th November 1652 (*Extracts from the Records of the Burgh of Edinburgh, 1642-55,* pp. 55, 297). He resigned his office into the hands of the Town Council on 20th April 1681, on the grounds of old age, having served the university for 37 years (ibid., 1681-89, p. 12). In a tribute to him, the Council recorded their great satisfaction with his work. "By his active and successful endeavours," they recorded, "he has been very instrumental in causing the College to flourish, and in training up many hopeful youths in virtue and learning" (ibid., pp. 26-7). He was voted a testimonial of 1,000 merks, and a few years later a payment of £100 Scots and a quarterly pension of £50 (ibid., p. 193). Pillans died in February 1689 and was buried in the Greyfriars churchyard (*Greyfriars Interments 1658-1700,* p. 517). He was married twice, and had several children who died in infancy.

5. J King Hewison (*The Covenanters,* 1908, Vol.II, p.414) takes issue with Alexander Shields' account of these events, on the ground that Renwick did swear an oath of loyalty to the king. What was signed by Renwick was however no more than a standard formula signed by all intending graduates, and was distinct from the Oath of Allegiance. The formula certainly included a promise of loyalty to the sovereign, but Renwick evidently felt that he could sign this without compromise of principle, especially since the promise was qualified by the words *in Domino* (in the Lord). There is no documentary evidence that Renwick signed the Oath of Allegiance as such. Indeed, the text of the Oath does not appear in the *Graduation Register* until 1683. However, Shields' account is not without its difficulties. One such difficulty is the Act of Council of 1666 requiring all intending graduates to sign the Oath of Allegiance. However, it is known that the university authorities were not always exact in enforcing this requirement, and on occasion they had to be called to account for their own remissness in subscribing the Oath. It would no doubt be easier for a sympathetic professor to dispense with the requirement when the degree was given in private. Again however there is a problem, since the *Graduation Register* does not specifically record that Renwick took his degree privately (though it names three others in his year who did). The *Register* however is not an infallible guide. When it was published by the Bannatyne Club in 1858 its editors were under the necessity of augmenting its information from other sources. Its list of graduates for 1681 was found to be particularly deficient, and had to be augmented by additional names culled from the published Theses. While it includes Renwick's name in the main list of graduates, this does not necessarily imply that he took part in the public laureation (as King Hewison maintains). The significant point is that the *Register* does not in itself disprove Shields' account. Shields was himself a graduate of the university (in 1675) and would be well conversant with the procedure. The fact too that he in all probability had the information from Renwick himself is sufficient warrant for its credibility. Amid all the allegations levelled at Renwick in later years not one of his critics attempted to cast doubt on the validity of his degree. The Government itself, in its various proclamations denouncing him, was always careful to prefix his name with the honorific "Mr", the recognised designation of a university graduate.

6. Renwick's movements between the end of his university studies and his first associations with the Societies are uncertain. It is not known for certain whether he was in Edinburgh throughout this time. In the *Records of the Burgh of Lanark* for 9th June 1681, there is found a request from one "James Renwick, indweller in Lanark" to be admitted a burgess of the burgh. It has been taken for granted by several writers that this was the future field-preacher

(cf. Robertson, *Lanark: The Burgh and its Councils 1469-1880*, 1974, pp. 114-5). The Town Council suspected that the applicant had been "in the rebellion" (i.e., at Bothwell Bridge) and they hesitated to admit him until he had accepted the king's indemnity and taken the bond for the peace, which he obliged himself to do. On the strength of this he was admitted, and took the burgess oath in the normal form. Some months later, after the Societies' declaration had been published at Lanark, ten men from the town were arrested and brought to Edinburgh on suspicion of having had a part in the affair. These included a James Renwick. After being held in the Canongate Tolbooth, on 7th April 1682 they were allowed their liberty on payment of caution of 100 merks (*Register of the Privy Council*, Third Series, Vol. VII, p. 388). Being unable to raise this sum themselves they borrowed the money from local money-lenders, binding themselves to repay it by 3rd May (*Register of Deeds*, Mackenzie's Office, 19th June 1682). The bond in their joint names survives, in which James Renwick is described as a "merchant there" (i.e., in Lanark). It is beyond reasonable doubt that the signature "James Renwick" in the bond and in the Town Council record is that of the same individual. It can also be granted that the signature bears a creditable resemblance, though perhaps no more than that, to the signature of the future field preacher. However, if it was indeed Renwick, it needs to be asked how, at the age of nineteen, he could have been admitted burgess of a royal burgh, and also how he could have earned the designation "merchant there" having only, that year, completed his university studies in Edinburgh. On the other hand, it can no doubt be argued that the choice of Lanark for publishing the declaration – in which Renwick was actively involved – does point to some association between the town and Renwick. Further research may throw more light on the matter.

7. The "Cess", as it was known, was imposed by a Convention of Estates, or emergency Parliament, on 10th July 1678. Its purpose, according to the appointing Act, was that "his Majesty may be the better enabled to raise more forces for securing this his ancient kingdom against all foreign invasions and intestine commotions". The Act however made it very clear what the specific immediate threat was considered to be: " . . . these dangerous field conventicles, declared by law rendezvous of rebellion, do still grow in their numbers and insolencies; against all which the present forces cannot in reason be thought a suitable security." The total levy amounted to £1.8 million Scots over the five year period from Whitsunday 1678 to Whitsunday 1683. In face of a continuing perceived threat from the same source the Parliament which met in July/August 1681 extended the levy for a further five years, to Martinmas 1688. The Cess proved a fruitful cause of dissension among the non-conforming Presbyterians, some of whom felt that to pay it was a duty owed to the civil authority (and so enjoined by Scripture) while others refused it on the ground that it had been plainly levied to bear down the Gospel.

CHAPTER 3 – IN THE BONDS OF FELLOWSHIP

1. The buried heads were discovered 45 years later, on 7th October 1726, and were re-interred on 19th October in the Greyfriars Churchyard, close to the Martyrs' Monument. The circumstances of the re-burial were very different from the first occasion. There were present, says Patrick Walker, "the greatest multitude of people, old and young, men and women, ministers and others, that ever I saw together." (*Six Saints of the Covenant*, Vol. 1, p. 327).

2. The records of the United Societies were collected by Michael Shields, who was Clerk to the Societies from 1683, and were published by John Howie of Lochgoin under the title *Faithful Contendings Displayed* in 1780. The records nowhere make reference to the appointment of Renwick as Clerk, but it is clear from other sources that Renwick was

appointed to this office at the first General Meeting. In his answers to the interrogations put to him after his capture Alexander Gordon of Earlston stated that the notice calling the second General Meeting (on 15th March 1682) had been "subscribed by Mr James Renwick who is Clerk to the Convention" (*Copies of the Informations and Original Papers relating to the Proof of the Horrid Conspiracy against the Late King,* 1685, p. 101) and Earlston's commission in Latin was signed by Renwick as Clerk on 10th April 1682 (ibid., p. 92).

3. In a dispatch of 21st January a Government agent noted intriguingly: "It was observable that four persons were the principal actors, the rest not appearing so zealous." (*Calendar of State Papers,* Domestic Series, 1682, p. 39). It is difficult not to believe that one of the four was Renwick himself.

4. Wodrow, rather oddly, does not give the text of the Lanark Declaration, though he reproduces faithfully the other testimonies of the period. Nor was the Declaration published by the Government, unlike those at Sanquhar and Rutherglen. As a result, it is now seldom to be met with, though the text can be consulted in the Societies' *Informatory Vindication* which reproduces this and the other testimonies of the time. See also Johnston, T*reasury of the Scottish Covenant,* 1887, pp. 144-7.

5. Renwick took no part in drafting the Declaration, and he was later to describe parts of it as "very exceptionable" (*Informatory Vindication,* 1687, p. 55). Alexander Shields says that, had Renwick had a hand in it, it would have been "more considerately worded" (*Life of Renwick,* 1724, p. 17). Who the authors were cannot now be proved.

6. *Register of the Privy Council,* Third Series, Vol. VII, p. 311; *Extracts from the Records of the Burgh of Edinburgh,* 1681-89, p. 37.

Chapter 4 — The Call to Service

1. The commission was one of the documents seized from Earlston at Newcastle in June 1683 and afterwards published with other captured papers (*A True Account and Declaration of the Horrid Conspiracy against the Late King,* 1685, pp. 91-2). The Latin of the commission was unkindly termed "wretched" by that prejudiced critic, Charles Kirkpatrick Sharpe (Law, *Memorials,* 1819, p. 248 note). At the same time it may be admitted that the Latin of the document is somewhat less than elegant. There are indications that, while having a competent knowledge of the language, Renwick was not altogether comfortable in the use of it and sought to avoid it when he could. When replying in later years to a letter in Latin from Jacob Koelman he wrote: "I received your letter in Latin, but knowing that you are well versed in English I need not write back to you in that same language."

2. Russell and Grant pointed out, correctly, that the need for reforming the names of the days and months had featured in the last testimony of William Cuthill, who was executed along with Donald Cargill and three others on 27 July 1681. The portion of Cuthill's testimony dealing with these matters was omitted by the compilers of the *Cloud of Witnesses,* on the ground that it was not relevant to the causes of his suffering, "these vain janglings and unprofitable strifes of words being ceased". However, it is also fairly certain that the compilers did not want to publicise the revelation in the suppressed part of Cuthill's testimony (preserved among the Laing MSS) that he had formerly been an associate of the notorious John Gibb. While Cuthill acknowledges, on hindsight, that he was "the worse of John Gibb's company" he nevertheless maintains that he had been "refreshed" by the spiritual exercises he had shared with Gibb and his associates.

3. *A History of the House of Hamilton,* 1933, pp. 701-2.

4. John Flint and William Boyd feature in the narrative. John Nisbet was a native of Northumberland who was educated in Edinburgh and moved thereafter to London. In 1683 he was arrested on suspicion of complicity in the Rye House plot and narrowly escaped with his life. Of the unsuccessful candidates, John Smith, who seems to have been a young man of considerable promise, died from a lingering illness in the spring of 1683. William Hardie, who had graduated at St Andrews in 1682, was eventually ordained and admitted to Crail, Fife, in 1690; he was translated to the Second Charge, St Andrews, in 1701 and to the First Charge there in 1712. He died in 1723 (*Fasti Ecclesiae Scoticanae*, Vol. 5, pp. 234-5).

Chapter 6 – A Time of Testing

1. It appears that Robert Hamilton suspected his brother-in-law of association with the plotters and sought, unsuccessfully, to dissuade him. In a letter to Earlston on 8th February 1682 he wrote: "Stand afar off from meddling with such a crew . . . remember how the Lord has helped you hitherto to contend and to state his cause, and be not cheated out of the good old way witnessed unto by so many faithful testimonies and noble warriors who have sealed it with their blood; but wait on him who has taken the controversy in his own hand and I think is crying to his poor ones this day to stand still, and behold his great salvation."

Chapter 7 – The Start of the Ministry

1. Many of the places frequented by Renwick and the other field-preachers retained their desolate moorland character until well into the twentieth century. In visiting the north of Galloway in the 1890s Rev John H Thomson spoke of the "empty, waste appearance" of the countryside, which he compared to a "vast wilderness" (*Martyr Graves of Scotland*, p. 384). From one vantage point he surveyed "a wild waste of treeless hills and dales that seemed to stretch away into almost illimitable space" (ibid., p. 386). The topography of those places is now very different. The blanket afforestation of the post-war period has enveloped many of the upland areas and changed the landscape irrevocably. Over a quarter of the land area of Dumfries and Galloway is now covered by forest, the great majority of it non-native species (*National Inventory of Woodland and Trees, Dumfries and Galloway Region*, 1999, p. 2). It is a pity that at least in the early stages little was done to blend in the massive forestry plantations with the character of the area and its historic associations. Of late, however, some effort has been made to open up the forests and to improve access to sites associated with the persecution.

2. Renwick's Testimony was addressed to Robert Hamilton, with whom he left it on his departure from Holland in 1683. He clearly took another copy with him, as he read it publicly at the Darmead meeting. In deference to Renwick's wishes, steps appear to have been taken to suppress the document after his death, and there are no copies among the Societies' surviving papers. However, one of the original copies fell into the hands of the publishers of Renwick's sermons, who published it as an appendix to the first collected edition in 1776. It also appeared in the second 1776 edition and in the editions of 1777 and 1804. In each of these there is a note saying that the original autograph signed by Renwick "is still preserved entire" and is available for inspection if desired. This however now seems to be lost. The publishers justify their action on the ground that Renwick had given Hamilton discretion either to suppress the document or to keep his final letter alongside it, and they reproduce the relevant part of the letter with their note. It seems however that they were not without some misgivings, for they add: "It is hoped that none will think the worthy author injured, or that his desire in the foresaid letter is crossed or wholly disobeyed." To

mitigate any offence, and to try to protect Renwick's reputation, they took out what they describe as "a few of the most tart phrases" and recorded the names of ministers only by their initial letters.

3. In the absence of the original testimony it is not now possible to know with certainty who the ministers were whom Renwick excluded from fellowship, since they are identified only by their initials in the published version. The relevant passage reads: "I testify and bear witness against people's joining in any part of their ministry with these men: viz. Messrs W.K., J.R., T.H. elder in Scotland, J.H. in England, T.H. younger at Utrecht, G.B. at Rotterdam, and that bitter and base reproacher J.W." However, it can reasonably be assumed that "W.K." was William Kemp, a field-preacher prominent since before Bothwell and formerly active against the Indulgence, but who was seen by many as not fulfilling his early promise. "J.R." appears to be John Rae, who continued field-preaching for some time after Bothwell but was arrested and sent to the Bass in November 1683. "T.H. elder" was Thomas Hog of Larbert (not to be confused with Thomas Hog of Kiltearn) who was also active in the fields but who died in 1680 or 1681. "J.H. in England" was John Hepburn, a native of Morayshire, who had been another active field-preacher but who was now seen as having deserted the testimony. "T.H. younger at Utrecht" was the younger Thomas Hog, son of the minister of Larbert, who again had been prominent against the Indulgence and at one time a close companion of Richard Cameron, but who again was viewed as a deserter. "G.B. at Rotterdam" was George Barclay, another field-preacher who had lingered on after Bothwell but had then gone to Holland; he was to figure later in Renwick's career. "That bitter and base reproacher J.W." was probably James Welsh, a cousin of John Welsh of Irongray, who had preached sporadically after Bothwell but had showed himself to be no friend of the Societies. Renwick also testified at more length against three individuals – "Mr T.D.", "that man Mr P." and "that man J.R." "Mr T.D." was Thomas Douglas, who had earlier been a co-adjutant of Hamilton and active against the Indulgence; however he had later opposed Hamilton and his associates in Holland and was seen by them as betraying the testimony. "That man Mr P." was Alexander Peden, who had continued field-preaching for some time after Bothwell but had maintained a strongly individualistic stance and had kept aloof from the Societies' public declarations. "J.R." was James Russel. Finally, Renwick's testimony declared his support for "that noble battle fought in Holland against Mr M. for his counselling (yea so peremptorily) to join with that church-rending man, Mr F." The "noble battle" was Robert Hamilton's dispute with Robert McWard ("Mr M") over McWard's willingness to countenance the minister of the Rotterdam Church, Robert Fleming ("Mr F") who had advocated an understanding with the indulged ministers. Renwick admitted afterwards that he wished McWard's name had never been mentioned in the testimony.

4. Michael Shields, the Clerk to the Societies, maintained that although the Societies had left it to Hamilton to draw up the Protestation, "yet never any such paper came from him to the Societies; and that Protestation which was afterwards drawn up and published, was written at home, and sent abroad to Mr Hamilton, who put it in print". This was directly contradicted by William Brakel, who later told the Societies: "Mr Hamilton composed that declaration, and about a year before it was published he showed the same to me, so that it is not so much your declaration as Mr Hamilton's, only approven by you." Much of the document is so obviously in Hamilton's style that Brakel's version of events is difficult to refute. Indeed in a letter to Renwick on 12th May 1684 Hamilton appeared to take personal responsibility for the document. He wrote: "I see this Protestation will make to me, in a special way, a new storm and a bitter one; neither dare I but prosecute it, cost what it will."

5. The quotation is from Psalm 64:3.

NOTES

Chapter 9 – Into the Abyss

1. The "Holy Linn", a waterfall on the Garpel burn, is still pointed out as the spot where Renwick and others preached and administered baptism.

2. So infamous was the tragedy at Wigtown that, since the earliest times, attempts have been made to disprove its credibility. Foremost in these efforts was Mark Napier in his *Memorials of Dundee* (1857) though he has not been without his present-day followers. Painstaking evidence in support of the historical account was presented by Rev Alexander Stewart of Glasserton in his *History Vindicated in the Case of the Wigtown Martyrs* (1869) and this has never been effectively challenged.

Chapter 10 – A False Dawn

1. Patrick Walker says that Barclay came to Scotland in April 1685, some weeks ahead of the main expedition (Six Saints of the Covenant, Vol.1, p.101). This however seems a mistake. Argyle did indeed send over some men in advance, as Sir Patrick Hume records: "Persons were pitched upon to be dispatched to several places and persons in Scotland and Ireland with messages, for preparing the countries against our landing, as we expected them to be concerned; and having at several times discoursed the particulars, it was concluded that such of us as had useful advices in any particular to give these messengers, should give them in private, and haste them away, since good opportunities for their passage then offered; and this last was quickly done, and they sent off." (*Sir Patrick Hume's Narrative,* in George Rose's *Observations on the Historical Work of Charles James Fox,* 1809, p. 35). However as regards the ministers Hume records: "Some of us went to Rotterdam, called the ministers together, and 13 having met, we proposed distinctly our design, desired their opinion of it, and that some should go along with us: they after advising together, declared their good liking and approbation of our undertaking, as a great duty, and offered to join us as we judged necessary. We pitched on some of their number to go along, who condescended, and after did accompany us" (ibid., p. 36). It is clear also from other sources that the selected ministers accompanied the expedition rather than preceded it. John Erskine of Carnock specifically records having heard Barclay preach on board ship during Argyle's passage to Scotland on 3rd May (*Journal,* Scottish History Society, 1893, p. 115).

Chapter 11 – Trial and Controversy

1. Adam Alcorn graduated at St Andrews in 1674 and was apparently licensed by a "field Presbytery" of the non-conforming ministers. He was for a time chaplain to Lady Douglas of Cavers, who also employed Richard Cameron. In 1678 he was prosecuted for attending field-meetings, and sentenced to be banished to the plantations. He had as a fellow-passenger Alexander Peden, who was banished at the same time (*Register of the Privy Council,* Third Series, Vol. VI, pp. 52-3, 59, 76). However, the deportees got no further than London when they were released through the unwillingness of the ship's captain to receive them. Alcorn returned to Scotland, and appears to have continued preaching occasionally. He was however opposed to Renwick and allied himself with Robert Langlands, with whom he traversed the country for a time. In 1692 he was ordained and admitted to the charge of Athelstanford, in East Lothian, but his ministry there was beset by indisposition and by difficulties with the Presbytery. He died in 1701 at the age of 46 (*Fasti Ecclesiae Scoticanae,* Vol. 1, p. 353).

2. Langlands accepted the Toleration in 1687. He became minister of the Barony parish, Glasgow, in 1691 and in 1696 was translated to Elgin in Morayshire. He died there later the same year and was buried in the Cathedral cemetery, where an elegant Latin inscription marks his grave (*Fasti Ecclesiae Scoticanae,* Vol. 3, p. 393; Vol. 6, p. 389).

Chapter 12 – The Controversies Deepen

1. Robert Wodrow unfortunately confuses Cathcart's paper with the one distributed by Gordon; he reproduces the latter under the title of the former (*History*, IV, pp. 393-4). Cathcart's paper is given in a somewhat abridged form by Shields (*Life of Renwick,* pp. 88-90).

2. It appears from Renwick's treatment of this subject in a separate letter that the author in question was Johannes Wollebius (1586-1629), an eminent Swiss theologian, of Basel. His *Compendium Theologiae Christianae* (translated into English as *Abridgement of Christian Divinity*) is a classic of Reformed dogmatics.

3. Thomas Russel had studied at St Salvator's College, St Andrews, where he graduated in 1680. He was ordained and admitted at Kennoway in Fife in 1690, where he remained until his death in 1714 at the age of about 54 (*Fasti Ecclesiae Scoticanae,* Vol. 5, p. 92).

4. Flint later accepted the Toleration, and was settled in a meeting-house at Lasswade, Midlothian, in 1688. In 1710 he was translated to the New North Church, Edinburgh, where he remained until his death in 1730. He is described in his later years as "a worthy, affectionate, zealous man, and of considerable learning as a linguist." (*Fasti Ecclesiae Scoticanae,* Vol. 1, pp. 143, 330).

5. *Journal of John Erskine of Carnock,* Scottish History Society, 1893, pp. 193-5.

6. In 1688 Barclay accepted the Toleration and became minister of a meeting house at Gargunnock, in Stirlingshire. He was translated to Uphall, in West Lothian, in 1690 and died in 1714 (*Fasti Ecclesiae Scoticanae,* Vol. 1, p. 233, Vol. 4, p. 308).

Chapter 13 – Testifying Amid Tribulation

1 The Forest, or Ettrick Forest, was a popular name for the district later comprising most of Selkirkshire and parts of the neighbouring counties of Midlothian and Peebles.

Chapter 14 – The Informatory Vindication

1. The standard work on Shields is Hector Macpherson's *The Cameronian Philosopher* (1932). For his account of Shields' interrogations Macpherson is closely dependent on Shields' own account in *A True and Faithful Relation of the Sufferings of the Reverend and Learned Mr Alexander Shields, Minister of the Gospel,* published anonymously in 1715. However, this is to an extent unsatisfactory in that it does not record the precise words of the oath taken by Shields before the justices, or the subsequent statement which he signed, both of which are preserved in the Justiciary Court papers. On 26th March 1685 Shields took the Abjuration Oath in the following terms: "I Mr Alexander Shields do hereby abhor, renounce and disown in presence of the Almighty God the pretended declaration of war lately affixt at several parish churches in so far as it declares war against his sacred Majesty and asserts that it is lawful to kill such as serve his Majesty in church, state, army or country." This was signed by Shields himself and by six of the judges. On 1st May, after the interception of his letter to

John Balfour, Shields was further interrogated and publicly retracted the oath, in token of which he tore his signature out of the earlier document. On 6th August, after further pressure was put on him, he agreed to subscribe the terms of the oath again, though this time merely as an unsworn statement. In doing so Shields demurred at the use of the phrase "in so far as" and asked permission to alter this to "if so be". The published account appears to imply that his request was granted, and this is clearly the understanding of Macpherson (op. cit., p. 37). What Shields actually signed, however, was in almost identical terms to the oath he had earlier taken, and made no concession to his scruples. Additionally, it contained a specific acknowledgement of the king's authority. It ran: "I Mr Alexander Shields do hereby abhor and disown the pretended declaration of war in so far as it declares war against his sovereign King James the Seventh, and asserts it lawful to kill such as serve his Majesty in church, state, army or country. And that he owns King James the Seventh to be his lawful king and sovereign."

2. Grant was an indefatigable pamphleteer. His productions included *The Nonconformist's Vindication* (1700), *Rectius Declinandum* (1709), *A Bond of Union* (1714), *A Letter to a Friend* (1716), and, most notoriously, *A Manifesto, or The Standard of the Church of Scotland* (1723). In all of these he asserted the right of private persons to assume representative power, a right which he claimed was inherent in the Societies' earlier Declarations, but which in his view had been compromised in the *Informatory Vindication*. Grant clearly saw Renwick as the prime instrument in this defection. Writing of the Vindication, he claimed: "The author denies that anything was done by a representative power, in affirming that the word representative is not to be taken in its strict and proper acceptation, viz persons formally invested with authority and delegation from those whom they represent; but only a poor people, some way representing the corporation that should have done it, or representing others who should deserve the same signature. This is most false, for I was both eye and ear witness to the contrary, oftener than once or twice, where the author was present as well as I, viz Mr Renwick, and did see it owned as a representative power, and was firm in that judgement near the space of three years, for no other ways could tyranny be cast off but by a formal representative power" (*Rectius Declinandum,* 1709, p. 6). For good measure Grant charged the Societies with "making everything therein [i.e., the Vindication] as a canonical rule, affirming that it was sealed by a minister and martyr; and therefore to be owned, although contradictory to Scripture, reason, and sound policy." (ibid., p. 9). The Societies, while belittling Grant and his influence, nevertheless saw him as a constant threat and felt obliged to answer his *Manifesto* with an elaborate *Confutation* (1724).

3. The *Informatory Vindication* was re-issued, with additional material, in 1707 by the continuing Societies who did not espouse the Revolution Settlement. It was reprinted in 1744 and again in 1791. John H. Thomson well observes: "It is much to be regretted that the *Informatory Vindication* should be so little known, as its ability, its catholicity, and its terseness and clearness of statement make it one of the most readable documents of that age, and altogether worthy of its title" (*Cloud of Witnesses,* 1871 ed., p. 481).

Chapter 15 – The Woeful Toleration

1. The Kilmarnock meeting was held at "Grugar Moor on the Powbeth Burn" between nine and twelve at night on Sabbath 16th January. Houston was described as "an aged man in a white night-cape" who had been heard to "exclaim against paying of the cess and locality". He had also baptised several children, requiring "that they should be brought up in the Presbyterian religion" (*Register of the Privy Council,* Third Series, Vol. XIII, pp. 129-30).

2. Thomas Lining, who was for a spell in Scotland in the autumn of 1687, later suggested another reason for Houston's disappearance. "I heard," he wrote to Hamilton, "that when he was coming to Scotland, there came a call to him from a people in a place of Ireland where he had never preached before, which he thought himself bound to accept." This is however uncorroborated. Houston was eventually arrested in Ireland in January 1688 and in June was brought back to Scotland for trial. While being led to Edinburgh he was rescued by force from the soldiers in charge of him, some of whom were killed. However, in the rescue he suffered injuries which, apart from their physical effects, appear to have exacerbated his mental condition. Shortly after the Revolution he returned permanently to Ireland, where he died some years later. Houston had his misgivings about the Revolution Settlement though he did not join those who actively opposed it. Patrick Walker says of him: "However far wrong that man was in his head, many of his sayings have had a sad accomplishment." (*Six Saints of the Covenant*, 1901, Vol. 1, pp. 301-2).

Chapter 16 – A Fearless Witness

1. Boyd appeared before the first General Meeting of the Societies after Renwick's death (7th March 1688) and affirmed that he was now satisfied that those ministers who had accepted the Toleration should be discountenanced. Some in the Societies remained opposed to him, and he earned further disfavour later in the year when he took it on himself to proclaim William III's Declaration at Glasgow without the Societies' knowledge or consent. However, he was accepted by Shields and Lining into their company and preached several times with them in the fields before all three were eventually accepted into the national Church in October 1690. Later the same year he was ordained and admitted to the charge of Dalry, in Kirkcudbrightshire, where he remained until his death in 1741 at the age of 82 (*Fasti Ecclesiae Scoticanae*, Vol. 2, p. 408).

2. Through the offices of Robert Hamilton, Lining was ordained by the Classis or Presbytery of Emden in Holland in or about August 1688. He then returned to Scotland, where he accepted a call from the Societies to be their minister. Over the next year or two he accompanied Alexander Shields and William Boyd in field-preaching around the country. With Shields and Boyd he was accepted into the national Church in October 1690. He was admitted minister of Lesmahagow in Lanarkshire in 1691 and remained there until his death in 1733, by which time he had been appointed a Chaplain to the King in Scotland. He was described by a contemporary as "one of the most eminent clergymen in his day, and an able defender of the rights and privileges of the Church; scrupulously honest in his principles, and well skilled in church discipline" (*Fasti Ecclesiae Scoticanae*, Vol. 3, p. 314). In 1706 Lining published a pamphlet left by Alexander Shields in manuscript, which he entitled *Church Communion Enquired Into, or A Treatise against Separation from this national Church of Scotland*. In this work, Shields asserts the duty of church unity and defends union with the Church of the Revolution Settlement in face of those in the continuing Societies who stood out against it. Lining contributed a preface, in which he strongly upheld Shields' views and attacked the dissidents for their "sinful schism". His actions aroused the ire of the continuing Societies, and on republishing the *Informatory Vindication* in 1707 they inserted a "Postscript" alleging that Lining had written the pamphlet himself in Shields' name. Patrick Walker, who admired the work, and who had been with Shields when he wrote it, duly denounced this "slanderous, fool, lying postscript" and upheld Lining's integrity (*Six Saints of the Covenant*, Vol. 1, p. 145).

3. Hugh Kennedy (*c.* 1621-1692) studied under Samuel Rutherford at St Andrews and was ordained to Mid Calder, on Rutherford's recommendation, in 1643. He was a strong supporter

of the Protesters in the controversies with the Resolutioners which so dominated church affairs in the later 1640s and 1650s. Ousted from his charge at the Restoration, he accepted the 1687 toleration and was installed in a meeting house in Edinburgh in that year. In 1689 he became minister of Trinity College Church in the capital and in 1690 was Moderator of the first post-Revolution General Assembly.

CHAPTER 17 – A PRISONER FOR CHRIST

1. Lockup's signature appears on a letter sent by the Societies to Earlston, then their Commissioner in Holland, on 12th October 1682 (Wodrow, *History* IV, Appendix, p. 503).

2. Interestingly, Thomas Lining recorded of his visit to Scotland in late 1687: "Though there be no liberty granted to our friends at home, yet I perceived this, that the great part were somewhat more secure than formerly, and less afraid of the adversary, which was the occasion of several being taken."

3. The £100 reward for Renwick was shared out between Justice and five others, Justice receiving £30 (*Register of the Privy Council*, Third Series, Vol. XIII, p. xliii).

4. Patrick Walker in typical fashion refers to him as "curst Peter Graham, that son of Belial" (*Six Saints of the Covenant,* Vol. 2, p. 98).

5. James Boyle had at one time been considered by the Societies as a possible student for the ministry, and was described by George Hill in a letter of 15th March 1684 to Hamilton as "a very hopeful lad". He is said by Shields to have been popularly referred to as Renwick's "reader", though the Act of 1690 which remitted the various forfeitures, etc., calls him his "precentor". The terms can probably be reconciled by an extract from a description of contemporary Presbyterian worship given by an English visitor: "First, the precentor, about half an hour before the preacher comes, reads two or three chapters to the congregation, of what part of Scripture he pleases or as the minister gives him directions. As soon as the preacher gets into the pulpit the precentor leaves reading and sets a psalm, singing with the people till the minister, by some sign, orders him to give over. The psalm ended, the preacher begins" (quoted in C.G. McCrie, *The Public Worship of Presbyterian Scotland,* 1892, p. 233). Renwick is known, from the testimony of witnesses, to have followed this pattern in his services in the fields (*Register of the Privy Council,* Third Series, Vol. XIII, p. 369). Boyle was arrested after Renwick's field-preaching near Paisley in September 1687, and was imprisoned in the Canongate Tolbooth. When questioned, he disowned the authority of the king and maintained that Bothwell Bridge, at which he was present, had been "a lawful war". He further asserted that Renwick and those with him were "the only lawful ministers in Scotland". On 7th November 1687 he was convicted of high treason by the Justiciary Court and sentenced to be executed on 7th December. However, a petition for clemency was submitted on his behalf, in which he was represented as deeply regretting his earlier statements and acknowledging the authority of the king. On the strength of this he received a royal remission on 22nd November (*Register of the Privy Council,* Third Series, Vol. XIII, p. xix). He continued however in prison, apparently because he could not afford the dues charged for processing the remission through the system. Some months later he petitioned for his release, pleading his impoverished condition and the fact that his wife was near death (ibid., p. 373). There is no record of a response, though from the absence of further reference to him it may be taken that his request was granted.

6. Sir John Lockhart was known judicially as Lord Castlehill; Sir David Balfour as Lord Forret; Sir Roger Hog as Lord Harcarse; and Sir Patrick Lyon as Lord Carse.

Chapter 18 – Preparing for Glory

1. Dalrymple was to be King's Advocate again, under William III, from 1689 to 1692. Created Earl of Stair in 1703, he held other important offices of state under William and Queen Anne and was an energetic advocate of the union of the Parliaments of England and Scotland.

2. *Lives of Helen Alexander and James Currie,* 1869, p. 11. James Currie was later the originator of the Martyrs' Memorial in the Greyfriars Churchyard, erected in 1706. A memorial to Renwick at Moniaive was erected in 1828.

Chapter 19 – The Final Testimony

1. Hamilton returned to Scotland at the Revolution, and at about the same time he fell heir to the family estate of Preston on the death of his brother William, to whom he succeeded in the baronetcy. Since however his entry to the estate would have involved an acknowledgement of the "uncovenanted" rule of William and Mary, he refused to accept possession of his inheritance, or to take to do with it in any way. Over the next few years he continued to stand out firmly against the Revolution Settlement, and he was involved, with some others, in publishing a declaration of protest at Sanquhar in 1692, on which account he was arrested and imprisoned. After being kept in custody for some eight months he was released, the authorities having apparently decided that his activities, though troublesome, presented no threat to the public peace. He persisted in his separatist position, supported by a small band of sympathisers, until his death in October 1701. A few weeks before he died he penned a "last testimony" in which he wrote: "As for my own case, I bless my God, it is many years since my interest in him was secured: and under all my afflictions from all airts, he has been a present help in time of my greatest need. I have been a man of reproach, a man of contention: but praise to him, it was not for my own things, but for the things of my Lord Jesus Christ. Whatever were my infirmities, yet his glory, and the rising and flourishing of his kingdom, was still the mark I laboured to shoot at; nor is it now my design to vindicate myself from the many calumnies that have been cast upon my name, for which his slain witnesses shall be vindicated, his own glory and buried truths raised up, in that day when he will assuredly take away the reproach of his servants, and will raise and beautify the names of his living and dead witnesses. Only this I must add, though I cannot but say that reproaches have broken my heart; yet in what I have met with, before and at the time of Bothwell, and also since, I had often more difficulty to carry humbly under the glory of his Cross, than to bear the burden of it" (*The Christian's Conduct,* 1762, pp. 59-60).

2. After Renwick's death Shields continued field-preaching for a time with Lining and Boyd and with them was received into the national Church in October 1690. After serving in Flanders from 1691 as chaplain to the Cameronian or 26th regiment of foot, he was admitted minister of the Second Charge at St Andrews in 1697. He was appointed chaplain to the third Darien expedition in 1699 and served there for a time, but as he was returning home after the failure of the expedition he caught fever and died in Jamaica, in June 1700, when only in his fortieth year. He was buried at Kingston, but his grave is not known. His death caused widespread sorrow, and a number of elegies were written in his honour. One, of somewhat more literary merit than the rest, contains the following lines:

> He with the truth did still adorn his Shield,
> Which made him boldly to maintain the field;
> His name shall be embalmed with the perfume
> Of sweeter spices than from Egypt come.

> Truth's balmy laurel shall surround his name,
> And Fame, that mighty herald, shall proclaim
> Those just encomiums that to him are due
> And every age his praises still renew.
> *Shields* shall not die, while there's an honest heart
> That loveth Truth, and Truth will still impart."

Shields' brother Michael, the former Clerk to the Societies, accompanied him to Darien and is reputed to have died at sea at around the same time.

CHAPTER 20 – RENWICK'S PLACE IN HISTORY

1. It has traditionally been held that Scotland was a relatively passive participant in the Revolution, merely following the lead of the English nobility and Parliament. The latest scholarship has however cast doubt on that view, drawing particular attention to the influential role played at this time by Scottish exiles in Holland who were in close contact with the Dutch authorities and reflected to them the growing discontent among prominent Scots at home (c.f., G. Gardner, *The Scottish Exile Community in the Netherlands 1660-1690,* 2004, pp. 178 et seq.).

INDEX

Airdsmoss, 20, 30, 116

Alcorn, Adam, 124, 269

Alison, Colin, 92-3

Amsterdam, 40, 64-7, 114, 139

Apologetical Declaration, 105-7, 112, 121, 155

Argyle, Earl of, 111-12, 114-18, 121-2, 124, 127, 134, 137, 182, 233, 269

Arnot, Samuel, 173

Auchengilloch, 97

Balfour, John, 155, 271

Bannatyne, Ninian, 203

Barclay, George, 62, 116, 122-4, 129, 133-4, 139, 163, 268-70

Blackgannoch, 120

Black Loch, 92, 97, 100

Bothwell Bridge, 19-21, 27, 29-30, 40, 44, 59, 74, 77, 79, 96, 100-01, 111, 115-6, 122, 265, 268, 273-4

Boyd, William, 46-7, 50, 53-5, 64, 89, 138, 157-8, 182-3, 225, 252, 267, 272, 274

Boyle, James, 157, 199, 206, 273

Brakel, William, 45, 51-5, 62-4, 87, 123, 139-41, 146, 268

Brown, John, 109

Cambusnethan, 92-3, 118

Cameron, Andrew, 65-6

Cameron, Richard, 20-22, 29, 40, 44-5, 49, 61, 65, 78, 81, 86, 93, 116, 119, 122, 127, 135, 146, 160, 179, 221, 224, 268-9

Cargill, Donald, 20-22, 30-33, 40, 44, 49, 78, 81, 86, 93, 116, 122, 127, 160, 192, 215, 221, 224, 266

Carrick, 124, 128, 132-7, 139, 149-50, 251

Carsphairn, 107, 121

Cathcart, Robert, 132-6, 139, 149, 270

Charles I, 14

Charles II, 15-16, 20-21, 28, 36, 111, 162

Cleland, William, 114-5

Corson, Elizabeth (mother of James Renwick), 12, 199-200, 205, 208-9, 211, 214-5, 227

Covenants, 16-17, 29, 33, 35, 45, 58, 106, 113, 116, 120-1, 126, 136, 159, 164, 166, 184-6, 197, 217, 220-1, 225, 253-6

Cuthill, William, 266

Dalrymple, Sir John, 197-8, 201-3, 207, 219, 274

Darmead, 78, 81, 85, 118, 177, 212, 267

Dick, John, 148

Douglas, Thomas, 268

Dungavel Hill, 98, 100

Dunnottar Castle, 109, 138

Durham, James, 14, 185, 220

Earlston (Berwickshire), 154

Earlston (Galloway), 40, 155

Farrie, David, 31

Fleming, Robert, 44-5, 87, 268

Flint, John, 46-7, 50, 53-8, 64, 74, 88-9, 138-9, 251, 267, 270

Forman, Patrick, 31

Friarminion, 133

Friesland, 45, 87, 246, 248

Glencairn, 11-12, 24, 96, 108, 263

Gordon, Alexander, 137, 139-40, 148-9, 270

Gordon, Alexander of Earlston, 40-44, 46, 48-9, 60, 66-8, 74-5, 76-7, 114, 251, 266-7, 273

Gordon, Lady Janet, of Earlston, 97

Graham, John, of Claverhouse, 19, 73, 96, 108-9

Graham, Peter, 195, 273

Grant, Patrick, 42-3, 48-9, 64, 88-90, 139, 166, 224, 266, 271

Grassmarket, 96, 119, 194, 203, 212, 216, 218

Groningen, 50-51, 54, 56, 59, 63-5, 99, 123, 132, 138, 182

Guthrie, James, 17, 23

Hamilton, Robert, 44-6, 49-60, 62-6, 68, 70-71, 75-6, 79-81, 86-90, 94-5, 97-9, 110, 113, 121-2, 128, 137, 139-43, 145-8, 151, 154-5, 158-9, 172-4, 212-3, 223-6, 245-7, 249, 252, 267-8, 272-4

Hardie, William, 46-7, 267

High School of Edinburgh, 25

Hill, George, 49, 59, 65-70, 75, 85, 273

Hog, Thomas (elder), 268

Hog, Thomas (younger), 62, 268

Houston, David, 157, 164, 174-5, 177, 194, 199, 271-2

Howie, John, 230, 251, 265

Indulged ministers, 44, 74, 83, 93, 118, 123-4, 149, 163, 199, 253

Indulgences, 18-19, 29, 44, 93, 131, 159, 163, 170, 268

Informatory Vindication, 137-8, 141, 155-67, 174, 182, 184, 207, 210, 224, 226, 252, 266, 271-2

James VI and I, 13-14, 26, 198

James VII and II (as Duke of York), 27-8, 32, 67

James VII and II (as King), 111-12, 120, 131, 169-72, 201-2, 218-9, 226, 271

Justiciary Court, 107, 155, 198, 200, 203, 270, 273

Kemp, William, 268

Kennedy, Hugh, 184, 272-3

Kennoway, Thomas, 108

Koelman, Jacob, 146-7, 266

Lachlison, Margaret, 109

Lanark, 35, 37-8, 94, 264-5

Lanark Declaration, 35-7, 43, 79, 165-6, 224, 265-6

Langlands, Robert, 62, 116, 122, 124-7, 129, 133-4, 137, 158, 163, 165, 269-70

Leeuwarden, 45, 49, 51, 62, 77, 87, 99, 246, 248

Lining, Thomas, 98-9, 158, 177, 183, 225, 252, 272-4

Linlithgow, Earl of, 200, 203-4, 219

Lockup, John, 193-4, 196, 273

Magdalen Chapel, 194, 218

Marck, Johannes, 54-5, 88

Mackenzie, Sir George, 76-7, 100-02, 207

McWard, Robert, 45, 80, 268

Moniaive, 11-12, 263, 274

National Covenant, 14, 33, 113, 126, 185, 217

INDEX

Nisbet, James, 119, 143, 180-1, 227-9
Nisbet, John (Student), 46-7, 66, 267
Nisbet, John, of Hardhill, 119
Peden, Alexander, 41, 43, 79, 125, 128-30, 268-9
Pentland Rising, 18, 35
Pillans, James, 26-7, 264
Priesthill, 38, 109
Privy Council, 24, 27-8, 37, 67, 73, 76, 93, 97, 100, 101-3, 107-9, 111, 113, 116, 118, 131, 151-2, 155, 168-9, 176, 195-8, 200-01, 203, 205, 207-9, 220, 224-5, 264
Proclamations, 97, 102-5, 108, 114, 151-2, 169-72, 176-7, 191, 264
Rae, John, 268
Renwick, Andrew, 12-13, 24-25
Renwick, James
  birth and background, 11-22
  education, 23-8
  at Cargill's execution, 30
  appointed Clerk to United Societies, 34
  at Lanark Declaration, 35
  contends with James Russel, 42-3
  selected to study in Holland, 46-7
  studies at Groningen University, 50-53
  ordained by Presbytery of Groningen, 59-60
  in Dublin, 70-2
  returns to Scotland, 75
  called by United Societies, 78-80
  begins his public ministry, 81
  pursued by forces of authority, 92-9
  denounced and declared rebel, 100-3
  prepares Apologetical Declaration, 105-7
  lives life of an outlaw, 109-10
  declines to support Argyle's expedition, 116-7
  emits second Sanquhar Declaration, 120-1
  has unproductive meetings with ministers, 122-7
  reconciled with Alexander Peden, 128-30
  disparaged by Societies in Carrick, 132-41
  visits England, 145
  faces continued enmity and opposition, 147-51
  reward offered for his capture, 152-3
  joined by Alexander Shields and David Houston, 155-7
  prepares Informatory Vindication, 157-67
  ordains ruling elders, 177-9
  emits Testimony against James VII's Toleration, 183-7
  preaches final sermons in Fife and Bo'ness, 187-92
  captured in Edinburgh, 194-5
  interrogated by Privy Council, 195-8
  tried and condemned for high treason, 198-204
  his testimony, 209-11
  his last speech and execution, 216-8
  his place in history, 220-7
Revolution (1688), 219, 225-6, 252, 271-5
Rotterdam, 44, 49-50, 59, 62, 65, 68, 114, 139, 155, 268-9; Scottish Church in 40, 44, 61; Protestation against 87-8, 122-3, 141, 159, 165, 268
Russel, James, 42-3, 48-9, 64, 88-90, 116, 138-9, 224-5, 266, 268
Russel, Thomas, 88-90, 138-9, 270
Russell, Alexander, 31
Rutherford, Samuel, 14, 40, 160, 185, 220, 227, 272
Rutherglen Declaration, 36-7, 266
Sanquhar, 120, 133, 142, 274
Sanquhar Declaration (1680), 20-21, 35-7, 105, 126, 140, 266
Sanquhar Declaration (1685), 120-22
Semple, Gabriel, 173
Semple, John, 107
Sharp, James, Archbishop, 16-17, 19, 42, 96, 133, 155
Shields, Alexander, 23-5, 31, 62, 68, 86, 91, 104, 109, 124, 127, 143, 147, 154-8, 164, 174-7, 179, 183-4, 193-5, 200, 207-9, 214, 218, 225, 245, 251-2, 264, 270-5
Shields, Michael, 174, 251, 265, 268, 275
Smith, John, 46-7, 74, 267
Solemn League and Covenant, 15, 33, 37, 113, 120, 126, 185, 217

Somerville, William, 201
Stonehouse, 143, 176
Stuart, James, 31
Swinabbey, 108
Test Act, 32-4, 36, 111, 118
Toleration (1687), 169-73, 175, 177, 182, 188-91, 197, 206, 211, 217, 233, 270, 273
  Testimony against, 173, 183-6, 210, 252
United Societies, 34-43, 45-6, 48-9, 51, 53-4, 58, 63-7, 70, 74-5, 77-80, 87-90, 97-9, 103-5, 112, 114-7, 119-128, 131-42, 146, 148-9, 151, 153, 155-67, 172, 174-5, 177-8, 182-4, 193, 199, 208-11, 221, 225, 251-60, 265-8, 271-3, 275

University of Edinburgh, 26-8, 154, 263-4
Utrecht, 45, 65-6, 154, 268
Vilant, William, 93
Walker, Patrick, 127, 129, 265, 269, 272-3
Welsh, James, 268
Welsh, John (Ayr), 14, 227
Welsh, John (Irongray), 151, 268
Wigtown, 109, 136, 149, 269
William III, 218, 272, 274
Wilson, Margaret, 109
Wilson, William, 230
Witsius, Herman, 45
Wodrow, Robert, 266, 270, 273